$28.00
01/10/2013

D1624689

UNCONSCIOUS
BRANDING

UNCONSCIOUS BRANDING

HOW NEUROSCIENCE CAN EMPOWER (AND INSPIRE) MARKETING

DOUGLAS VAN PRAET

palgrave
macmillan

UNCONSCIOUS BRANDING
Copyright ©, Douglas Van Praet, 2012.
All rights reserved.

First published in 2012 by PALGRAVE MACMILLAN® in the United
States—a division of St. Martin's Press LLC, 175 Fifth Avenue, New
York, NY 10010.

Where this book is distributed in the UK, Europe and the rest of the
world, this is by Palgrave Macmillan, a division of Macmillan Publishers
Limited, registered in England, company number 785998, of Houndmills,
Basingstoke, Hampshire RG21 6XS.

Palgrave Macmillan is the global academic imprint of the above
companies and has companies and representatives throughout the world.

Palgrave® and Macmillan® are registered trademarks in the United
States, the United Kingdom, Europe and other countries.

ISBN: 978-0-230-34179-1

Library of Congress Cataloging-in-Publication Data

Van Praet, Douglas.
  Unconscious branding : how neuroscience can empower (and inspire)
marketing / Douglas Van Praet.
    pages cm
  ISBN 978-0-230-34179-1 (hardback)
  1. Consumer behavior—Psychological aspects. 2. Marketing—
Psychological aspects. I. Title.
HF5415.32.V36 2012
658.8'342—dc23

2012014890

A catalogue record of the book is available from the British Library.

Design by Letra Libre Inc.

First edition: November 2012

10 9 8 7 6 5 4 3 2 1

Printed in the United States of America.

To my parents,

Marie-Louise and Robert

CONTENTS

INTRODUCTION

When Freud discovered his sense of the unconscious, it had a vast effect on the climate of the times. Now we are discovering a more accurate vision of the unconscious, of who we are deep inside, and it's going to have a wonderful and profound and humanizing effect on our culture.

—David Brooks, TED, March 2011

SEVERAL YEARS AGO, IN SANTA MONICA, CALIFORNIA, I stood at the front of a large hotel conference room filled with marketing executives and advertising professionals and told them that consumers were not in control of their brand choices. The audience looked at me as though I had two heads. But what was mind-boggling to marketers was a no-brainer to any cognitive scientist, because to a certain extent, my colleagues were right: We do all have two heads.

Though Freud popularized the psychological distinction between the conscious and unconscious minds nearly a century ago, only in recent decades has science begun to unravel the biological mysteries of the human brain. Humans operate from two separate and often contentious cognitive systems and the mind that drives most of our behavior is ironically the one unbeknownst to our selves. A deluge of research in recent years about the emotional, irrational, and unconscious dimensions of decision making has vindicated my controversial stance: consumers, i.e., humans, make most of their decisions in life quite unconsciously. We are just beginning to understand how this research applies to the choices we make in everyday life, but what science is finding will fundamentally change both how we sell and how we buy.

For too long, marketers have been asking the wrong question. If consumers are making their decisions unconsciously, why do we persist in asking them directly through market research why they do what they do? It's like asking the political affiliation of a tuna fish sandwich. It's not that consumers are intentionally trying to deceive or are even reluctant to share their opinions. They simply can't tell us because they don't really know.

Before marketers develop strategies, they need to first recognize that consumers have strategies too . . . human strategies, not consumer strategies. These ways of thinking lead to a set of neurological and behavioral steps with a process, sequence, and structure rooted in our biology and evolution, not just in our culture and marketplace. And they are steps that can be uncovered and harnessed at will to guide and inform marketing and advertising strategy. As marketers, we need to go beyond asking why and begin to ask how. We need to shift from just measuring the outward expressions of beliefs and attitudes to better understanding the inward processes and real behavioral causes behind them. That is, how do the minds of people process information, structure their experience, and form the often-unconscious beliefs and motivations that drive their behavior?

When my mother goes to the supermarket and pulls one of the last boxes of Tide powder from the shelf, she is demonstrating what cognitive scientists have long theorized: that the moment she stands in the detergent aisle and reaches out for that box, her brain is processing decades of memories, nostalgia, the scent of her children's clothes, and the day she did her husband's laundry in their first new home. She doesn't buy the same brand just because it works or because it's cheaper; she buys it because it triggers a deep and neurologically seated process of behavior.

Unfortunately, businesses have long based their marketplace knowledge on culture and economics and not on the truths of biology and brain evolution. They have borrowed heavily from the social sciences while virtually ignoring the natural sciences, leaving so much fertile ground with woefully few farmers. This new shift from a cultural to a biological view of behavior is one of the most exciting and promising opportunities in the history of humanity. In fact, as this book will demonstrate a majority of the most outward, pervasive, and economically significant manifestations of our culture—such as our media, the television shows we watch, the movies we love, the advertising that moves us, and the products and services we buy every day—have clearly explainable neurobiological determinants.

Throughout my career in marketing and advertising, I have worked on every side of the market research and strategic planning industries, most recently at Deutsch LA, the award-winning, nationally leading advertising agency. Our clients include premiere industry marketers such as Volkswagen, Target, Sony PlayStation, HTC, Dr Pepper, and Snapple. What I have seen is that those advertisers and campaigns willing to take risks, to make creative leaps beyond the instruction of market research, and to act with instinct and intuition have proven the most fruitful. While these marketers discovered that we couldn't rely on the research alone, they also couldn't articulate the process of their gut feelings and their imaginative insights.

In addition to being a marketing practitioner, I supplemented my understanding by becoming a behavior change therapist working with clients of a different sort. In the age of technology, marketers are at risk of becoming out of touch with the real-life, flesh-and-blood needs and challenges of people—not consumers. I learned how to help everyday people like you and me who were interested in changing their lives and their behavior . . . not because of emotional illness but because of a desire for self-improvement and a more fulfilling life—the same things people seek in brands. And through that work, I noticed firsthand how the unconscious was the key to that change.

I became fascinated by the deeper worlds inside people. I became intrigued by how, unlike marketers, therapists always sought the hidden meaning, never hanging on the words of their customers as gospel truth. I learned to discern the subtleties of nonverbal communication, body language, and unconscious micro-expressions of emotions. Having studied at a college and clinic of behavioral science specializing in understanding unconscious motivation, I became certified as a hypnotherapist. I gained access and profound insight into behavioral-change techniques that often entail a fraction of the time and effort of other traditional psychological methods. Many of these esoteric, intuitive, revolutionary techniques were corroborated and deepened through my investigations of the neurosciences, including cognitive science, neurobiology, evolutionary psychology, and behavioral economics. So I began reverse engineering what I learned from all these disciplines, starting with the things that were proven to yield real results quickly in real people. I created a seven-step process to change behavior, one that I have been applying to marketing and advertising strategies with remarkable success ever since.

Much of what I have to say may seem like an indictment on the state of marketing today. This is not a judgment. It's a firsthand observation. Having worked many years helping marketers plan strategies and conduct research, I became acutely aware of the shortcomings of my own efforts and the tools of my trade. Far too many marketers have ignored the elephant in the room—the role of unconscious decision making—despite the continually amassing evidence of its importance. Far fewer have adopted any pragmatic means to integrate this learning into business operations. My frustration and curiosity for the truth led me to search for better answers. I found them not in market research but rather in the research of cognitive and behavioral authorities.

Most of the ideas in this book are not my own ideas. They originated in the minds of some of the world's most brilliant behavioral scientists. My contribution is to build a practical bridge to, and explain the manifestations of, their observations in our cultures, markets, and economies. Most marketers are still unaware of these scientists' insights, which is why I find it so important to espouse their truths to the marketing and advertising world. The lessons they teach have revolutionary implications on how we do business at a time when economic improvement and better business models are so desperately needed.

And though massive amounts of money are spent on marketing today, the predicament that department store merchant John Wanamaker posed a century ago remains. He is purported to have said: "Half my advertising budget is wasted. Trouble is, I don't know which half."[1]

In 2010, businesses spent $31.2 billion worldwide in market research, conducting quantitative and qualitative surveys and focus groups, often asking consumers to reveal insights they themselves didn't know.[2]

Yet, countless marketing expenditures are being wasted, because what people say in these surveys and focus groups usually does not reliably predict how they will behave in the real world. Not surprisingly, only an abysmal 2 out of 10 products launched in the United States succeed.[3]

Today cognitive neuroscience is proving that humans make decisions irrationally, perception is illusory, and our minds are designed for self-deception. As creatures who pride ourselves on being honest, level-headed, logical, objective thinkers sharing our uniquely human capacity for free will, these truths are hard to accept and even more difficult to apply.

The fact is, we humans live our lives on autopilot and we don't even realize it. Socrates said "know thyself," but the greatest irony of the human mind is that it doesn't really know itself at all. According to one of the world's leading neuropsychologists, Chris Frith, "The way the brain works is that it hides from us most of the work that it does. Something like 90 percent of brain activity never reaches consciousness at all."[4] And "as much as 95 percent of consumers' thinking occurs in their unconscious minds," according to Harvard marketing professor Gerald Zaltman.[5]

As consumers, we make choices without understanding their foundations, and as marketers, we sell and brand products without understanding how to truly connect them with people. We are all playing a game, and we don't even know how that game is being played. It's time to throw out the old playbook. It's time to reveal the hidden depths below our behaviors and to see how our most basic instincts, emotions, innate predispositions, and unconscious learned behaviors can be used to better connect brands with humanity.

This book is about the human side of business. Many consumers see marketing as an attempt to separate them from their money, not as a way to connect with them and satisfy their needs. And they have good reason to think this way. If you are interested in manipulating minds, please don't bother reading this book. People today are too savvy, cynical, empowered, and vocal to fall for irresponsible pandering to the most intimate and powerful parts of their decision-making process. While they might not understand their own intentions, they are very clear on the intentions of companies that try to sell them things.

Businesses and brands that succeed are those that generate real value. By better understanding the real motives of our decisions and beginning to appreciate consumerism from both sides of the fence, we can help facilitate this symbiotic exchange, creating both powerful brands and satisfied customers, prompting industry to change for the better, and driving the competitive forces that shape progress in free markets.

PART I
THE SCIENCE BELOW
OUR DEEPER BEHAVIOR

1
THE MYTH OF MARKETING

The rational mind is the humble servant, the intuitive mind the faithful gift. We have created a society that honors the servant, and has forgotten the gift.

—*Albert Einstein*

IN THE SUMMER OF 1957 IN THE NEW YORK CITY SUBURB OF Fort Lee, New Jersey, a polio scare frightened residents away from public swimming pools. Wary of what might be lurking in the pools and looking for ways to escape the heat of the afternoon sun, they headed in droves to the air-conditioned comfort of the darkened Lee Theater to watch *Picnic,* starring William Holden and Kim Novak. Looming behind the scenes, market researcher James McDonald Vicary was conducting an unusual experiment, one that he hoped would be a boon to consumers and advertisers.[1]

During the film, words were repeatedly flashed on the silver screen for $\frac{1}{3,000}$th of a second, urging moviegoers to "eat popcorn" and suggesting they "drink Coca-Cola." Vicary contended that these "invisible commercials," which were shown so rapidly that viewers couldn't actually see them, allowed for more entertainment time and eliminated bothersome ads. He maintained that his innovation also saved advertisers the money and resources required to produce regular commercials. Over the course of six weeks 45,000 people visited the theater, and the results surprised even Vicary. Purchases of popcorn soared by an astonishing 57.5 percent and sales of Coca-Cola jumped an impressive 18.1 percent.[2]

On September 16, 1957, *Advertising Age* unveiled Vicary's secret weapon of subliminal projection, reporting plans to extend the idea to television viewers. But the naïve market researcher was taken aback when the findings of his experiment ignited widespread public outrage and paranoia about ill-intentioned possibilities. The ensuing mass hysteria would later find him unlisting his phone number and shunning public appearances in fear for his life. That very same year also saw the introduction of Vance Packard's highly influential book *The Hidden Persuaders*. The book's central thesis was that we were being monitored and manipulated by marketers and advertisers without our conscious awareness.[3] A year later, a government investigation by the CIA led to a ban on these subliminal cuts in the United States. The reports concluded that: "Certain individuals can at certain times and under certain circumstances be influenced to act abnormally without awareness of the influence."[4] Fortunately, the public was now not only aware of the real dangers of subliminal advertising but could also rest assured knowing that laws were in place to protect them from corporate mind control. Except there was one problem: The experiment was a hoax. Vicary admitted to the fraudulence in a 1962 interview with *Advertising Age,* saying that the original market research study was "a gimmick" and indicating that the amount of data was "too small to be meaningful."[5] But the damage had been done and the urban legend lived on. Even to this day some people remain concerned about hidden messages and images in ads. But embedding a phallic symbol in a cluster of foliage or a naked body in a pool of water is not really a good way to make anyone buy liquor, cigarettes, or anything else for that matter.

The word "subliminal" comes from the Latin roots "sub" meaning "below," and "limen" meaning "threshold," referring to perception that happens below the threshold of consciousness.[6] And even though a failed and deceitful market research study over half a century ago had the entire nation barking up the wrong tree, we now know, with a certain ironic twist, a disturbing truth that has profound implications for both consumers and companies. Most of the business of life happens below the threshold of consciousness. And while we were so worried that others might be controlling our minds, what we really should be wondering about is whether we ourselves are ever in control.

THE TIP OF THE ICEBERG

We are living a delusion. We think the conscious or rational mind is in control because it's the part of our mind that talks to us, the voice inside our heads as we silently read the words on this page. Because we believe that this part of our mind is running the show, we also believe that the conscious minds of consumers must similarly be driving behavior. For marketers, this leads to a false pretense that purchase behavior is a conscious choice, but, science shows, the exact opposite is true.

In 2008 startling evidence to support belief in the role of the unconscious in decision making was demonstrated in an experiment by a group of scientists led by John-Dylan Haynes from the Max Planck Institute for Human Cognitive and Brain Sciences in Leipzig, Germany. Using brain scans, these researchers were able to predict participants' decisions about seven seconds before the subjects had consciously made the decisions. As the researchers reported in *Nature Neuroscience* on April 13, 2008, "Many processes in the brain occur automatically and without involvement of our consciousness. This prevents our mind from being overloaded by simple routine tasks. But when it comes to decisions, we tend to assume they are made by our conscious mind. This is questioned by our current findings."

The decision studied was a simple choice of whether or not to push a button with one's left or right hand. Participants were free to make the decision whenever they wanted, but had to indicate at what point they made the decision in their mind. By observing micropatterns of brain activity, the researchers were able to predict the subjects' choices before they were "known" to the participants themselves. "Your decisions are strongly prepared by the brain activity. By the time consciousness kicks in, most of the work has already been done," says Haynes.[7]

This unprecedented prediction of a free decision raises profound questions about the nature of free will and conscious choice. For decades marketers have been talking to themselves instead of speaking to the real desires and motivations of consumers. They have been rationalizing the effectiveness of the wrong marketing tools aimed at the wrong target and the wrong mind. It's not their fault. They were unconscious of their own delusion.

Think of the human mind as if it were an iceberg. Just the tip is visible, or "conscious," while the vast majority lies concealed from perception, or "unconscious." Most of our thoughts, beliefs, and even our decisions occur without our own awareness. Marketers need to go deeper to really understand the true nature of our behavioral causes. Fortunately, science is now plumbing these depths at a revolutionary pace and, in turn, illuminating mysteries that have long eluded us. Below the surface is where our intuitive, emotional, and unconscious mind hides. This is the part of our mind that drives almost all of our behavior.

Albert Einstein once said, "Imagination is more important than knowledge." He understood the power and importance of the unconscious mind, developing the theory of relativity by imagining what it would be like to ride on a beam of light. The neuropsychological technique called dissociation enables us to look at a problem from a different perspective by getting outside of our own head. Einstein embraced the "mysterious," saying, "It is the source of all true art and science." He probably could have predicted the neuroscience revolution of today!

Einstein's greatest gift was his inordinate ability to make the leap beyond imagination to create what others couldn't see—by integrating conscious, logical thought with unconscious, intuitive insight. He lived not just above the surface of the iceberg but also in the part not visible to the eye, pulling from the depths of his intuition to guide his research and theories. By honoring the whole of the iceberg, we too can help revolutionize our understanding of how markets behave.

MEASURING UNAWARENESS

Today you'll find evidence of what Einstein referenced as the forgotten gift of our intuitive mind in the language, tools, and metrics of marketers.

One of the greatest ironies is that "awareness" has always been the gold standard for guiding and measuring campaign and brand success. Marketers spend a disproportionately large percentage of their primary research budgets evaluating and measuring brand, advertising, message, and product awareness. But the quantitative copy tests, concept tests, and advertising tracking studies that make up the majority of this evaluative research only skim the surface. They fail to recognize and understand the underlying unconscious causes that often evade awareness. One marketer who didn't believe in consumer research was Steve Jobs. When a reporter once asked how much market research was conducted to guide Apple in the launch of the iPad, he famously quipped, "None. It isn't the consumers' job to know what they want." The iPad, according to some measures, would become the most successful consumer product introduction in history.[8]

Our brains experience and know more than our minds can ever possibly report. Self-reported data in market research surveys simply can't measure the implicit, nondeclarative memories that unconsciously prime our brains' receptivity to brands and messages. These memories are complex sets of neurological associations that lie deep in the brains' emotional systems and become anchored to the brand but hidden from view. When researchers try to investigate brand affinity and loyalty, they often find themselves recording the conscious relationship one has with the brand, not the deeper, intuitive connections formed over a lifetime.

For instance, when someone is presented with the option of a Coke instead of a Pepsi, autobiographical memories and culturally learned associations are being fired deep within the brain—outside the awareness of the would-be soda buyer. These associations link a present brand stimulus with experiences from the past. This personal "data" is summarized in consciousness as a feeling. But consumers usually cannot consciously access most of these thoughts or the origins of their emotions.

The real answers exist in the domain of the unconscious, emotional mind, a part of the brain that speaks in feelings, not words. The unconscious mind is like a device that has recorded all of the data of all of your life's events. If the unconscious could talk, it would perhaps ramble illogically and boundlessly. It would conjure up all the deep imprints, episodes, thoughts, emotions, and associations spanning one's entire life, the sum total of which would represent the true value of the brand. The list would go on and on and on, filled with episodic memories and autobiographical life events that, while no longer easily accessible by the conscious mind, remain stored in the vast memory banks of the intuitive mind.[9]

When asked about preference in market research surveys, the respondents most often post-rationalize and make up evidence, offering up some logical reasoning that seems plausible. Our conscious minds are designed to think up stories to try to explain and make meaning of the hidden forces and hardwired neural programs that guide our behavior. "I prefer Coke because I like the taste better," they say, and that is the so-called factual response that is coded and entered into the data table and reported in the key findings of the report. Some marketers would look at that data and develop advertising about a great-tasting carbonated beverage. Fortunately for Coca-Cola, their marketers have not gone down this path, and Coca-Cola has their market share dominance to show for it.

Coke's focus has always been establishing an instantly recognizable and appreciated brand. Through the classic, consistent logo, the iconic contour of the bottle's design, the mellifluous alliteration of the brand name, its investment in world-class, heart-warming advertising, and a pervasive retail presence, it became not only the first truly global brand but also the most recognized trademark in the world.[10] In 2011 the Coca-Cola brand was worth an estimated $74 billion—more than Budweiser, Pepsi, Starbucks, and Red Bull combined—a position maintained by spending $2.9 billion in advertising in 2010, more than Microsoft and Apple's advertising budgets put together.[11]

SINGLE-MINDED IS WRONGHEADED

For years, we have lived under the adage "advertising must be single-minded," but this reasoning is fundamentally flawed: there is an inherent "duality" to the structure of our minds. Influence is born by appealing to the emotions while overcoming rational restraints. This conflict between unconscious emotionality and conscious rationality creates the opportunity for effective brand promises. When the mind accepts a brand story as told in advertising and marketing communications, it is both believing the story's rational tenets and bonding to its emotional meaning.

Before marketers develop strategies they start with a description of the target as a single person, typically called "a persona," which is based upon traditional self-reported research. This individual, often described along current cultural, product, category, and media usage dimensions, represents a discrete demographic and psychographic segment of a population. But by focusing on how this persona is different from the rest, we ignore the universal similarities: the human insights that we share, regardless of gender, age, income, geography, or culture, and that also prompt our actions. Knowing that someone is a 35- to 44-year-old loyal owner of a domestic sedan who indexes high on watching reality TV, claims to work out two plus times a week, says that reliability is the number one reason they choose to buy a particular car, and lives in Midwestern America neglects that person's deeper, more meaningful, universal human desires and aspirations.

Once when I was conducting focus groups, I asked a cross section of cost-conscious compact sedan owners who had just seen the redesigned Jetta, "What would your friends think of you if they saw you driving this new car?" They responded defiantly, saying things like "I don't care about what others think of me, I just want to get from point A to point B!" Shortly thereafter, these same panelists were shown several concepts to describe the new Jetta and asked which they preferred. "I like *Head-Turning Good Looks!*" they concurred.

Their "persona" had fabricated a smart, responsible image, but deep down they really desired recognition and attention. The irony is that if we fall for their self-deceiving trap, they won't be happy and neither will Volkswagen. We arrived at a strategy that afforded them a level of sophistication that they had always wanted at an attainable price, and an ad campaign summarized by the expression: "Great. For the Price of Good." This effort helped the new Jetta attain its best sales year ever in the United States.[12] Both minds were satisfied, and their conflict resolved by conferring status and not just promising practicality. Deep down each and every one of us wants a little more social status. If you are the exception to this rule, you are most likely lying . . . to yourself.

But marketers often get so caught up in the outward cultural expressions of the persona, they ignore the humanity that binds us all. Ironically, psychologist Carl Jung coined the term "persona" to describe the façade designed by people to make an impression on others while concealing their true nature! The persona plays an important evolutionary role in human behavior, helping us to adapt to our cultural group, to fit in with and be accepted by others. This has aided us in our survival for many thousands of years, and still does so today. It is this social mask that each of us wears to shield and conceal our authentic yet more vulnerable inner self.

The persona is the mask of overconfidence that invents stories to color reality in our own favor. This creates a dilemma for market researchers. For instance, in survey research, 95 percent of professors report that they are above average teachers, 96 percent of college students say they have above average social skills, and when *Time* magazine surveyed people in the United States and asked "are you in the top 1 percent of earners?" 19 percent of Americans indicated that they are in the top 1 percent of earners![13] Social science experiments reveal that people are inherently self-righteous and consistently overrate their abilities, contributions, generosity, and autonomy. We chalk up success to skill and failures to bad luck. We say that advertising does not influence us, even though the data says otherwise. We swear that our partners take out the garbage less than we do, even though it's really about the same. Our beliefs distort our realities, and we are programmed by our very nature to look out for number one. People even maintain these self-serving delusions when they are wired to a lie detector, which means they are lying to themselves and not intentionally to the experimenters![14] And, we do this as an adaptive function, to lead better lives and to insulate ourselves from depression. In fact, people who lie to themselves tend to be happier and more successful in life and business.[15]

The persona shows up to focus groups and filters one's responses in a manner acceptable to fellow panelists, modifying opinions in deference to authority. People are intimidated by the moderator, who is strategically and symbolically positioned at the head of the table, or they are influenced by the know-it-all panelist who hijacks the discussion in an effort to impress the group. Like a chameleon adapting to the requirements of the environment, the persona is the part of one's identity that often yields to groupthink while concealing deeper personal thoughts, the thoughts that make up the dark mass of the iceberg below.

Suspicious of the unknown, the persona is wary of the faceless, nameless observers behind the two-way mirrors. I recall an incident when I was conducting an in-depth interview about perceptions of mortgage lenders with a subprime home mortgage loan candidate in Los Angeles. The man believed that his bank had secretly arranged the so-called research interview as part of his approval process. Needless to say, it was almost impossible to break through his paranoid defense shield. Despite my constant reassurance to the contrary, he kept up the self-serving image of financial responsibility. Quite frankly, I don't blame him. What is more important, getting your home mortgage loan approved or giving your opinion about an annoying online banner or a piece of junk mail?

If people present themselves differently from who they are and believe their own lies and confabulations, we need to find out how to go deeper to reach their truer selves. As Carl Jung put it, "In each of us there is another whom we don't know."[16] The "inner self" is a term Jung used to describe the totality of the psyche that includes our deeper, more unconscious desires and intentions, or in essence, "the real you." The self and its hidden intentions is where the actual truth and opportunity lie for marketers.

THE LIMITATIONS OF TRADITIONAL MARKETING TOOLS

A group of ten people sit in a brightly lit room. The fluorescent lights above feel more appropriate for an interrogation space. They shift in their seats, unsure of the questions they will be asked, and appear uneasy about offering the "right" responses. One of them taps his fingers annoyingly on the conference room table they are all situated around, a sound picked up by the not-so-cleverly concealed microphones. Cameras are recording the session through the mirrored glass that separates them from hidden observers. The group watches as someone emerges from the back room, passing a suspicious note to the moderator who has just joined them, as a giant two-way mirror looms in the background. The participants in this focus group laugh and talk nervously, sometimes avoiding eye contact as the session begins. This environment practically demands that their inauthentic personas be on display and that their more intimate "real selves" be kept concealed from the superficial scenario they are in.

Is it reasonable to expect deeper, more emotional and deeply personal responses in such a contrived and clinical environment? If consumers can lie to themselves, wouldn't they just as easily lie to moderators in a focus group setting? Certainly. This is why we must understand the "tells" of their lies.

Behind the glass in the back room, observers clack away at the keyboards like stenographers at a trial, recording evidence to support their own predispositions and confirmatory biases. Amidst the hours of dialogue and often contradictory reports, they pay attention and hang on to the content of the words, while ignoring the context, the part of communication that actually determines the meaning. The answers can be found not in the words themselves but in how they're said and in what isn't said. Instead of focusing on the words, we need to focus on the inner self of the person: the body language, the linguistic hints and slips, the intonation shifts, the micro facial expressions, and the behavioral incongruities that often belie the meaning of consciously reported behavior.

Ironically, qualitative research is the one place where we can really investigate what is going on below sea level. Being able to look into the eyes of consumers as well as to observe their bodily reactions is a distinct advantage over larger-scale quantitative surveys conducted by phone or the Internet. It is not just about whether a person says they prefer Coke or Pepsi, or one advertisement over another, it's also about observing and analyzing how they respond to those choices.

But this can only happen with a highly skilled moderator practiced in the nuances of body language and the art of detecting subcommunication. Like psychologists and therapists—a skilled few—moderators must not accept the words of people on face value but seek the story behind the story. They know and can comprehend their panelists better than the panelists can even understand themselves. These moderators look for the meaning beyond the words. Though truly great moderators are rare indeed, they often succeed in using qualitative research in spite of the structure of the focus group, not because of it.

Professor emeritus of psychology at UCLA Albert Mehrabian conducted a study on human communication and found that 7 percent of a message was derived from the words, 38 percent from the intonation, and 55 percent from the facial expression or body language. It is only reasonable to conclude that a majority of communication is not captured in the words per se, the verbatim notes of the top-line report, or even the full one. How full can the report be if it is missing the majority of insights from the parts of the mind that guide behavior?

While quantitative surveys have more robust, stable, and projectable sample sizes, these tools, as currently structured, often fail to reach the deeper emotional unconscious. Because of the manner in which the data is obtained—the level of personal detachment and the inherent limitations of self-reported data—the findings are often reduced to what the participants are saying and not how they really feel. To make matters worse, a majority of current quantitative research is conducted online, allowing for anonymous feedback and a feeding ground for role-playing personas, if not carefully controlled.

Before we can develop better market research tools we need to first develop a better understanding of how the human brain works to change behavior. To do this we must first shift the focus to the unconscious.

THE POWER AND FUNCTION OF THE UNCONSCIOUS MIND

As Einstein knew, the processing power of our unconscious mind is immensely more powerful than that of our conscious mind. Timothy Wilson, professor of psychology at the University of Virginia and author of the book *Strangers to Ourselves,* indicates that our senses take in about 11 million bits of information every second, but we are only consciously aware of about 40 bits of that information! Which means the remainder of those 11 million bits of information is being processed without our ever knowing. Looking at the world through consciousness is like looking at life through a tiny keyhole[17]—our critical mind can perceive only a tiny sliver of the vastness of information that is being processed by our bodies and absorbed by our senses.

Not surprisingly, the dominant unconscious easily overrules our conscious side. To demonstrate this point, try a little experiment on your own. Sit in a chair and extend your dominant leg. With that leg, make small clockwise circles with your foot. While performing this motion, draw the number 6 in the air with the index finger of your dominant hand. What happened? Everyone who attempts this task usually has one of two reactions; their foot will either freeze in mid-air or reverse directions while the hand easily completes the task of drawing the number 6.

What's going on here? Drawing the number 6 is an unconscious motor program. You have done it so many times in the past that you do it automatically without thinking. It is a learned behavior. Making a circle with your foot is a conscious activity that requires thought-focus and energy because it is not likely a behavior that has been previously learned. Instead, the learned behavior overrides our conscious effort. This happens throughout our lives more often than not. We defer to our autopilot learned responses, instead of adapting to a new process or pattern.[18]

But even though our powerful unconscious mind dominates, the conscious mind is actually the gateway to our unconscious. Repeated conscious activities and experiences are eventually turned into capable, hardwired intelligence deep within our brain, residing comfortably and effortlessly beyond our awareness. Much of what is ingrained in our unconscious minds, including the brands we know, love, and to which we are so loyal, began life in the conscious mind. Like drawing the number 6 over and over again in a penmanship exercise, or seeing ads over and over again on television, brands and their messages are now second nature to you. Over time, these lessons have become infused in our brains and bodies as learned behaviors.

The unconscious is the domain of our emotions—the feeling of good or bad that we assign to things. When Shakespeare's Hamlet says, "There is nothing either good or bad, but thinking makes it so," what he really meant was that "feeling" makes it so. Value judgments are made on the basis of emotions and feelings, not thinking or logic. When the waiter brings over a tray of desserts and your eyes fixate on the Belgian chocolate truffle cake, your emotional systems light up with the good feelings and memories of all things chocolate. Your rational mind tries to dissuade you, pointing to the facts that cake is fattening, high in calories, and unhealthy, but try as it might your logic falls victim to feelings of intense pleasure that assign value to the cake. Your brain values the feelings, not the facts.

Brands are like people. The value you assign to someone is based largely on how the individual makes you feel. For instance, your natural attraction to mates and partners is driven by unconscious emotions, decision rules that have already made the choice for you. It happens at a deeper level. Throughout millions of years of evolution your brain has become preprogrammed with preferences for characteristics like tall men or curvy women. There's nothing you can do to consciously change that. That's why you can't logically convince yourself to fall in love with someone when there simply isn't any chemistry. No amount of reasoning will change how you feel because feelings weigh in before and irrespective of logic and conscious choice.

When we go to the local market, we find that the brands we buy are the same from week to week. Though a specific offer or coupon might tempt us to contemplate All detergent if we are a Tide loyalist, we will most likely walk out of the store with our preferred brand. Emotions not only make judgments, they also generate automatic physical reactions. They determine Crest vs. Colgate, Toyota vs. Honda, Nike vs. Adidas, blondes vs. brunettes, and short vs. tall. Our emotions drive preference, choice, satisfaction, and loyalty, determining what products are chosen from the shelf and which people and activities we engage with in life.

The unconscious, quite literally, runs the body. It controls all of our sensory perception and the myriad continuous bodily functions that thankfully go off unnoticed and without a hitch. Right now, the unconscious is keeping your balance, instructing your heart to beat, commanding your lungs to breathe, growing your hair and nails, replacing the cells in your body, and removing toxins from your bloodstream. It not only constantly monitors your internal state but also what's happening around you, always alert for potential threats and opportunities such as predators, food sources, and mating partners.[19] The main goal of our unconscious minds is self-preservation, the survival and replication of our genes and selves. It is the home of our natural instincts and learned habits, those repetitive behaviors that include the loyalty to a product or brand.

Think of the unconscious mind as a vast repository of all our past experiences and lessons learned, as well as the natural instincts that our forebears have taught us through the instruction of the information encoded in our DNA. Many of these memories are referred to as implicit or nondeclarative memories since we no longer can explicitly recall them, like the feeling of a cold Coke on a hot summer day in fifth grade. In all of our behavioral responses we automatically and often unknowingly reference these learned and innate impressions. In essence, we are never really living in the present alone. We are always making largely unconscious comparisons to our past in order to predict what will happen in the future.

Unlike the conscious mind, which is linear in thought, focusing more on single tasking and logical facts, the unconscious mind is holistic, highly perceptive, and multisensory. It is constantly multi-tasking and parallel processing many levels of information. For example, the conscious mind hears the words coming out of someone's mouth, but the unconscious mind takes into account the inferences, the credibility, and authority of the speaker, the extent to which that person is aligned in their words with their deeds and actions, the feelings and associations evoked by their presence, and the judgments and reactions of others.

The unconscious responds to the context or structure of a message not just the actual content, aware of how the information is delivered and not just what is said. As the advertising great Bill Bernbach once said, "Telling isn't selling."[20] Because of this, the best ways to reach the unconscious parts of our minds often involve embedding the message in structural devices that evoke emotion and require internal, personal, and divergent interpretation. This is why we use stories, poems, songs, jokes, pictures, symbols, characters, roles, and metaphors. They are particularly ripe marketing tools, effectively bypassing critical analysis to evoke feelings that strike at the heart and gut. They speak to that deep and powerful unconscious, the man behind the curtain to whom we normally pay no attention.

BRANDS ARE EXPECTATIONS BASED ON MEMORIES

To begin to really understand the definition and role of a brand in the lives of consumers, we need better research tools. Thankfully, neuroscience is beginning to provide some.

Neurobiological evidence of how branding actually works was brought to light in a seminal study done by a team of pioneering neuroscientists led by Read Montague, director of the Brown Human Neuroimaging Lab at Baylor College of Medicine. This study took the marketing tactic known as the Pepsi Challenge into the laboratory.

In the famous Pepsi Challenge, most people prefer the taste of Pepsi in blind taste tests, that is, when they don't know which brand they are drinking. Yet Coke is still purchased more often by the majority of cola drinkers in the real world. How does one reconcile these observations? How can one brand be preferred in taste and the other preferred in purchase? It seems only logical that we buy beverages that taste better.

To answer these questions the team of neuroscientists set out to repeat the experiment of the Pepsi Challenge with a new twist. Volunteers would drink the beverages while having their brains scanned with an fMRI (functional magnetic resonance imaging) machine, a harmless, noninvasive approach to visually observe the mind, that is, the brain in action. This scanning technology works by demonstrating the dynamic flow of blood in the brain, thus signaling what parts and functions of the brain are being activated.

To accomplish this, participants were placed in an fMRI machine and the beverages were delivered through carefully designed strawlike tubes. In the first part of the experiment they would be unaware of the brands they tasted, replicating the design of the Pepsi Challenge. In the second phase of the experiment, volunteers would be exposed to an image of the can of Pepsi or Coke prior to receiving each drink to determine the effect of brand knowledge on preference and brain activity.

When the participants were aware of the brand, they stated a greater preference for Coke and brain scan imagery revealed significant differences in neurological activity. When the test was "blinded" and they were unaware of what brand they were drinking, preference levels and neurological responses for Coke and Pepsi were similar.

But when those tested expected Coke, there was significantly greater activation of the frontal area of the brain called the dorsal lateral prefrontal cortex, an area involved in decision making, working memory, associations, and higher cognitive thinking. The prefrontal cortex is also involved with our personality and our perception of self. Additionally, there was also greater activation within parts of the limbic system, which is the emotional center of the brain, and the hippocampus, which plays an important role in memory.[21]

As Montague puts it, "there is a huge effect of the Coke label on brain activity related to the control of actions, the dredging up of memories, and things that involve self-image."[22] This experiment demonstrated that when exposed first to an image of the Coke label, participants thought about the brand via the prefrontal cortex, the part of the brain that plans behavior.

Humans plan future behavior by relating present experiences to memories, past experiences, and learned associations. In other words, brands reside in our brains and not just our culture. They activate unconscious thoughts and beliefs. As Montague concludes, "We live in a sea of cultural messages. Everybody has heard of messages, and in the case of Coke, those messages have insinuated themselves in our nervous system. There is a response in the brain which leads to a behavioral effect—in this case personal preference."[23]

BRANDS ARE CHEMICALLY DRIVEN SHORTCUTS

Decision making is about making predictions, and our brain does this largely through the release of dopamine. This "gimme more" neurotransmitter is responsible for wanting, craving, and motivating us to do nearly everything, including sex, drugs, gambling, playing video games, and even shopping. The dopamine system also has a close relationship with the opioid system of the brain, which produces pleasurable sensations. "You're probably 99.9 percent unaware of dopamine release," says Montague, "But you're probably 99.9 percent driven by the information and emotions it conveys to other parts of the brain."[24] Dopamine also plays a key role in memory because it is one of the neurotransmitters that controls brain plasticity and learning.[25]

Merely seeing the Coke label was enough to activate the brain's pleasure centers without even taking a sip, by elevating the levels of dopamine, a naturally occurring chemical produced by the brain that signals feelings of reward.[26] There is a dopamine link between the prefrontal cortex and the pleasure systems in our brain. The way we plan future behavior is based upon present feelings: The more rewarding it feels, the more likely we are to engage in that activity.

Dopamine is also the feel good "drug" of anticipation. We do not need to experience the product to get the rush of dopamine. We only need to imagine and anticipate it in our minds by activating our prefrontal cortex, the part of the brain that lets us envision future possibilities. Montague's team used magnetic resonance imaging of the brain to fairly accurately predict participants' preferences before they would even take a sip! "We were stunned by how easy this was," Montague said. "I could tell what they were going to do by looking at their brain scans."[27]

On a logical, side-by-side product comparison, people might prefer Pepsi, but brand preference has very little to do with rationality. Dopamine is also the chemical responsible for making value judgments that guide decisions. This choice just "feels better" than the other choice. Preference and enjoyment of Coke is derived from not just the sweet taste but more so the "sweet" anticipatory emotions. Marketers are in the business of selling what it means to "feel good." We love the brand, not just the sugary, effervescent liquid.

Clear historical reminders of the emotional (not rational) nature of brand preference are the failures of Crystal Pepsi and Coke Clear. These introductions sparked a marketing fad in the early 1990s, an attempt to link purity with the new colorless beverages. Rational consumers would choose the product without the artificial brown coloring, and opt for the purer clearer cola, right? After all, caramel coloring occurs when you burn sugar, and any biologist will tell you that burnt sugar is actually a carcinogen.[28]

As it turns out, our unconscious minds prefer the brown shade because this brand property is strongly steeped in our memories of the brand. Without the rich, brown coloring it just doesn't seem like the Coke that we have always enjoyed. Instead, the beverage feels like an imposter, lacking the positive emotional valence we have come to associate with its caramel hue. The color colors our experience, not just the soda. In fact, it doesn't even taste the same because our beliefs about what we are drinking change our actual experience and our perception of taste.

To demonstrate this effect of visual perception and expectation on taste, a group of experimenters at the University of Bordeaux in France gave 54 professional wine tasters white wine that had been colored with a tasteless, odorless red dye. When asked to describe the wine all of these experts described the white wine using terminology typically used to describe red wine. Even the most astute connoisseurs can be duped by their own brain chemistry. Whether you are an everyday consumer of cola or an expert in tasting wine, your unconscious mind is processing information on parallel tracks, at many levels and with many senses. Often it can create meaning when there is none, creating a real experience based on a false illusion.[29] As cofounder of the field of evolutionary psychology John Tooby explains, "All sorts of things that we think are matters of the external world are in fact these matrix programs playing in our heads and structuring the world for us. And there really is an external world and it corresponds sometimes to some of these elements, but we're lost in this video game that we mistake for reality."[30]

Brands are subjective, not objective, experiences. They are symbols that signal expectations of outcomes based upon our past beliefs and impressions. The color of Coca-Cola, McDonald's golden arches, the scent of Tide—these are brand properties anchored in our past experiences. These sensory cues trigger unconscious memories, thoughts, patterns, and experiences that are manifested in consciousness as feelings sensed by the body. This conscious output is our brain's way of summarizing unconscious information. Emotions inform our interpretation and guide future behavior, prompting our motivation to buy before we even become aware of them. Neuroscientist David Eagleman likens the conscious mind to that of a newspaper, "by the time you read a mental headline, the important action has already transpired, the deals are done."[31]

Brands are learned behaviors: unconscious automatic intelligence acquired through experience. Learned behaviors are conditioned responses that have been internalized. They simplify our lives by generating choices and action without requiring us to think.

When the brain is overwhelmed with thought—often triggered by outside stimuli—it is forced to juggle more balls than it is capable of juggling. Classical studies in experimental psychology have confirmed the limitations of our conscious working memory at about seven units (plus or minus two), which is why there are seven digits in a phone or license plate number.[32] Currently, our brains are exposed to far too much information each day to consciously process all of our decisions.

Metabolically speaking, conscious thought also requires significantly more energy. This is why too much mental activity makes us tired, inducing us to crave high energy, sugary snacks and caffeine as ways to help us pay attention and maintain clear thinking. Instead of working overtime to consciously process these outside influences, it's much easier and efficient to let the automatic feelings and responses do the thinking for us. It's like using a calculator instead of having to figure out the math, or programming your car's navigation system instead of having to read directions. We end up taking the easy route, the path of least resistance. And brands are the road signs we follow. They are judgmental heuristics—or mental shortcuts—allowing us to respond without significant thought or energy. This not only brings us enjoyment and pleasure in the brands we choose but also relief from confusion and effort in the process of purchasing them.

THE PROMISE AND PITFALLS OF NEUROMARKETING

Neuromarketing is a new field of market research that promises to quite literally get inside our heads. These market research studies explore consumer response to marketing stimuli by using techniques such as EEG (electroencephalogram) brain sensors, fMRI brain imaging, and galvanic skin response (measuring stress responses through changes in skin moisture). A primary goal of this research is to narrow the "say" versus "do" gap, the divide between what people say they feel and how they really feel. The number of neuromarketing companies has risen from only a handful a few years ago to about a hundred worldwide today.[33] While this technology promises to deliver much needed insight into the unconscious, it is still very much in the nascent and exploratory stages.

But measuring brain responses is already helping marketers break through the shield of the persona and get at the real feelings of consumers. Frito-Lay chief marketing officer Ann Mukherjee says brain imaging tests can be more accurate than focus groups. This technology helped to evaluate a Cheetos television spot, an ad that featured a woman who takes revenge on a laundromat patron by putting the orange-colored cheese snacks in her dryer full of white clothes. In focus groups, panelists expressed socially acceptable disapproval for the prank and dislike for the ad because it was too mean-spirited. But brain tests revealed that the women actually loved the commercial; our inner selves are not as politically correct as our personas. The marketer chose to air the spot, which seems like solid reasoning since likability is generally a good thing and there is evidence to suggest that it correlates with persuasion. The ad can be a mediating variable: I like the ad therefore I like the brand.[34]

But is this really or always the right approach? There are instances when likability doesn't translate into sales success. The dotcom era yielded some of the funniest, most entertaining, and likable ads but generated abysmal business results. Most notably, the beloved pets.com sock puppet (a dog mascot with button eyes, flailing arms, and a microphone in his paw) gained widespread popularity and cultlike status. The puppet appeared in Super Bowl ads and as a guest on *Good Morning, America,* was interviewed by *People* magazine, and there was even a giant balloon in his image at the 1999 Macy's Thanksgiving Day Parade. But that was not enough to save the company from liquidation less than a year after its IPO.[35]

And there are instances when unlikable ads worked exceptionally well. Anyone who lived in the environs of New York City in the 1980s will likely recall the very effective psychopathic rants of Crazy Eddie, the electronic retailer whose "prices [were] insane!" His irritating diatribes annoyed millions of television viewers but helped earn the 43-store chain more than $300 million in sales at its peak, despite Crazy Eddie's later fiscal problems.[36]

In addition, evoking an emotion that entertains is not the same as generating a desired buying response. Marketers are not aiming to entertain; they ultimately want the prospective consumer to consider the product, not just laugh at the commercial. When choosing the right health insurance company, do I want to feel amused or charmed, or do I want to feel secure and safe? And not all emotional responses need to be positive. As a behavior change therapist, I have learned that negative emotions, like anger, outrage, disgust, hatred, fear, and dread, can be some of the most powerful ways to rally someone into action.

People are hardwired to avoid pain more than to seek pleasure. The fight-or-flight response, for example, is perhaps the deepest, most highly ingrained behavioral pattern in human evolution because it keeps us out of harm's way. The brain often learns on the basis of painful emotions. It is said: "We suffer our way into wisdom." When we touch a hot stove, we learn very quickly not to do it again. And it's often the sting of losing that best teaches us how to win. The twin pillars of pain and pleasure motivate all behavior and there are instances when employing either or both can work well in marketing.[37]

The brain is too complex to find a magic bullet. For instance, the amygdala, a part of the brain that controls anger and hate, is also responsible for lust and attraction.[38] There is no single buy button in the brain. Describing brain response in a laboratory setting is far from explaining how those neural responses will impact behavior in the real world and how they can inspire actionable marketing solutions.

Good insights in the wrong hands can lead to bad advertising. For example, according to NeuroFocus, a leading neuromarketing company, placing images on the left and copy on the right helps the brain process this information faster. This is because items in the left field are processed by the right frontal lobe of the brain, which processes images, and items in the right field are processed by the left frontal lobe, which processes language. This very insightful observation is especially helpful in designing optimal user experiences. But if every marketer applied this insight as a rule to all advertising, everything would eventually look similar and nothing would stand out.[39]

The brain, much like the humans it commands, is inherently paradoxical and conflicted. Establishing sets of rules or making bombastic claims is destined for failure and will hinder inspired thinking and creativity, the engine that drives marketing innovation and success. When we design products, packages, advertisements, communications, displays, websites, and marketing experiences all by the same set of rules, even if they are rooted in how the brain processes such experiences, the outcome will be a sea of sameness, the death knell of any brand.

The fact of the matter is that anyone can do neuromarketing without ever scanning a single brain. I'm not suggesting we ignore the possibilities of testing marketing materials with brain scanners, sensors, and biometrics. These technologies offer intriguing, exciting possibilities and promise, but they should also be approached with guarded optimism. We are only at the edge of what promises to be deep and meaningful research, and this process will evolve as we learn more about the mysteries of our brain.

My objective is to provide you with an actionable framework that can help marketers today as well as inform the development of neuromarketing in the future. As the evolutionary behavioral scientist and marketing professor Gad Saad argues with regard to the rapidly emerging fields of neurobusiness: "The neuroimaging paradigm will largely remain a fishing expedition for pretty brain images as long as no organizing theoretical framework exists to guide the research and provide coherence to the otherwise disjointed findings."[40]

TOOLS, NOT RULES

There is nothing in the world more complicated and humbling than trying to solve the mysteries of the human brain. We need tools, not rules. We need a system that puts these insights into perspective . . . one that explains the full spectrum of behavioral change influences from multiple angles, considering the process that the unconscious and conscious minds undergo when forming beliefs, evaluating choices, and purchasing brands. From there, we will be able to encourage divergent thinking and novel solutions.

As W. Edwards Deming, the world's foremost authority on quality control management, once said, "If you can't describe what you are doing as a process, you don't know what you are doing." Deming, an American statistician and consultant, was responsible for revolutionizing postwar Japan's industries and reviving the Ford Motor Company in the 1980s. At the heart of his 14-point management philosophy to transform an organization was this principle: "Improve constantly and forever the system of production and service, to improve quality and productivity, and thus constantly decrease costs."[41] In order to improve the marketing process, we need to first shift the focus from within the walls of companies and unveil the process of behavior change within the depths of the minds of people.

While the brain may be a noun, the mind and behavior are verbs. You can't put the mind or behavior into a basket or a shopping cart because it is a process. And how the brain processes behavior change is like any other process. Much like baking bread, there are key steps that must be accomplished in a specific sequence. If you use the wrong ingredients and mix them together in the wrong order, you don't get bread and you don't get a change in behavior. Once the sequence and structure are uncovered, they can be guided, measured, and adjusted accordingly. When you uncover the unconscious processes of the mind, you can observe it in full awareness and strategize the most effective ways to modify behavior. You can then conduct actionable, effective market research because you know where to measure by making the unconscious conscious.

It's like the story about an old boilermaker who was hired to fix the steam engine of a giant ship. After listening to the engineer's description of the problem, he asked a few questions and then checked out the boiler room. Carefully inspecting the maze of twisting pipes, he listened closely to the hissing and thumping sounds, occasionally feeling the pipes with his hands. He then reached into his tool bag, grabbed a small hammer, and tapped once on a valve as the boiler system lurched back into perfect action. A week later the steamship owner received a bill for $1,000. The ship owner complained because the boilermaker barely did anything and spent a mere fifteen minutes of his time fixing it. When the owner asked to see an itemized bill, this is what the repairman sent him:

Tapping with hammer:	$ .50
Knowing where to tap:	$999.50
Total:	$1,000.00

It's important to make an effort, but knowing where to focus your resources makes all the difference. By knowing where to tap, we can dislodge chunks of the iceberg and float them up to the surface to be examined in full view. As Carl Jung once said, "Until you make the unconscious conscious, it will direct your life and you will call it fate."[42]

Without conscious awareness of the process, sequence, and structure of the largely unconscious nature of the mind, you are much like a blind watchmaker—a term that British ethologist and evolutionary biologist Richard Dawkins used to describe the accidental nature of natural selection and evolution. Or, in marketing parlance you are just "throwing shit at the wall to see what sticks." Your outcomes and results are largely happenstance, lacking direction, focus, and the effectiveness necessary to compete in today's marketplace.

Every day, we wake up wearing two hats: marketer and consumer. We sell ourselves at work, we sell our products in the market, and we participate as consumers practically every minute of our lives. We can do that unconsciously, failing to see the powerful mind at work behind all of our choices and actions, or we can understand why and, more importantly, how we really make the decisions to do the things that we do.

2
HUMANS, NOT CONSUMERS

Consumers are statistics. Customers are people.

—*Stanley Marcus, former president,*
Neiman Marcus

EVERY DAY WE COMMUNICATE THE WAY WE THINK BY THE way we speak. Whether through spoken dialogue, written communication, or symbols and gestures, language is one of the most important ways to create and share meaning of the world around us. The name we give something frames our perspective, even changing the meaning by the label we assign it. This is why every time I hear the word "consumer," a term so common in our everyday language, a part of me winces.

The use of the word "consumer" is almost unavoidable in marketing. But to most businesspeople a consumer is an entity that promotes economic advancement through the purchases of goods and services, not a real-life person with feelings, dreams, goals, and aspirations. If you told your "average consumers" they were being defined that way, they would be irritated, not allured. This "consumer" label is often assumptive, counterproductive, and terribly misguided. And, reducing people to other marketing labels that strip them of their humanity and diminish empathy—such as "buyers," "laggards," or "eyeballs"—is equally unhelpful. Perhaps the greatest offense is that it presupposes a behavior that has yet to be earned by the marketer. For marketers, the first step in better understanding the target audience is to better define them, recognizing that people do a lot more than consume. If we continue to sell to people merely as purchasers of products and not as the perceptive, essentially human beings they are, we will be the ones demonstrating poor communication skills before the advertising is even created.

Unfortunately, marketers spend an inordinate amount of effort identifying and tracking *consumer and cultural* trends that are often fleeting and dynamic, instead of understanding the constant and relatively unchanging, innate *human* needs that are behind those trends. As the American biologist Edward O. Wilson put it, "The genes hold culture on a leash. The leash is very long, but inevitably values will be constrained in accordance with their effects on the human gene pool."[1]

Because evolution happens at an imperceptibly gradual pace, it is often the oldest parts, not the new and improved advancements, of human cognition that drive our daily decisions. Human insights are the enduring truths that can unify marketing efforts and cut across a broad array of varying segments, widening appeal while providing ongoing relevance over time. Unlike *consumer* needs, *human* needs run much deeper and have primary influence on behavior change.

The goal of most humans is to satisfy their own needs and drives, not to consume your product. By using the term "consumer," marketers are suggesting a company-out perspective that implies hubris on the part of their strategy. It precludes a deeper understanding of why people are motivated to buy and what it takes to gain their trust and make the sale. This marketers' perspective violates the prime directive of marketing strategy by emphasizing corporate interest over customer benefit. This may seem counterintuitive at first. So much of marketing is aimed at making the specific sale, but, as I aim to demonstrate, to gain a more in-depth understanding of *consumer* behaviors, we need first to raise our sightline and define our potential customers more broadly. After all, we are not always consumers of certain brands but we are always Homo sapiens—regardless of the product category under inquiry.

STONE AGE MINDS

After the inception of the genus Homo around 2.4 million years ago, our ancestors lived for approximately 84,000 generations as hunter-gatherers. By comparison, there have been only a mere 7 generations of the industrial age. Our species lived for well over 99 percent of our evolution in hunter-gatherer societies.[2] Our wants and needs are many millennia in the making, long before the product, brand, or category ever existed. Our minds were designed to solve the problems hunter-gatherers faced, not the problems of modern day consumers. This is why when we narrowly define people as consumers, we draw attention to the present relationship between a target audience and product category, ignoring all of the evolutionary influences that have shaped our brains and behavior, and which still influence so much of that relationship today.

Around 200,000 years ago, and following millions more of evolution, modern humans first appeared during the Pleistocene epoch, living in small nomadic bands foraging the savannas of eastern Africa.[3] Life for these early humans was like being on a camping trip, although a lot more arduous, one that lasted a lifetime without the ability to buy much-needed supplies at REI.[4] Our advanced industrial age, in which we live sedentary lives in climate-controlled houses, shopping at supermarkets, eating fast foods, and watching television, is not even a century in the making. This lifestyle that feels so permanent is nothing but a tiny blip on the radar screen of humanity. To put our times into even greater perspective, the digital age has been with us for a mere two generations. We have gone from aim-and-throw hunters to point-and-click shoppers in an instant, but that doesn't change the fact that our brains remain better suited to Amazon-like rainforests than to amazon.com-like websites. As evolutionary psychologists put it, "Our modern skulls house stone age minds."[5]

That's because as much as we might be in the twenty-first century, the cognitive structures and mental programs that evolved and adapted throughout the Pleistocene environments live on within us today. These brain mechanisms have primary influence on how we

behave in our world even though they were designed for very different environments and circumstances. Though we no longer live in an
environment for which our minds were designed, our brains behave
much as though we do. Natural selection, or what we commonly
refer to as evolution, moves at a glacial pace even if our lifestyle is
changing at light speed. It is a very slow process, and it hasn't had
enough generations to design circuits adapted to a postindustrial society. But since the environment in which we live continues to rapidly
change, the problem remains: We are in fact moving faster than our
own brains.[6]

This is why instead of simply charting what people buy, we need
to begin to examine the real motives behind why they buy. Although
shopping for goods and services is a relatively new behavior for our
species, the ancient brain circuits that guide us to select the right
nutritional options and resources remain intact. In essence, the basic strategies for foraging on the plains of the Serengeti are much
like those used today at Wal-Mart. When people choose only *their*
brand of cereal, for instance, it is not unlike picking familiar roots,
fruits, tubers, nuts, grains, and seeds while foraging. These are the
safe choices, proven to avoid pain and predict pleasure.

Though it may seem ironic that anxiety and fear are the primary
motivators of our pursuit of well-being, the evolutionary process is
largely driven by harm avoidance. Back in the Pleistocene, choosing
unusual and potentially poisonous fruits or plants meant possible
sickness or, in the worst case, death. Even if the stakes aren't as high
today, the behavior remains. We don't like to stray from the safety
of our daily routine. The trusted, proven products we choose and
our loyalty to those brands are in part modern day artifacts of our
Pleistocene past.

EVOLVED PSYCHOLOGY

Like brand new automobiles, humans come with a built-in set of
stock features that are standard from the factory, traits and characteristics with which we are all born. All humans have what evolutionary psychologists call *evolved psychological mechanisms*—inborn

behavioral capacities that drive automatic, unconscious decisions. These cognitive mechanisms, such as *reciprocal altruism, rituals, territoriality, collective decision making, coalition formation, predator avoidance, food selection, mate choice criteria,* and *intrasexual competition,* play primary roles in a vast array of our enduring behaviors. These evolved psychological mechanisms often generate immediate behavioral responses that occur without thinking, based upon a narrow slice of information, much as catching a glimpse of a snake will make your body jump before your head even has time to consciously process what just happened.

For decades much of the social sciences have subscribed primarily to a tabula rasa view of human behavior. That is, the mind is born as a blank slate, without any rules for processing data, whose structure is formed by experience, through parenting, socialization, culture, etc. Marketers have followed suit in their approach, focusing their attention almost exclusively on cultural and marketplace factors, putting their eggs in the nurture basket while virtually ignoring the natural influences and the biology with which we are born. Advertisers predominantly obsess and become distracted by the hottest new trends in social media, technology, fashion, music, entertainment, and by what is currently selling in the market, paying little-to-no attention to the deeper, enduring truths of our basic human wants, needs, and desires. But as Tim Mahoney, executive vice president and chief product and marketing officer at Volkswagen of America, points out, "As marketers we sometimes get preoccupied with new shiny things. That can be dangerous. Above all, marketing is about tapping into human insight."[7]

There is so much more to our behavior than culture alone can explain. As Allen D. MacNeill, a senior lecturer in biology at Cornell University, puts it, "Contrary to the assertions of many social scientists, human behavior is not infinitely malleable nor explainable in purely cultural terms."[8] In fact, more recent discoveries in neuroscience, cognitive science, and evolutionary biology do not support a blank slate point of view. It now appears that virtually all behavior has both innate and learned components. According to Harvard evolutionary psychologist Steven Pinker, author of *The Blank Slate: The*

Modern Denial of Human Nature, "the newest research is showing that many properties of the brain are genetically organized, and don't depend on information coming in from the senses." Pinker adds, "Behavior may vary across cultures, but the design of the mental programs that generate it need not vary. Intelligent behavior is learned successfully because we have innate systems that do the learning."[9]

HUMAN AUTOMATICITY

In many ways treating people as otherworldly, separate from and unrelated to other animal species, has impeded our discovering a more in-depth, empirical understanding of our own behavior. Ethology, the study of animal behavioral patterns in natural environments, has offered revelatory insights into human behavior because it makes no such assumptions. Though marketers do not need to become zoologists in order to understand human behavior, we find that by observing natural patterns in other animals we can begin to learn key insights into our own evolution. Charles Darwin's theory of natural selection, for example, was largely inspired by the variety and change in the dogs he observed in childhood and the finches he encountered on his trip to the Galapagos Islands.

The renowned psychologist and expert on the science of influence Robert Cialdini introduced marketers to the unconscious catalysts of consumer behavior in his seminal book *Influence: The Psychology of Persuasion.* By first drawing a comparison to what ethologists refer to as "fixed action patterns"—automatic, preprogrammed behavioral responses in animals to certain stimuli—he was able to show how humans often work from similar fixed patterns. In Cialdini's example, he writes of an experiment in which a mother turkey hen, who typically exhibits a tendency to huddle, warm, and care for *any* nearby baby chick when she hears its cheep-cheep chirping sounds, is thrown into confusion when the protection trigger is exploited. To study this phenomenon, scientists equipped an inanimate stuffed polecat, the turkey's natural enemy, with the electronically recorded sounds of a chirping turkey chick. In Jekyll-and-Hyde fashion, the mother would huddle and tend to the polecat when the cheep-cheep sounds were emitted, but when the sounds were turned off she would violently attack the stuffed animal. The thin slice of information provided by the sign stimulus of the chirping sound, the essential feature needed to trigger the response, was enough to override all other sensory input, making the turkey literally blind to its own enemy.

The question remains: If an animal can be preprogrammed to react to a specific environmental feature, can humans be preprogrammed in a similar fashion? For instance, is it possible that humans respond to certain essential features in marketing? And can we reject an advertisement that violates these rules or accept one that recognizes and leverages them? Are there unconscious triggers that both marketers and consumers are unaware of? And if so, what are they and how can they be recognized and utilized to create stronger bonds with brands? Can we begin to recognize the presence of evolved psychological mechanisms in our marketing programs, such as the coalition formation and territoriality of brand clubs and loyalty programs, or the predator avoidance phenomenon of angry bloggers who warn their digital tribes of the perilous deception of unscrupulous marketers?

As it turns out, humans have automaticity, too, derived from both nurture and nature: that is, involuntary innate tendencies and learned social norms in response to environmental stimuli that occur without the awareness and effort of consciousness. As our lives become busier and more complex, we are more likely to blindly obey these stereotypical rules of thumb that make our decisions for us. A process that happens all the time, it will happen more often in an increasingly complex environment.

For example, the power of market leadership and #1 brand status is largely explained by the prevailing human truth of our herd mentality—*when in doubt do what everyone else is doing,* or what Cialdini calls "social proof," the tendency to follow the lead of others. This proclivity has been reenforced over thousands of years of evolution within hunter-gatherer societies, among groups of people whose opinions mattered to each other's survival. The reason Toyota Camry continues to be the best-selling passenger car in America is largely due to the fact that so many owners have demonstrated their commitment, a trust that persists even despite recent safety concerns and product recalls for the brand.[10]

Another such mental heuristic is the social norm *expensive equals good*. Much like the turkey hen's belief that a cheep-cheep sound is a signal to protect, humans will believe that when you want to get the best, you should get the most expensive. Not surprisingly, this thought process, if we are not careful, can result in cozying up to a polecat. We think we are getting one thing when really we are getting another, but experience has taught us that "you get what you pay for," and so we are seduced by the cheep-cheep of a not-so-cheap product. This heuristic can make us pay as much as 85 percent more for a brand-name drug than for the generic, even though the FDA requires generic drugs to have the exact same quality and performance.[11]

Stella Artois leveraged this heuristic to great ends, counterintuitively highlighting its higher price point as an advantage, positioning the otherwise run-of-the-mill beer in Belgium as a premium import in the US. The brand grew tremendously in America while touting the tagline developed by Lowe and Partners Advertising, "Perfection has its price."[12] Not a bad thing for consumers or for Stella, since "average" by Belgian standards is in fact quite premium for American tastes. But this generalization also makes us pay more for a bottle of wine from a premium winemaker even though it sells virtually the same wine under a second label for much less. It makes us feel sophisticated about our more expensive choice to opt for the high-end Vera Wang gown as opposed to simply feeling smart for buying the more approachable and casual Simply Vera counterpart available at Kohl's retail stores. Whether it's a handbag or a pair of shoes or even a box of cereal, we feel better about our decision because we pay a higher price. Conversely, if you are wearing a fake Rolex watch, it doesn't really feel as good to you because you know you paid only $50, not $5,000. Your awareness counts. Our views of the world and brands are based on beliefs often informed by these cognitive shortcuts.

These mental shortcuts were designed to help us navigate a complex and often precarious world where we constantly needed to make decisions without taxing our conscious mind. But there are instances when following the convention or the herd can backfire, like the turkey that cuddles her enemy or the consumer who selects the wrong brand.

RECIPROCAL ALTRUISM

Perhaps one of the most potent human-compliance triggers is reciprocation, *to repay in kind whenever possible for what another person has done or provided for us.*[13] Charles Darwin believed that reciprocity was the foundation of moral behavior in humans. From social grooming in primates ("I'll scratch your back if you scratch mine"), to religious doctrine ("Do unto others as you would have others do unto you"),[14] when we are given something or something is done for us, we feel naturally compelled to return the favor. The origins for this altruism lie deep in our evolutionary history. Infants as young as 18 months old display altruistic behavior, and our closest living relatives, the chimpanzees, also show evidence of rudimentary helping behavior. According to German researchers in a study reported in the journal *Science*, altruism may have evolved about 6 million years ago among a common ancestor of humans and chimpanzees.[15]

Reciprocal altruism can also drive market economies, like the massive uptick in sales due to holiday gift-giving, which is largely a function of this genetic predisposition. Marketers have also been exploiting this trigger seemingly forever in the guise of the free sample or the trial offer. By giving you that small tube of toothpaste, there is a small part of us that feels obligated to consider that flashy new whitening formulation. When the nice woman at the grocery store offers us a free sample of cheese, we feel guilty eating and running, and sometimes relieve that anxiety by finding our way over to the cheese section to comply with the suggestion. Kapil Bawa of Baruch College and Robert Shoemaker of New York University have reported empirical findings that suggest that, "unlike other consumer promotions such as coupons, free samples can produce measurable long-term effects on sales."[16] To illustrate how pervasive and natural this tendency is, a university professor sent Christmas cards to a group of complete strangers, and holiday cards came pouring back to him even though he had never known or met these people.[17]

Throughout evolution, people bond with or reject people, not companies. Based on their past interactions with the representatives of the goods and services they wish to obtain, they will reward the good and punish the bad. It is this human truth that drives the success of customer service standouts like Nordstrom and Ritz-Carlton. Whether company representatives are nice to customers or whether they treat them poorly, people will automatically repay them in kind as a form of today's checks and balances in free market economies.

While evolutionary biologists refer to this tendency as reciprocal altruism,[18] cultural anthropologists call it the web of indebtedness. Either way, this unique adaptive mechanism binds individuals into efficient collective units with a division of labor, allowing for diverse, mutual exchanges of goods and services.[19] In all foraging societies, sharing was a universal characteristic that regulated access to things like food, material goods, and land. These reciprocal exchanges among people are the hallmarks of all human civilization and the antecedents to the trade and commerce of the industrial age enjoyed today.[20]

These mechanisms can also guide brand and product choices. For example, the green or eco-friendly movement can be largely explained by a similar evolved tendency that evolutionary psychologists call competitive altruism. This predisposition for cooperative, procommunity behaviors such as philanthropy, buying a Prius, or installing fuel-efficient light bulbs confers the benefits of good reputations among our social peers. Studies have shown these altruistic individuals are more likely to achieve higher status, especially those who display their altruism publicly.[21]

Instead of focusing on ephemeral cultural expressions and product category trends, i.e., consumer behavior, we need to first step back and understand these human universals. What are the enduring tendencies of all human life and not just the lifecycles of our products and marketplace categories? How do these tendencies cross cultures and span the history of our species? And how do they direct choice today? How can we use that understanding to best connect with these aged instincts and evolved minds to form powerful brands?

Brands that own claims to fundamental human truths can experience immeasurable growth and market share dominance. AT&T in the 1980s, despite its monopoly and stranglehold on the telecommunications industry, fondly found its way into the hearts of Americans through a campaign that reminded people to "Reach out and touch someone." This long-standing effort branded the behemoth by not just connecting our phone calls but plugging into our inherently social nature and deep-rooted need for human connection. And more recently, in 2010 *Adweek* declared "Get a Mac" (also known as "Mac versus PC") to be the best advertising campaign of the first decade of the new century.[22] This long-running series of 66 television spots helped make Apple the world's most valuable brand by 2012.[23] Apple, once a niche player for creative types, established its core via the territoriality and coalition formation of different thinkers and status quo rejecters, creating an exclusive community of independent-minded people who prided themselves on this distinction. The brand grew to be mainstream by appealing to the universal human need for social status, by personifying Apple face-to-face with the competition. Who would you rather hang out with, the unflappably cool Mac hipster or the bumbling, boring PC dolt? "Get a Mac" positioned the brand not just as a better product with its endearing yet competitive product proof points but also as an ever-expanding cooler club of people.

ONE BRAIN, MANY MINDS

Two of the founders of the field of evolutionary psychology, Leda Cosmides and John Tooby from the University of California, Santa Barbara, describe the rapidly growing field of evolutionary psychology as "based on the recognition that the human brain consists of a large collection of functionally specialized computational devices that evolved to solve the adaptive problems regularly encountered by our hunter-gatherer ancestors. Because humans share a universal evolved architecture, all ordinary individuals reliably develop a distinctively human set of preferences, motives . . . and specialized interpretation systems—programs that operate beneath the surface of expressed cultural variability, and whose designs constitute a precise definition of human nature."[24] Evolutionary psychologist Robert Kurzban explained to me in a 2011 interview that the human mind is a lot like a smartphone preloaded with many discrete apps with narrow specific functions that run simultaneously, often without our awareness and at times in conflict with each other. These mental apps are designed to drive us to do things like seek food, strive for status, stay fit, avoid predators, be honest, or trick people.[25]

To ignore these universal mental programs is to overlook some of the most fundamental ways to understand and change behavior. We all share a universal biology or "evolved architecture," in part because we all share common ancestry. As the anthropologist Curtis Marean indicates, "The genetic record shows us that we are all descended from a small population of approximately 600 breeding individuals." While there may be disagreement about when and how many, it does seem that everyone on earth today is descended from a small original population in Africa.[26] It may sound trite, but it's true: We are all one. The more you go back in time, the closer the relationship gets. So if we really want to accurately chart the demographics of our target audience in the United States, perhaps we should net together the subcategories of Caucasian, Hispanic, Asian, and Other into one larger all-inclusive grand net labeled "African Americans," because everyone in the world originally came out of Africa. There really is only one race: the human race.

EVOLVED PRODUCT PREFERENCES

Have you ever wondered why we really love and derive so much pleasure from eating food? Though food is perhaps one of the most important resources in sustaining life, so is oxygen, and yet we don't love or crave air. We value food not just because it's important but also because for most of our species' history it has been very difficult to obtain. Air on the other hand is abundant and everywhere.[27] Those circumstances form the basis of our emotional desires. We want that which is both important and that which is scarce, which explains why the essence of every good brand strategy is importance plus uniqueness—or, stated another way, motivation plus differentiation.

Driven by evolutionary need, we are influenced by the things we want and the preferences we inherit. For example, in our history, humans who were highly motivated by their emotional desire for obtaining food were conferred an advantage over those who were less driven to endure the expenditures needed to obtain this critical resource. These individuals were most likely to survive and pass on their culinary love affair to their children, a trend that was reinforced generation after generation. It's no surprise that today we still think of "needing" food when more often than not we really just "want" to eat.

In 2010, hamburger giant McDonald's generated more than $32 billion in US sales.[28] The tremendous success of the fast-food industry is not solely based on the marketing prowess of heavyweight advertisers like McDonald's Corp. Much of the food offered at these restaurants is based on our inherited preferences developed over evolution's timeline. As David Buss, one of the founders of the field of evolutionary psychology, says, "We have not evolved any genes for McDonald's, but the foods we eat there reveal the ancestral strategies for survival we carry with us today."[29]

These taste preferences are based in foods high in fat, sugar, and salt, because in most of our evolutionary past these were essential nutrients to our survival. Early humans' daily activities consisted of procuring food and water, interacting socially, escaping from predators, and maintaining shelter and clothing, all of which required significant expenditures of energy. These everyday toils involved navigating miles of arduous and often challenging terrain, requiring sugar and fat to meet these physical and mental demands. Humans' high metabolic requirements for these high-energy foods were a result of not just intense physical demands but also intense cognitive requirements. That's because compared to other species, primates, especially humans, have more highly developed nervous systems that require glucose, a type of sugar. Our cognitive abilities may be more advanced but they also demand more sustenance. Weighing only about 3 pounds, our brains constitute a mere 2 percent of our weight but use about 20 percent of the body's energy.[30] This is why so much of our behavior is done without consciously thinking. Our minds are lazy out of necessity and seek to make shortcuts in an effort to save energy.

Similarly, our desire for salt is also explained by our ancestors' requirements. Sodium or salt has always been an essential ingredient to our cellular health, especially for muscle cells and the cells of the nervous system, but was incredibly scarce in Pleistocene environments, where rainfall tended to leach it from the soil and rocks, washing it away into the salty ocean. Since plants do not take up sodium from the soil, it was more adaptive for humans to eat animals, which is why our desire for meat and our craving for salt were passed down from our hunter-gatherer ancestors.[31]

Individuals who were highly motivated to seek out sugars, fats, and salt were more likely to survive and pass on these same taste preferences to their children. Thousands of generations later, we crave sweet, fatty, and salty foods even though they are no longer scarce or as important to our modern diets, and in many ways, are counterproductive, causing diseases like diabetes and heart disease. Nonetheless, we are still so steeped in our hunter-gatherer mindset that we share these taste preferences, even when these junk food sensibilities spell trouble. An adaptive function has become potentially life threatening, but our instincts continue to take precedence over our rationalizations.

We see this in marketing success stories all the time, although it is often used to unfortunate results. McDonald's savvy but controversial "Supersize me" campaign was a prime example of how to use human instinct to increase market value. This sales tactic was based on an evolved unconscious decision rule that one should consume fat, sugar, and salt *wherever and whenever* possible. This strategy is especially adaptive in an environment with limited and competitive access to resources. As much as reason tells us that these resources aren't scarce, our instincts remind us that if we don't have them, we risk starvation of vital nutrients, harkening back to a time when we were forced to cover almost 12 miles a day in search of food.[32] Today, pulling up to a fast-food drive-through in the convenience of your automobile with a few bucks in your pocket is a relatively effortless endeavor, but though our lives have changed, our taste preferences have not. The brain circuits that were elegantly designed to solve the problems our ancestors faced have backfired on modern man.

Our penchant for overindulgence is not just limited to fast-food restaurants. The best-known slogan for Lay's potato chips, "Betcha can't eat just one," helped elevate the brand to international sales success. Lay's snacks are deliciously high in fat and salt, and the insightful slogan led a supersized sales tactic, not because it was based on consumer insight, but because it was based on one of the oldest truths of humanity. When your target audience is *all* humans who are *all* highly motivated, you have the foundation for an extremely pervasive and profitable business model or ad slogan.

Suppressing our biological drives and overcoming innately programmed behaviors, while possible, is much easier said than done. Menu calorie labeling is rapidly becoming the law of the land, but studies have shown that simply providing caloric information is not enough to reduce consumption. A Washington state study tracked food purchases at a fast-food chain for a year after it began posting calorie counts on menus, and it concluded that sales were unaffected by labeling. In New York City, the first major city to mandate the posting of fast-food calories, there are conflicting research results. When customers were asked if they believed the labeling influenced their decisions, their self-reported responses showed a dramatic effect; an overwhelming 88 percent majority said they purchased fewer calories as a result. But when actual behavior was measured by examining purchase receipts before and after calorie labeling, there was no difference. Our guilty indulgences transcend our wishful reporting.[33]

Advertisers can choose to better understand these triggers and customers can choose to recognize and resist them, although evolution in these instances has stacked the deck in the marketers' favor. If you find yourself thinking about stopping for a 7-Eleven Super Big

Gulp or ordering a Burger King Triple Whopper with Cheese, pause for a moment so that you can consciously contemplate the power of marketing tactics driven not just by thirst or hunger but by that little biology gizmo inside your head that commands your behavior. Likewise, only through conscious awareness can marketers understand the powerful and instinctual nature of these deeper drives and their very real impact on market economies.

SOCIAL BRAINS AND STATUS-CONSCIOUS MINDS

To understand the human brain is to understand that we are profoundly social creatures. Our biology has driven us to commingle, and those interactions have in turn molded our biology toward even greater social strivings. The human brain evolved not just in reaction to the physical environment, but perhaps even more importantly in reaction to the social environments in which humans lived. As neuropsychiatrist Louann Brizendine states, "Our brains have been shaped by hundreds and thousands of years living in status conscious hierarchical groups."[34]

Humans are essentially pack animals who have lived, and continue to live, in relatively small groups of people. These groups were and remain today *dominance hierarchies* consisting of social systems that have a pecking order of relationships based on rankings and mutually beneficial social interactions. Yet in order to prosper, we walk the delicate balance between being both altruistic and selfish, cooperative and conflicted. We are constantly seeking to assert our self-interest while remaining firmly within the good graces of the tribe.

Human nature is therefore inherently polarized and paradoxical. We are violent and aggressive yet also empathetic and moral creatures. We are hardwired both to care for others and to pursue self-interest. The hierarchies in which we've always lived have collectively endeavored toward the common good, in part because what was good for the group was often good for the individual as well as one's kin. As much as the tribe was important, its main function was to ensure the survival of each individual member. We are kind to others because it serves us and ours well.

Today we work much the same way within our modern tribes. You may recognize these same tendencies in office politics. We all share the common lofty mission of corporate success to improve sales and markets and espouse the desire to treat each other with reciprocal altruism, but the hidden plot and the real goal is often one of individualistic competition and self-advancement. These devices are not unlike the evolved psychological mechanism of intrasexual competitions among men who undermine their pals for the prize of a promotion or a beautiful woman and perhaps a handsome son, or women who contrive their way into the protective hands of a high status male who will care for her and her children. Whether we know or acknowledge it, our noblest inclinations often arise from the insidious ploys of our DNA.

The daily dramas of human endeavors are the story within the story. The real purpose of the tale is to survive, flourish, protect one's kin, and eventually proliferate our genes successfully into the next generation. To this end, we push and pull our way up and down the hierarchy, maneuvering to maintain, challenge, and lift our status through both subtle and overtly aggressive competition in which some members become submissive to higher status individuals.

Status is so important because it enables greater access to physical resources like food, shelter, material goods, clothing, and mates. Though hunter-gatherer societies seemed egalitarian in the way they distributed goods and resources, they were actually quite status conscious—although in their times, the currency was not a market share or a dollar bill, but rather the access to meat.

One of the benefits bestowed on the best hunters was having the most wives. These wives shared in the high profile fortunes of their hunter counterparts with reassuringly plentiful access to meat.[35] In 2009, researchers from the Max Planck Institute for Evolutionary Anthropology in Leipzig, Germany, reported that wild female chimpanzees were more likely to have sex with males that regularly gave them meat. "These results strongly suggest that wild chimpanzees exchange meat for sex, and do so on a long-term basis," they wrote in an article that appeared in the journal *PLoS ONE*, shedding light on the time-honored tradition of the dinner date.[36]

Beyond the sexual, physical, and nutritional benefits, high status individuals also enjoy the emotional payoffs that come with the territory. It feels good to be important and recognized by others as having higher status. As Nobel laureate economist John Harsanyi says, "apart from economic payoffs, social status seems to be the most important incentive and motivating force of social behavior."[37]

Experimenters Robert Deaner, Amit Khera, and Michael Platt, at Duke University's department of neurobiology, demonstrated this need for status through a study involving other primates such as macaque monkeys. These primates actually paid currency by sacrificing the fruit juice they love for a chance to look at pictures of high status individuals in their groups. Access to information about high status members is important because it's necessary for social maneuverings that may impact one's own status. As a result, we, like the macaques, have evolved a feel-good response to obtaining such information.[38]

This helps explain our own deep-seated preoccupation with celebrities, television shows like *Extra* and *TMZ,* and print publications like *People Magazine* and the notoriously popular tabloids. We love paying attention to high status individuals because it confers an evolutionary advantage. We lunch with important clients and movers and shakers because we want to share in their secrets as well as their company, much as we carefully choose the right spokesperson or brand ambassador so that our target can share in the social currency of their equity. Whether it's the person on the fast track in the field of business or the field of play, we buy Air Jordan Melo sneakers or stay at Trump Tower because there is a part of us that wants to know what it's like to be a Michael Jordan or a Carmelo Anthony or a Donald Trump.

This deep-seated motive also explains the allure of being in the know. Tried and true marketing strategies offer this privilege through such tactics as first-to-know loyalty programs for the inner circle of valued customers. It also drives the viral buzz of the mainstream as the asymmetry between insiders and outsiders pursues balance when those in the know seek to share and those left out seek to know. Campaigns that leverage and facilitate this natural feel-good response and the behavioral inclination derived from this exchange of information can efficiently spread brand messages while satisfying their customers' needs for information in the form of social currency.

REJECTION REALLY HURTS

Our preeminent need to be social goes back to our deepest evolutionary need to survive and replicate. Back in the Pleistocene epoch, if you became alienated from the group, you risked losing the safety, protection, shelter, food, and sex that living in the group ensured. Rejection and subsequent ejection from the tribe would be akin to a death sentence from lack of these resources. In other words, if you got kicked out of the group, you would likely die and your genes would be effectively weeded out of the gene pool. Our goal to be social is rooted in our genes' goals to survive. Our values are our genes' values. To truly understand the importance of rejection to humanity is to understand the play within the play of our daily dramas.

Just as status seeking is guided by the pursuit of positive emotions, the avoidance of rejection is driven by the fear of painful physical feelings. In 2009 UCLA psychologists discovered that a gene linked with physical pain sensitivity is also associated with social pain sensitivity. They demonstrated that the mu-opioid receptor gene, which regulates the most potent pain relievers in the human body (mu-opioids), is also involved in socially painful experiences, according to the study's co-author Naomi Eisenberger, professor of psychology and director of UCLA's Social and Affective Neuroscience Laboratory.

Eisenberger and her colleagues conducted an experiment using functional magnetic resonance imaging (fMRI) to examine subjects' brain activity during an interactive game of virtual ball toss. Participants believed that they were playing a game in which they would virtually (over the Internet) toss and catch a ball back and forth with two other participants, who were purportedly also in fMRI scanners at other locations. In reality, the subjects played against a computer with predetermined outcomes. Initially the subjects were included in the game, but later they were excluded as the two virtual participants stopped throwing the ball to them.

The researchers found that when participants believed they were being snubbed by their virtual playmates, the dorsal anterior cingulate cortex and anterior insula, areas of the brain that are often associated with physical pain, were activated, and individuals with a specific variation of the mu-opioid receptor gene showed greater activity in these regions. As Baldwin Way, the lead author on the research paper puts it, "The feeling of being given the cold shoulder by a romantic interest or not being picked for a schoolyard game of basketball may arise from the same circuits that are quieted by morphine."[39] These findings support the common belief that rejection "hurts."

The overlap of social pain and physical pain makes sense. "Social connection is linked to survival," Eisenberger indicates, and thus "feeling physical pain by not having social connections may be an adaptive way to keep them. Over the course of evolution, the social attachment system, which ensures social connection, may have actually borrowed some of the mechanisms of the pain system to maintain social connections."[40] In a follow-up study, Eisenberger and her team found that taking Tylenol reduced neural sensitivity to the pain of rejection.[41] If you get stood up on a date or haven't been invited to a party, try taking Tylenol instead of drowning your sorrows in Budweiser or a pint of Ben & Jerry's.

Brands are not just products; they are the means to acceptance in social groups, whether their power is in high-end brands like Mercedes that provide entry into the elite, or low-priced options like Target and Ikea that uplift the populace with a sense of style and cachet typically afforded to the more privileged. This underscores the importance of building brands from the core, nurturing the religious-like zeal of hard-core Sony PlayStation gamers, Ducati motorcycle loyalists, or Grey Goose aficionados, whose dedication to their brand is not only driven by their deep-seated need for acceptance by aspirational groups but also the avoidance of real physical pain.

MONKEY SEE, MONKEY IMAGINE

One of the most important neuroscience discoveries in the past two decades has been that of mirror neurons. In the early 1990s, Italian neurophysiologist Giacomo Rizzolatti and his team of graduate students at the University of Parma, Italy, were investigating the motor system of the brain, the part of the central nervous system involved in movement, when they came upon a surprising find.[42]

To better understand the human brain, they were studying the electrical activity of the motor neurons of a macaque monkey. Using needle-thin electrodes, the researchers were researching the activity of the premotor cortex, the part of the brain involved in the planning and initiation of movement. As expected, these motor neurons would fire when the monkey moved an arm to grab an object.

One hot summer day something completely unexpected happened. The team left for lunch and they forgot to turn off the equipment, leaving the monkey hooked up while they were gone. When they returned, one of the graduate students working with Rizzolatti began licking an ice cream cone he had brought back, while the monkey watched longingly. To the surprise of the scientists, every time the researcher licked his ice cream, the electrodes signaled a spike in activity of the motor neurons of the premotor cortex of the macaque, despite the fact that the monkey remained motionless. It was "monkey see, monkey do" but, instead of physically doing the action, the macaque was imitating the same activity in its own mind by firing the same motor neurons and imagining eating the ice cream cone.

Rizzolatti's team serendipitously discovered that day that empathy, that is, putting yourself in someone else's shoes, is mediated by neurons in the brain's motor system. These "mirror neurons," as Rizzolatti named them, give humans the capacity for shared experiences by enabling us to project ourselves into the minds, feelings, and actions of others. He explained, "We are exquisitely social creatures. Our survival depends on understanding the actions, intentions, and emotions of others. Mirror neurons allow us to grasp the minds of others not through conceptual reasoning but through direct simulation. By feeling, not by thinking."[43]

Mirror neurons help us form the basis for what behavioral scientists refer to as "theory of mind." This is the ability to understand the motives, intentions, and actions of others in an effort to develop theories about what they will do and why they will do it. They let us be both altruistic and competitive, not only giving us empathy to feel others' pain, but also an understanding of their truer, and sometimes more deceptive, intentions. They make us tear up with sorrow for the misfortunes of our comrade or see through the thinly veiled kowtowing of our enemies. Mirror neurons are the key to building empathy and understanding, which comes from observing and interacting with individuals whether via the media or firsthand.

RITUALS, COALITIONS, AND REALITY

Mirror neurons give humans not only the capacity for shared experiences and better understanding but also the ability to learn through imitation, enabling the cultural transmission of ideas and experiences. This process automatically helps us pass along valuable information and abilities to others by facilitating the infectious mimicry of brand rituals, fads, and trends that marketers hope to spread throughout culture. Because we are hardwired to mimic these actions, these repeated reflexes become learned behaviors. Playing the game Punch Buggy or Slug Bug by lightheartedly jabbing your friend every time you see a Volkswagen Beetle, or squeezing a lime into the neck of a Corona bottle, or eating the middle of an Oreo cookie first are all examples of hardwired brand rituals of imitation lubricated by the contagious reflexes of our mirror neurons.[44]

These neurons help explain the meteoric growth of reality television, which now comprises more than half of the network programming in the United States and nearly three-quarters in the world market according to Nielsen Media Research.[45] That's because the more real the characters appear and the less contrived the plot, the more we actually feel those same experiences and those same feelings.

Survivor leveraged human insights on many primal levels to become one of the most watched, influential, and enduring reality shows, rating in the top 10 during its first eleven seasons in America.

Through real people and unscripted storylines, *Survivor* reconnects modern, sedentary TV audiences to their nomadic tribal past, transporting the viewer via the automatic reflexes of our mirror neurons to relive the dramas of our ancient competitive and cooperative tribal rituals. Ordinary people like us are left in remote places to create their own primitive dominance hierarchies through the evolved psychological mechanisms of coalition formation, territoriality, and collective decision making.

Burger King capitalized on this human insight to prove to America just how much people loved the Whopper when it introduced the "Whopper sacrifice": Delete ten friends on Facebook and receive a free Whopper. Two hundred thousand friends were sacrificed in just over a week and 35 million free media impressions challenged the concept of Facebook, which ultimately forced Burger King to take it down in a short-lived but convincing demonstration of the attention-getting allure of social rejection.[46]

The power of mirror neurons has also captivated the big screen with the original reality horror movies *Blair Witch Project* and *Paranormal Activity*. Ironically, these movies increased both viewer engagement and revenue while decreasing production costs. The choice of using hand-held, grainy black-and-white video and stationary surveillance cameras made these movies more believable and more real, as if it was truly happening to us. Launched in the summer of 1999, the *Blair Witch* social media campaign was one of the first viral Internet campaigns. Forbes.com recently rated this campaign as the best social media effort of all time. Web users speculated whether or not the story of young documentary makers lost in the woods was really true. Fake newspaper postings and police photos of their missing car had people wondering and waiting for more, pulling them into the digital media frenzy as if it were an unfolding live news story.[47]

Despite a pittance of investments to make these motion pictures, they had a huge return on investment. *The Blair Witch Project* made it into the *Guinness Book of World Records* for "Top Budget: Box Office Ratio" (for a mainstream feature film), costing a mere $22,000 to make and generating $240.5 million, a ratio of a single dollar spent for every $10,931 made. *Paranormal Activity* was shot for a reported $15,000, yet has raked in $194 million worldwide with limited marketing.

Paranormal Activity's success was driven largely by online buzz and word of mouth. "On the social networking sites, everybody's talking about how freaking scary this movie is," said Paul Dergarabedian, box office analyst for Hollywood.com. He added, "This does not happen every day. This is literally capturing lightning in a bottle." As Paramount vice chairman Rob Moore said, "This movie doesn't lend itself to a big, giant marketing campaign. This movie is an old-fashioned word-of-mouth movie." When you leverage human truths as well as these movies did, humans do the marketing for you.[48]

Similarly, our team at Deutsch LA reintroduced Americans to the game of Punch Bug with a twist and renamed it Punch Dub with a new set of rules. That is, if you see any V-dub, not just the Beetle, give someone you know a playful punch. Within months after launching the campaign, over a third of the adult population reported having played the game.[49] If brand equity is essentially positive memories, triggering these recollections unleashes its power. By dusting off and reigniting a beloved brand ritual, we were able to fondly make the brand top of mind, culturally relevant, and have people do the marketing for us. In 2010, Sands Research, a leading neuromarketing firm, using electroencephalography (EEG) recordings and eye-tracking data gathered from study participants, found our Super Bowl commercial to be the most effective of all the ads tested from Super Bowl XLIV using its proprietary Neuro Engagement Factor (NEF)™. As Dr. Stephen Sands, chairman and chief science officer at Sands Research stated, "Volkswagen's 'Punch Dub' was our top scorer this year with a commercial that engaged viewers in virtually all of the frames. The company turned viewers into 'Volkswagen detectors' by having them look for and anticipate the cars—VW really maximized their entire 30 seconds."[50]

TWENTY-FIRST-CENTURY TRIBES

Part of the popularity of the reality boom is the extent to which people identify and bond with similar others. The tribal groups in which we evolved consisted of individuals who were a lot like ourselves and many of whom were kin. When we see people like us on television programs or in advertising, for instance, we relate more closely to the ebb and flow of their daily dramas. We share more in the tension of their conflicts and rewards of their successes. Today we still long for the physical connection to others that we so long enjoyed in close-knit hunter-gatherer societies. Today's brands and new media provide the means to satisfy some of these sensibilities, even if they are as much a part of our imagination as they are part of our real life.

So strong is our need for social attachment that it builds the structure of our societies and markets. This innately social tendency extends out, moving from our instincts to our families to our tribes, city-states, nation-states, and beyond. It creates the relationships between friends and communities. It is the mortar between less intimate groups like the religion we practice, the political party we support, the digital communities we visit, and the brands that we buy. We are all seeking identity and identification with social groups, which is why, especially in technology, marketing a sense of community has become the brand imperative. We are not PC users, we are part of the Dell community; we are not just players of PlayStation or Xbox, we are a part of those gaming communities.

But how can a faceless corporation create a common connection with people when human bonds are rooted in identifying with a face and a real person? Marketers have learned to bridge this chasm by focusing their efforts on the creation of brands that engender identity meaning and tribal attachment. Our purchase affiliations with strong iconic brands like Apple, Harley-Davidson, Target, and Nike are not just a reflection of our interest in a product or service, but also an identification with a group of like-minded people bound by a common sense of purpose—Apple for the *creative-minded*, Harley for the *free-spirited*, Target for the *smartly hip*, and Nike for the *achievers*, to name a handful. Evolutionary psychologist Geoffrey Miller indicates that brands are modern day manifestations of our need to "display traits" and flaunt "fitness indicators" that advertise our biological potential as mates and friends.[51] We all want to be part of the winning team and the in-crowd, and brands hold the passage beyond the velvet ropes of the social clubs of today's markets and today's societies.

The Internet now enables the connection to far-flung virtual tribes way beyond the social circles of our hunter-gatherer origins. These online communities provide marketers with a robust social-science laboratory that provides an unprecedented view and measurement of marketing effectiveness. The evidence to date strongly suggests an evolution-inspired viewpoint of behavior change in market economies. We need to build on the powerful unconscious patterns of behavior throughout human history, recognizing how our minds are designed to solve problems of the past. The paradox of human behavior in the digital age is that we are changing more quickly than we could ever imagine, but we are also repeating the same predictable patterns that have dominated most of our species' existence. To say that the Internet is changing our behavior is perhaps the biggest of understatements, but despite these changes, it's ironic how remarkably similar our behavior remains in the digital realm to that of the old hunter-gatherer past.

For example, eBay is one of the first and most successful online businesses. What eBay did was provide a modern digital translation of one of the most deeply ingrained human behaviors throughout history: our need to share and exchange resources. Quite literally, eBay is a web of indebtedness, a self-monitored community that enables individual people, givers and takers, to share through "social proof," "reciprocal altruism," and "collective decision making." Vendors can rise up the ranks to a position of trusted status through mutual exchanges of satisfaction and the reciprocal exchanges of approval or disapproval of buyers and sellers in the social group.

Social media is among the hottest topics and the fastest growing media not just because of advances in digital technology, but because our brains are designed to be social. Today, Facebook is used by 901 million people[52] in 70 languages worldwide.[53] The tremendous success of Facebook is largely because it is the most direct online interpretation of the concept of *tribe*. Through virtual alliances and a series of back and forth friend requests, we can discover and create our own digital tribe. We can explore our place in

the pecking order based on those who accept or reject our friend-
ship, the thumbs-up approval of ideas and thoughts we might share,
and the positive or negative commentary in response to our posts.
Talking to someone privately by email is one thing, but wall postings
let us have public conversations with a member of our tribe, introducing a social dynamic into interpersonal interaction. The dialogue
becomes a message to the collective tribe as much as it is a communication to an individual tribesperson. The online acceptance or
rejection of a tribe's member is made powerfully simple through the
click of button.

Facebook evolves the human need to seek alliances and form
coalitions unbounded by geography or proximity. It reunites our old
tribe members and enables heretofore impractical and impossible
new associations with new groups we aspire to join. Facebook helps
those feeling the pain of alienation in the real world by connecting
them through the virtual world, allowing people to advertise their
potential as friends and mates through personalized content and user
profiles.

The growth and success of mobile apps like Twitter now enable
our affiliations to become truly nomadic. Twitter raises our deep
need to feel constant attachment to others, even when we're on the
go, while empowering our own bid to position ourselves atop the
pecking order of the dominance hierarchies that we create virtually.
Deep down we all want others to acknowledge, admire, or better
yet follow our lead. So deep is our need for status that when the
prestigious One Club, whose mission is to acknowledge excellence
in advertising, invited top digital creative types to award the best
of the digital decade from 2000 to 2010, heading the list was none
other than the infamous Crispin Porter + Bogusky's "Subservient
Chicken" for Burger King. This app enabled web users to dominate
a lowly man dressed in a chicken suit through text commands that
made the obsequious birdman do just about anything you asked.[54]
Why just order chicken when you can simply order one around? And
Foursquare, a location-based social networking site, enables users to
prove their attendance at high status happenings by checking in at
concerts, parties, and sports events so that they can display badges of

their experiential achievement in the real world to their tribe in the digital world.

We are human. And being human, we are driven by our enduring instincts and prepackaged proclivities. To narrowly define a person as a consumer is to neglect our deepest strivings. When marketers tempt someone's biology with a free sample of Häagen-Dazs, when people display their in-crowd whereabouts on Foursquare, or when some people don't just talk on their phone and instead choose to signal the proud badge of an iPhone . . . take a moment to recognize the ancient circuitry of our Pleistocene past living within all of us much like it did thousands and thousands of years ago.

3
THE BIOLOGY OF BEHAVIOR

We share the same biology, regardless of ideology.

—Sting

RECENTLY, I STOPPED AT MY LOCAL ROTISSERIE CHICKEN restaurant after a busy day at work. Just steps from my house in a beach city of greater Los Angeles; this is my idea of fast food. I pause for a moment on the sidewalk-facing side of the building to take in the brand new, imposing, and colorful promotional display painted proudly on the plate glass window. It boldly pronounces "Got Chicken?" Much to my simultaneous amusement and annoyance I think to myself, "Really? Can we be a little more original?" But despite my objections or anyone else's, these self-serving adaptations of the virulent catchphrase show little evidence of abating nearly two decades after the famous "Got milk?" campaign was created by the talented Goodby Silverstein & Partners of San Francisco. What is it about certain ad messages that they seem to take on a life of their own? The answer lies in the base of our brain and the origins of our evolution.

In his book *The Expression of the Emotions,* Charles Darwin insisted that the brain grew and evolved naturally over time by gradually adding newer systems of neurons on top of the older ones to form the collective whole of the brain. In order to understand the human brain you have to take this evolutionary perspective, appreciating that the brain is the only organ in the body that exists in evolutionary layers. Derived from Darwin, this metaphor of the brain as archaeological sites buried from old to new presents a realm that needs to be carefully excavated and deeply mined to understand the true depths of humanity.[1]

In the 1960s neuroscientist Paul MacLean, who later became chief of the Laboratory of Brain Evolution and Behavior for the National Institute of Mental Health, popularized this notion by proposing the highly influential triune brain theory, the idea that the brain is actually comprised of three distinct brains that evolved over time. These layers formed one on top of each other, and each brain has its own distinct drives and subjectivities. Nerves interconnect these three brains, which seem to operate as separate biological computers, simultaneously cooperating with or contradicting each other. These three brains form the three planes of consciousness from which we experience the world: the physical, the emotional, and the rational minds. MacLean's three-part brain theory simplifies the brain's design, but it remains a useful model for marketing applications.

THE REPTILIAN OR PHYSICAL BRAIN

The physical brain, which evolved first, is situated deep at the base of the skull, emerging from the spinal column. This part of the brain is the oldest and smallest remnant of our prehistoric past, and is often referred to as the reptilian brain because of its similarity to the brains of reptiles, which preceded mammals by roughly 200 million years.[2] The physical brain, using sensory input, helps to monitor and physically respond to the environment, ensuring self-preservation and mobilizing the body when the fight-or-flight stress response is triggered.[3]

The physical brain is the domain of our natural instincts, our deepest ancestral memories that guide fundamental life functions, including many of our automatic behaviors. These habits and life-sustaining routines—such as breathing, circulation, digestion, sleeping, waking, eating, sexual reproduction, foraging, and hoarding food— are resistant to change because they are essential for our survival and bodily maintenance. The physical brain is designed for taking action, guided by the part of the brain we know as the cerebellum, which means little brain.[4] This appears as a separate structure at the bottom of the brain below the cerebral hemispheres and is in charge of the coordination of bodily movement through sensory feedback, and the modulation of emotion.[5] Because it lacks rationality and intellect, the physical brain has no ability to learn from experience, often repeating the same automatic patterns over and over without change, and generating behaviors that are impulsive, rigid, obsessive, and ritualistic.

Since it operates mostly out of fear and anger, the physical brain drives an anxious, paranoid, and often darker temperament, sometimes resulting in aggressive and even violent behavior. These response repertoires include territoriality, deception, prejudice, social dominance, pecking order behavior, status maintenance, awe for authority, and tendency to follow precedent.[6] Though it is located at the bottom, or foundation, of the brain, and is completely unconscious, it still sits atop the motivational hierarchy, driving some of our strongest, most basic instincts and primal urges. In order to provide handles to marketers who seek to understand and tap into these powerful drives, I refer to them as the "Six S's": survival, safety, security, sustenance, sex, and status. A variation of these themes is what evolutionary biologists sometimes refer to as "the four F's": fighting, fleeing, feeding, and fucking. If you ever happen to box out your space in a crowded elevator, get a little carried away in a friendly game or sport, become uncontrollably enraged by a careless motorist, crane your neck to get a better look at a horrible car crash, or simply crave a Krispy Kreme doughnut, your body is being commandeered by the survivalist instincts of your physical, reptilian brain.

In marketing, because the physical brain drives the unconscious need for survival and sustenance, it often gives way to the unwitting obsessive and repetitive inclination to spread advertising catchphrases like "Got milk?" In the 1980s, the advertising agency Lowe and Partners discovered that the availability of food, even if it is simply a condiment, especially when coupled with a message of economic status, is able to drive a brand to widespread awareness and cultural interest. The campaign generated national attention when two British chauffeur-driven aristocrats politely shared a jar of the fancy mustard, punctuated by the phrase "Pardon me, but do you have any Grey Poupon?" and the tagline "One of life's finer pleasures." These physical drives are responsible for the endurance of other slogans, such as the tagline "Mmm . . . mmm good," which helped Campbell's become one of the world's largest food companies, and for the infectious appeal of Life cereal's famous "Mikey, he likes it!" commercials.

The physical brain also galvanizes our attention toward messages of security, which efforts such as American Express's legendary "Don't leave home without it" sentiment captured so perfectly, or Allstate Insurance's long-standing claim of safety and confidence underscored by "You're in good hands with Allstate." And anyone alive in the late '80s and early '90s will likely remember the commercial for an obscure brand that worked the infamous cry "I've fallen and I can't get up" into the everyday American vernacular. This ad featured an old lady whose survival was jeopardized as she lay helplessly injured on the floor in her own home only to be saved by the Life Alert medical alarm, an approach the brand continues to use to this day.

THE LIMBIC SYSTEM—THE EMOTIONAL BRAIN

The next neurological stratum to evolve was what MacLean called the "limbic system" or the emotional brain, which is also referred to as the paleomammalian brain. This emotional brain establishes bonds with people, tribes, groups, and brands, controls our emotions, memories, social bonding, and attachment. It includes key brain structures such as the amygdala, the hippocampus, and the hypothalamus, regulates involuntary nervous system functions that lie below consciousness, and acts as a control system that regulates homeostasis, the biological processes that maintain our life balance and stability, e.g., the regulation of our body temperature and blood pressure.

At the center of the limbic system lies the amygdala, a set of two almond-shaped structures that serve as the gateway to our emotions.

The amygdala is poised deep in the brain and acts like an alarm, which in a nanosecond can set into motion programs of action, initiating the fight-or-flight response when needed. In the face of threat or adversity, the amygdala alerts the hypothalamus, the part of the brain that regulates involuntary functions, which then commands the brainstem in the physical brain to spring into action.

The words "emotion" and "motivation" share the Latin root *movere,* meaning to move, which suggests that inherent in every emotion and every motivation exists the tendency to take action.[7] It is the amygdala that imbues experiences with emotions, associating a feeling to a thing or event. For example, touching a hot stove connects painful feelings and emotions with the learned response to steer clear of hot stoves in the future. Likewise, it is also the amygdala that alerts people when they get burned by marketers who make false promises or fall short of expectations. This emotional sting causes customers to flee from the brand or in some instances fight back on the blogosphere or in the marketplace. But that sting also can be used to the advantage of advertisers through the tried and true problem-solution format of many effective ads that provide the means to move away from the "pain" toward the pleasure of the brand's solution.

In conjunction with the adjacent hippocampus, the amygdala is responsible for learning through a process called associative memory.[8] First, the hippocampus encodes the details and facts of an experience, converting information into long-term memory, and then the amygdala tags that event with a specific emotion. As the accomplished neuroscientist Joseph LeDoux illustrates, "The hippocampus is crucial in recognizing a face as that of our cousin. But it is the amygdala that adds you don't really like her."[9] This two-part memory process in which the hippocampus gives rise to the cognitive representation and the amygdala gives rise to the emotional response seems to originate unconsciously. As LeDoux states, "These two things happen simultaneously, the amygdala memory is triggered unconsciously, you don't have to be aware of the stimulus in order for that to be triggered. Hippocampal memory is probably triggered unconsciously as well, but you become aware of the memory when it's triggered because that's what a hippocampal memory does, it creates a representation of conscious experience."[10]

This learning process demonstrates why brand or ad recall is not enough to change behavior. Marketers must not only engage the hippocampus to encode and recall the characteristics and facts about the brand and advertising message, but they also need to assign emotion in order to determine the brand's utility and worth. The implications for marketers indicate the need for not only arresting visuals but also and perhaps more importantly stimulating emotions. The limbic system assigns value, sorting events as agreeable, disagreeable, or indifferent on the basis of past patterns of memory. For instance, the hippocampus recognizes the product as Coke from its iconic shape, red-and-white color scheme, cursive font and classic logo, but it's the amygdala that tells you "I like Coke." The emotions associated with the Coke brand determine that you will in fact "enjoy Coke," thereby generating the behavior to choose that brand. This limbic system assigns value to objects, events, and experiences by attaching emotion, relating them to past memories, and in turn identifying patterns in our lives. This part of the brain is unconscious and involuntary, but at times we can gain conscious access to these emotions through feelings and physical sensations.

The emotional brain also determines what we choose to pay attention to. The more emotionally charged, the more likely your brand will stick out or break through the clutter, forcing people to notice your message. Emotional arousal occurs when our brains create vivid memories of a particular experience, establishing importance and attracting attention to environmental stimuli.[11]

If the movie *Titanic* made you cry, or you've enjoyed the joy of a reunion of family or friends, or have been moved by an old song, admired an inexplicably beautiful work of art, or simply felt the feeling of comfort in choosing a familiar brand or the excitement of trying a new one, your emotional brain has been activated deep within your central nervous system. In marketing, tapping into our limbic system results in some of the most effective and memorable ad campaigns. A study done by the UK-based Institute of Practitioners in Advertising analyzed the effectiveness of ads chosen from a large database of advertising award competition entrants and found that campaigns with primarily emotional content performed about twice as well as the approaches that focused on rational content.[12]

Emotion moves people to buy. Whether it's how a toilet tissue in the UK linked their Andrex Puppy to our universal adoration for man's best little friend, or how a brand of film captured the special, fleeting "Kodak moments" of life, or how the slogan "When you care enough to send the very best," one of the most recognized and trusted lines in advertising, made Hallmark the largest manufacturer of greeting cards—when you lead with emotion, you often lead in the marketplace.

THE NEOCORTEX—THE RATIONAL BRAIN

The most recent and outermost brain layer to develop is the neocortex or the rational brain. The neocortex is both the crown and crowning accomplishment of our brain's evolution as well as the seat of our free will and conscious awareness. It is home to our higher cognitive functions such as language, speech, writing, problem solving, and analytical and mathematical thinking. The neocortex, also called the cerebral cortex (or cortex for short), consists of the commonly recognized wrinkly outer folds that are divided into the famous left and right hemispheres. The right brain is more spatial, artistic, and abstract and the left brain is more linear, rational, and verbal. While the emotional brain assigns value, the neocortex makes rational meaning of the feelings and emotions generated by the deeper, unconscious brain structures, attempting to explain the reasons and implications of why we feel a certain way.[13]

MacLean referred to the neocortex as "the mother of invention and the father of abstract thought."[14] This area of the brain includes the prefrontal cortex, the most advanced and evolved part of our brain, which uniquely distinguishes humans from all other species. The prefrontal cortex gives us the ability to plan behavior or create new possibilities, functioning like a mental simulator of different realities by giving us the capacity to imagine and anticipate the consequences of our actions in the future. The prefrontal cortex lets us know before we need to try it that a heavier-than-air flying machine is possible or that liver-flavored ice cream is a bad idea.

It also enables our ability for conscious reasoning and comparative analytical thought, which is illustrated by the self-talk that goes on inside our heads. It is that voice that deliberates "should I or shouldn't I" as one peruses the aisles of a store. Because it lets us envision positive and negative outcomes, it gives us the ability to take voluntary action by making considered choices and guides our moral decisions, such as suppressing inappropriate physical urges. It also allows us to think twice before acting, applying the rational brakes of restraint before we lease a convertible BMW, spring for a $2,500 Gucci handbag, or polish off another tray of Godiva chocolates.

In addition, the prefrontal cortex is where the perception of self and identity is located, our conscious awareness of who we are. It is the part of the brain that recognizes the image in the mirror is actually you, and is the domain of our personality, identifying where we fit into the social hierarchy and how we express ourselves to the world around us.[15]

The rational brain might have come last in the evolution of our brain, but it is the most important part in terms of higher order thought. It makes sense and order of the world, rationally interprets things, and creates conscious subjective meaning of our feelings and unconscious responses. Though it is the crowning accomplishment, it is also less influential on many of our behaviors, and it is not always recruited or required for action.

When you are filling out a crossword puzzle, or comparing the facts on brand labels, or learning a language with Rosetta Stone, or deciding to skip the weekend trip to Vegas, you are actively engaging your neocortex or rational brain.[16] We often engage the neocortex in marketing when we provide the audience with figures and facts like comparisons with other brands. While these logical facts per se may not be the primary drivers of motivation, they do serve an important role in giving oneself permission to act on our emotions and physical urges. Rational information therefore plays a secondary, but nonetheless important role in advertising and marketing. Having said that, there are times when rational approaches like a single-minded focus on price savings can work wonders for challenger brands that don't own the emotional high ground of their established counterparts. As a strategy planner on the MCI (now Verizon) account at Euro RSCG in New York years ago, I observed firsthand how smart, rational efforts like "Five-cent Sundays" and "Friends and family," an early type of loyalty program that offered savings to frequent callers, effectively challenged and greatly undermined AT&T's monopoly. AT&T owned the comfort of being the dominant, familiar brand that facilitated social connection, but MCI laid claim to the importance of cost savings.

FEELING DRIVES BEHAVIOR

Through his important work and early hypothesis about what the triune brain might mean for human cognition and action, MacLean fundamentally changed the way we think about brain functions. Prior to his model, it had been assumed that the neocortex, the newest, rational part of the mind, dominated over the older brains in top-down fashion. But MacLean proposed that it was just the opposite. Often, the lower physical and emotional systems could hijack the higher rational brain from the bottom-up. In essence, our feeling brain serves as the primary driver of our behavior and the seat of our value judgments, while our rational mind acts as a backseat observer that more often than not goes along for the ride.[17] We don't really have free will but rather free won't. We can apply the brakes of restraints to the forces of feeling, but we also can often fall short of stopping in time.

Have you ever struggled with a decision in which part of you felt one way and another part of you felt another? Perhaps you have experienced the powerful urge to indulge in a decadent slice of the aptly named devil's food cake with sinfully rich cream filling. You were experiencing the competing conflicts of your three-part brain: the physical brain, which loves food because it knows that you can't live without it; the emotional brain, which has learned so many past pleasurable emotions and memories involving cake; and lastly, the rational brain, which has its reasons for resisting but often succumbs to the urges and feelings of the other parts of the mind. Even though the rational brain understands the facts of the choice—that too much sugar, fat, and calories are unhealthy—all that matters is that eating cake is the quickest way to feel really good. Feeling trumps logic. Two out of your three brains have overruled your rational one. Similarly, have you ever jumped to buy something that was a bit too rich for your blood—perhaps a car, a handbag, a new watch, or a pair of athletic shoes? The decision was made long before you rationalized the benefits of the exorbitant price tag.

The adage "Life is short, eat dessert first" rings true because our brains are literally wired for short-term gain. And back in the Pleistocene era, lifespan was indeed shorter, in great part due to impending everyday hardships and threats. Short-term strategies kept us out of harm's way, avoiding starvation, and ensuring our survival and the survival of our genes. We jumped from predators much as we avoid brands we don't trust. Similarly, we leap today at the opportunity to overindulge in food or engage in sexual encounters as we did in the past. Response without thinking might have saved and produced lives in our foraging past, but today it can get us into a lot of trouble, and it has. The massive credit crisis, the snack food epidemic, the burgeoning pornography industry, and rising rates of teen pregnancy are the direct results of our "feeling brains'" (physical and emotional) abilities to hijack behavior.

Today neuroscientists are coming to understand that our brains are even more complex, intertwined, and conflicted than the triune-brain theory suggests. For instance, some neuroscientists believe that the concept of a limbic system is outdated, since brain imaging technologies have demonstrated that emotions tend not to exist in any single part of the brain for very long but are rather distributed throughout the brain. We also now know a linear view of the brain's evolution as proposed by the triune brain model seems rather fanciful. In reality, the forces of evolution don't just pile layer upon unchanged layer. Natural selection both modifies what it finds as well as works with what is there.[18]

But despite these sophisticated and complex processes, the brain remains an inelegant series of ad hoc solutions heaped like ice cream scoops over millions of years of evolutionary design. This intricate patchwork is not without its flaws, yet somehow it works, and it does so unfathomably well.[19] MacLean's three-part brain theory remains a powerful organizing theme to simplify the brain's design, and is also a useful model with rich practical applications for marketers. Much as Freud's suggestion that the three competing parts of the human psyche—the id, the ego, and the superego—had a vast effect on our culture and the climate of the times, MacLean's suggestion of three competing biological layers of the brain has inspired scientists and laypeople alike, and can now help marketers, too, in better understanding how we buy.

All human experience, behavior, and brain function can be grouped into these simplified neurological buckets. On the deepest levels are the low road systems of the basal ganglia and cerebellum, the physical brain. In the middle lies the limbic or emotional system. And last is the neocortex, the high road of rational, deliberative thinking. This three-tiered approach is also a helpful metaphor and mnemonic for understanding the extent to which our behaviors are unconscious or conscious. The deeper or lower in the brain, the more unconscious the behavior.

Because our beliefs are formed largely on the basis of our past experiences, we can compartmentalize these dimensions of experience as threefold. In other words, our decisions, which are derived from our beliefs, are based upon: (1) the physical experiences of our body, (2) the emotions and feelings of our heart, and (3) the rationalizations or logic of our head. Against these three planes of consciousness, we can begin to prioritize and better develop marketing strategies that address the full range of human existence. In a nutshell, marketers need to create engaging emotionally and physically stimulating brands that also satisfy our rational concerns of resistance.

THE PHYSICAL BRAIN'S MARKETING GOLD

Since the more primitive emotions, feelings, and motivations, especially those of the physical, reptilian brain, are primary to driving action, hitting upon these primal triggers can create strong and consistent behavioral responses. This observation helps explain why some marketing ideas are more prolific and viral than others. By dissecting the drives of the physical brain, marketers can better develop ideas that spread and influence behavior change, generating repeated engagement with a brand and igniting the obsessive loyalty that every marketer wants.

In his highly influential, revolutionary book *The Selfish Gene,* famous British ethologist and evolutionary biologist Richard Dawkins coined the term "meme"—a unit of cultural information that is transmitted from mind to mind through imitation and replication in a manner analogous to the transmission of genes.[20] Memes include tunes, slogans, catchphrases, fashions, styles, and rituals that seem to spread throughout cultures as if they had a mind and intention all their own. I will demonstrate that most of the memes in our culture reflect our deepest, unconscious biological drives, or those Six S's— survival, safety, security, sustenance, sex, and status. These themes are so often at the roots of many of the most prolific meme's because they are both completely unconscious in origin and utterly important to survival.

THE POWER OF FOOD

Our brain is quite literally a "survival organ." There's no coincidence that arguably the two most pervasive marketing memes of all time piggybacked on one of our most basic survival needs: having enough to eat. Both of these memes cautioned and queried people about the scarcity of basic food staples through their simple slogans. I am referring to Wendy's "Where's the beef?" and the California Milk Processor Board's "Got milk?," two advertising taglines identical in structure and equally potent in effect.

In the 1980s the catchphrase "Where's the beef?" quickly found its way into the breadth and depth of American culture, capturing the mood of the time and the straightforward attitude of the brand. The slogan showed up everywhere from water cooler conversations to presidential debates, making the diminutive octogenarian Clara

Peller, who was featured in the ad, a national icon. Today, roughly three decades later, the classic slogan returns to television to celebrate the launch of Wendy's latest revamped hamburgers. The ubiquitous presence of that slogan and its influence in advertising and culture was perhaps surpassed only by another campaign for yet another basic food source with an uncannily similar inquiry, "Got milk?" This catchphrase began in the early 1990s and remains an active meme and international icon, becoming what few would argue is the most imitated and parodied slogan in American advertising history.

Like selfish genes whose sole purpose is replication, memes appear also to be guided by their own viral intentions, evolving organically through clever and not-so-clever variations. "Got milk?" continues to spawn countless co-created mutations as people, publicity seekers, and businesses substitute for "milk" virtually any other conceivable product, service, or concept, adapting the meme to fit their own devices. "Got milk?" and "Where's the beef?" were exemplary ads brilliantly executed in their own right, but because they were built strategically on primal pillars, they were empowered to organically spread, launching them to the top of their craft and the fore of our culture. Under the obsessive inclinations of our physical brains, these memes perpetuate effortlessly without regard for rationality. As Dawkins puts it, we humans are merely "lumbering robots" programmed in service of the replication of our selfish genes, or in this instance, our selfish memes.[21]

If you think this is all just one big coincidence, think again. If you want further proof of the power of food memes, ask, as many others have, "Why the hell do we take pictures of food and post them online?" The next time you are on Facebook, scroll down your list of posts. Chances are you have at least one photograph of a seemingly random entrée, dessert, or snack. And this phenomenon is far from limited to Facebook. One of the largest and most active Flickr photo-sharing groups is called "I Ate This," and similar trends can be found on Twitter, MySpace, Foodspotting, Shutterfly, FoodCandy, and Chowhound.[22] Displaying our food to our digital tribe comes from that nonsensical, irrational part of our brain that has nothing to do with logic and everything to do with the most basic of human instincts: the need to eat in order to survive.

As an advertising strategic planner, I have long endured the complaints of copywriters and art directors while developing advertising for restaurant accounts. The creative team often bemoans the obligatory, formulaic inclusion of the hackneyed beauty shots of food that the client demands—the steaming cheese pulls of pizza, or the exaggerated portion of delectably delicious sandwiches and grill-marked steaks. But argue as the creative team might, the marketer is right about this one. When we see food in all its glory, we take notice. The emotionally charged instincts of our cerebellums motivate us off the couch and into the local Burger King, Pizza Hut, or Taco Bell.

REPRODUCTION SELLS

We all know the power of sex. But its value extends beyond the physical attraction to potential mates, and into the consequences of those sexual encounters: the next generation. This is evidenced by our utter fascination with babies and children. And why shouldn't we be engrossed? From the standpoint of evolution, having children and perpetuating our genes is the purpose of sex. This explains why kids and babies are everywhere, from the hilarious E*trade baby commercials[23] to the computer-generated Evian babies on roller skates who break-danced and back-flipped their way to what the *Guinness Book of World Records* declared was the most viewed online ad in history.[24] And those are babies we *don't* even know. On Facebook, parental displays of people's children are even more commonplace than plates of pasta or bowls of beef. Some parents even choose a picture of their kid instead of their own profile shot. People post these pictures of their children because it arouses deep emotion, conferring status and pride in what is most important—the replication of our genes. According to the esteemed neurologist Antonio Damasio, social emotions like pride and admiration "exist as prepackaged arrangements in the biology of your brain."[25] These emotions are biological preconditions of evolutionary intelligence. In other words, we are born with them.

LEVERAGING PRIMAL TRIGGERS

The mathematics on this one is simple: When you stack primal triggers you multiply the effect. This is why, when celebrities get pregnant, they automatically jump to the top of the Internet search charts. The event of their pregnancy not only sends a message about sexual reproduction, but also speaks to our innate obsession with status. *America's Top Chef* has run on the cable network Bravo for nine seasons and counting, spawning two spinoffs (*Top Chef: Masters* and *Top Chef: Just Desserts*) with two more planned, because it combines *status* with *sustenance*. *World's Deadliest Catch* combined triggers for *sustenance, safety, security,* and *survival* to make a group of crab fishermen one of the most successful shows on cable in 2007. The 2010 episode about the demise of one of the boat captains became the third most viewed broadcast in Discovery Channel history. We are all stopped dead in our tracks by messages of death because our number one goal is to live.

Unconscious branding amplifies exponentially when ads stack these primal triggers, such as food on top of sex. Carl's Jr. and Hardee's hit the jackpot when they featured 2012 *Sports Illustrated* swimsuit cover model Kate Upton steaming up the drive-in movie theater. Upton is seen chowing down on a spicy Southwest Patty Melt in a commercial created by the ad agency 72andSunny, sweating down her cleavage, and stripping off her pink sweater, an effort that quickly snagged the advertisers over a half billion impressions worldwide and rising.[26]

The famous Michelin tires baby and corresponding ad slogan, "Because so much is riding on your tires," is an iconic and effective advertising creation that owes the roots of its success to the nature of our biology. "We are so proud of the impact the baby campaign has had over the years," remarks a Michelin brand manager. "It's rare for an advertising campaign to have this kind of longevity and influence."[27] But when you cleverly execute great ads on evolutionary pillars, such as *safety, security,* kinship and children *(sex),* you have the power to commandeer minds and persistently move people because they are steeped in primordial emotion. Harvard business professor Gerald Zaltman says the ad showing a child sitting in a tire evokes the deep unconscious, universal metaphor of a container that keeps the family safe. Zaltman employs a market research technique using images to get at consumers' nonliteral, nonconscious metaphorical drivers of brand selection. He cites how the last version of the commercial, featuring a child positioned within a tire on a wet surface, surrounded by pairs of stuffed animals, invoked the secure imagery of Noah's ark, the famous biblical container that withstood a catastrophe.[28] By identifying the deeper meaning behind brands and ads, by mining for these unconscious metaphors through projective techniques like picture sorts and storytelling, marketers can consciously create ads directly aimed at these otherwise hidden drivers.

During the halftime show of the 2004 Super Bowl, a single exposed breast created a national debate. The infamous Janet Jackson and Justin Timberlake wardrobe malfunction with its fleeting flash of flesh reportedly became the most digitally recorded and replayed moment in television history at the time according to TiVo, and the most talked about and controversial halftime event in Super Bowl history.[29] Why do we care so much about something so trivial? Because to the physical brain, sex is a matter of life and death.

Nike is certainly one of the most lauded brands in modern day marketing because of an advertising campaign that challenged people to achieve their goals and aspirations, instructing them to "Just do it." Before the campaign launched, the expression "do it" already existed as a pervasive meme and cultural euphemism for "having sex." In 1968 the Beatles released the song, "Why Don't We Do It in the Road?" on their highly acclaimed White Album. McCartney reportedly wrote the song after he saw two monkeys copulating on the streets of India.[30] In more recent decades, people have displayed all sorts of tribal affiliations using the same catchphrase, touting their sexual prowess through bumper stickers and T-shirts reading, "Ham radio operators do it with greater frequency," "Ultimate Frisbee players do it horizontally," and "Conservatives do it right," etc. In 2008 a book was published called *Just Do It,* which chronicled the trials and tribulations of a man and his wife seeking to have intercourse for

101 consecutive days. Whether out of conscious foresight or unconscious intuition, Nike's decision to bootstrap their brand expression on a preexisting meme for sexual reproduction was a smart move, putting the brand at the pinnacle of marketing and at the height of public consciousness.

FIGHT, FLIGHT, AND FEAR

No Fear, a niche market brand of extreme sports clothing made by an unknown designer, infectiously spread throughout American culture despite a pittance of advertising budget relative to mainstream apparel brands. Created in 1989 and popularized nationwide by the mid '90s, this lifestyle-based clothing line rapidly became the existential catchphrase for the radically minded. Rebellious youth displayed hats, shirts, and accessories that expressed contempt for social norms and their resolve to triumph over one of our most basic of human tendencies.

No Fear is primal unconscious branding par excellence because the name itself is its marketing, intrinsically speaking to their target audience's universal desire to feel dominance over submission. The name played into the innate human tendency toward self-deception, outwardly refuting the feeling we all have but cleverly conceal, and displacing fear with the more empowering side of the same coin, choosing fight over flight.

In 1998 the movie *Titanic,* about the ill-fated maiden voyage of the world's largest steamship in early 1912, earned $1.8 billion, becoming the highest grossing film of all time, a distinction it retained for over a decade. After a 12-year run, it was dethroned at the box office by *Avatar,* which earned $2 billion, a movie about extraterrestrial tribal warfare. Whether it's at the hands of others or against the forces of nature (or aliens from outer space), humans love to gaze through the lens of war, disaster, and destruction, because we are so deeply programmed by the darker, more violent nature of our reptilian brains. We all slow down to check out the roadside accident, both in our lives and on the screen, because we are so powerfully gripped by moving pictures of conflict and primal emotion.

Titanic leveraged one of the most memorable disasters of the twentieth century, the sinking of a large passenger ship, just as *Avatar* intimated associations with one of most memorable disasters of the twenty-first century, the destruction of the World Trade Center towers of 9/11. When the towering Na'vi Hometree falls after a missile attack, blanketing the landscape with floating embers, for many viewers it was impossible not to think of the September 11, 2001, attack, a day that will forever remain imprinted into the minds and memories of every American. When asked about the scene's resemblance to the World Trade Center, James Cameron, who wrote and directed both *Titanic* and *Avatar,* replied that he had been "surprised at how much it did look like September 11th."[31] Whether by conscious design or unconscious intuition, Cameron, whose resume also includes *Terminator, Rambo,* and *Aliens,* is a master at making blockbuster action films that move us deeply at both the core of our being and the core of our brain.

The interest in death and destruction helps explain why today's media consistently gives us the ability to connect and even interact with our more physical and violent nature without having to hurt ourselves or anyone else. This might explain the strong demand to experience warfare virtually, driving the success of video games like Call of Duty: Black Ops and Call of Duty: Modern Warfare 3, which both broke the record for the biggest entertainment launch in history.[32] The video game industry is now so pervasive that *Late Night with Jimmy Fallon* dedicates an entire week to it, interviewing not just actors and entertainers but game developers, designers, and industry leaders. As recurring guest Eric Hirshberg, CEO of Activision Publishing, said in a June 11, 2012, interview, "there would probably be about as many people playing Call of Duty tonight in multiplayer as could fill about 400 Madison Square Gardens."[33] Whether watching the battles in *Avatar* from the perspective of an extraterrestrial humanoid, or playing a game of Killzone or Modern Warfare 3 from the viewpoint of the killer, or just enjoying the ritualized warfare of smashmouth football from the safety of the sidelines or the living room couch or the Internet-machinations of our own fantasy teams and leagues, many people like to engage in violence at arm's length.

Not surprisingly, violence and destruction can also make for compelling advertising. But because of the heightened scrutiny that advertisers find themselves under, this is often better done tongue in cheek. The Blendtec Total Blender proved how a relatively unknown household appliance could destroy everything from a baseball to a camcorder or even an iPad in a series of online videos called "Will it blend?" Consumers were enthralled by the series of destructive shorts, as was a unanimous panel of judges who rated the effort as the second most effective social media campaign ever, according to Forbes.com, trailing only the break-out success of the *Blair Witch Project*[34] and increasing sales by a whopping 700 percent.

But finding entertainment in violence is nothing new. Harvard experimental psychologist and cognitive scientist Steven Pinker provides compelling evidence for this, citing sixteenth-century Paris where a popular form of entertainment was cat burning . . . lowering a basket or sack of live cats into the flames of a bonfire as dozens of onlookers would shriek and jeer with delight. Today abusing animals can make you the object of scorn and moral outrage, as well as get you sentenced to prison—just ask pro-football player Michael Vick. Instead, we watch *Hannibal, Dawn of the Dead,* or *Drag Me to Hell,* or play a casual game of Thrill Kill, Resident Evil, or Dead Rising. Today news media understand the benefits of focusing on the reptilian side of violence—pain and suffering boost ratings and engagement. Despite the daily global reports of terror, war, and revolution, and those ongoing stories of local murder, rape, and robbery, our present society is far less violent than it has been in previous history. According to Pinker, there is a worldwide trend toward decreased violence. He explains, "If the wars of the twentieth century had killed the same proportion of the population that die in the wars of a typical tribal society, there would have been two billion deaths, not 100 million."[35]

Perhaps the reason for this seemingly counterintuitive trend relates to our modern media usage and the role it plays in satisfying an innate thirst for violence. Could the decreased violence in the real world be due to the increased violence in the media, offering far more opportunities to sublimate our darker thoughts in dissociated or virtual bloodshed? Some conclude that it is the media that causes violence, but is it possible that the critics have it backwards? The videogame industry does not appear to turn virtual violence into real violence. More than a generation has now been raised on violent video games and there is no evidence that there are more sociopaths and snipers today. According to Lawrence Kutner and Cheryl K. Olson, founders of the Center for Mental Health and Media and members of the psychiatry faculty at Harvard Medical School, the rate of juvenile crimes has actually decreased as the usage of video games in the past two decades has skyrocketed.[36]

Young children are impressionable and impetuous, lacking the ability to filter and restrain impulses because their frontal cortex, the part of the brain that does this, is still forming. But can the media in our society actually help some people vent their more violent impulses in manners that are less harmful and more socially acceptable? Can a child sublimate his primal urge to bully and dominate others by playing a video game instead? Can violence in the media play a therapeutic role in helping us face our own mortality, an awareness we humans uniquely share? I say this not to condone violence in the media but only to help explain its function and growing prevalence, and our increasingly insatiable appetite for more and more. Like it or not, violence sells because it's in our DNA and our biology. All humans have a dark side, or what Carl Jung called "the Shadow," an unconscious reservoir of negativity that deepens without an outlet. And based upon the glacial pace at which our brains evolve, it's not going away any time soon.

SEEING WITHOUT SEEING

An experiment led by Professor Beatrice de Gelder, from the University of Tilburg in the Netherlands, demonstrated that a man left completely blind after multiple strokes was still able to successfully navigate an obstacle course using his sense of where the impediments were. As de Gelder said: "This is absolutely the first study of this ability in humans. We see what humans can do, even with no awareness of seeing or any intentional avoidance of obstacles. It shows us the importance of these evolutionary ancient visual paths.

They contribute more than we think they do for us to function in the real world."[37]

This phenomenon known as blind-sight exemplifies the influence of our reptilian legacy, providing peculiar evidence for the existence and importance of the unconscious as a driver of perception and human behavior. Blind-sight appears to be a seemingly lizardlike ability to react to the environment reflexively, enabling us to move rapidly and appropriately without having to think about it.

In de Gelder's experiment, a blind patient known only as TN was able to safely maneuver through a random obstacle course made up of boxes and chairs without so much as bumping into a single object. Authorities believe that blind-sight demonstrates that even though our eyes cannot identify the object, there is a part of the brain that can respond on an unconscious level.[38] For example, a man who is completely blind demonstrated that he was still capable of seeing and responding to facial expressions registering emotions like anger and joy, even though the regions of his brain involved in processing visual information remained totally inactive.[39] That's because the brain has thirty different areas involved with the processing of visual information that are processed along two pathways: the old and evolutionarily ancient low road from the brain stem, which is unconscious, and the new higher pathway that leads to the visual cortex in the back of the brain, which is conscious.

Acclaimed neuroscientist V. S. Ramachandran, director of the Center for Brain and Cognition and distinguished professor with the Psychology Department and Neuroscience Program, University of California, San Diego, explains the contradiction of "seeing without seeing" in describing a patient who can detect motion in a visual field to which he is completely blind. "It's almost as if the patient is using ESP. He can see, and yet cannot see. So it's a paradox. It turns out from the eyeball to the higher centers of the brain, where you interpret the visual image, there is not just one pathway, there are two separate pathways that subserve different aspects of vision, one of these pathways is the evolutionary new pathway, the more sophisticated pathway if you like, that goes from the eyeball through the thalamus to the visual cortex of the brain."[40]

One needs the visual cortex in order to see something, but the other pathway—the one that is "evolutionarily older and more prominent in animals like rodents, lower mammals, birds, and reptiles—goes to the brain stem, the stalk on which the brain sits, and [from there, information] gets relayed eventually to the higher centers of the brain. This older pathway going through the brain stem is concerned with reflexive behavior," Ramachandran says, making you pay attention to something important in your visual field, controlling your eye movements, and directing your gaze. As Ramachandran describes it, "In these patients, one of these pathways alone is damaged. The visual cortex is damaged. And because that's gone, the patient doesn't see anything consciously. But the other pathway is still intact. And he can use that pathway to guess correctly the direction of movement of an object that he cannot see."[41]

He adds that in some ways we all experience blind-sight in our daily lives, such as when we drive a car. When you are driving and having a conversation with a passenger, for example, you are occupying conscious attention to the conversation, and at the same time you are unconsciously responding to the activity on the road. Only if something unusual happens, such as a big truck passing by, will you actually notice it. In a sense, blind-sight enables you to navigate through the world, whether on the road to work or on the path to sales closure in the cluttered purchase funnel, you're on autopilot while still being consciously active in the present.[42]

For marketers this means we are always processing information on both levels and we can't disregard the level that we can't see. Neuromarketing seeks to identify and understand the responses we can't see or articulate by studying bodily and brain reactions.

MIND EMBODIED, NOT JUST EMBRAINED

William James, the father of American psychology, first drew our attention to the physical nature of emotions in the 1880s. James offered a prescient look at the sequencing of emotional and rational processing, proposing that emotions are actually mental interpretations of physiological states. For example, James believed that when we experience fear, we first feel the bodily response of emotion—the increase in heart rate, the tensing of muscles, the sweaty palms—and then, and only then, as a reaction to these body states of panic do we have the awareness of that emotion.[43] Later, neuroscience would support James's theory, helping to reverse a widely held belief that rationality is the driving force of human cognition and decision making.

Joseph LeDoux, professor of Neuroscience and Psychology at New York University, pioneered the study of emotions as a biological phenomenon. LeDoux's research on fear and anxiety demonstrated how our bodies take action without our minds even knowing. We take action based upon the emotional processing of an event, often ignoring rational processing altogether. "The conscious brain may get all the attention," says LeDoux, "but consciousness is a small part of what the brain does, and it's slave to everything that works beneath it."[44]

LeDoux's findings showed us that the amygdala can literally hijack our mind and body, causing us to respond while completely bypassing our cerebral cortex, the seat of our conscious awareness. He indicated that there are two key neural pathways in reaction to environmental stimuli. There is a quicker, more impulsive, unconscious response, or the low road, and a slower, more considered, and conscious response, the high road.

The high road includes both an emotional and a rational component, a recursive feedback loop between the feeling and thinking parts of the brain. If you can recall or imagine the experience of unexpectedly encountering what appears to be a snake, you can see how these neural pathways function. You might see a frightening object and immediately jump—the fast route—and then a moment later recognize that it was only a garden hose—the slow route.

The overactive amygdala was essential in our hunter-gatherer past, where impending threats from saber-toothed tigers or competing tribes required quick, life-saving, response-without-thought behaviors. As a result, the wiring of our brains today still heavily favors rapid-fire emotional reactions that bypass conscious logical thinking. That's because the neural circuits of information flows from the amygdala to the cortex are like superhighways, while the pathways traveling from the rational systems to the emotional systems are like country roads. Since the prefrontal cortex is the part of the brain that enables us to consciously choose our behavior, low-road decisions that bypass these higher cortical functions are made unconsciously for us by the brain's emotional systems.[45]

In other words, our emotions influence our thinking much more than our thinking influences our emotions. As LeDoux puts it, the "human brain (like every other part of the body and every part of life and biology) is a work in progress." Because evolution is such a slow, ongoing process, LeDoux says, "At this point in our evolutionary history, the systems involved in thinking, reasoning [conscious], planning, and decision making are poorly connected with the brain systems involved in controlling our emotions." This explains why emotions tend to control us, and why it is often hard to control our emotions.[46]

The implications for marketers are clear: to move people quickly and with the least amount of resistance, we need to focus much of our effort on low-road physical and emotional processing, which are the superhighways to the consumer unconscious.

LEARNING WITHOUT KNOWING

Because these emotional systems can function independently from the cortex, memories and response repertoires can be formed without us ever knowing. It's like no one was home when we were out living and learning. Our conscious minds, seated in the neocortex, are often oblivious to the fact that memories and learned responses are being formed in the present.

Joseph LeDoux gives an example of how this might happen. "Let's say we were having lunch one day and there's a red-and-white checkered tablecloth, and we have this argument. And the next day I see somebody coming down the street and I say, I have this gut feeling about this guy, he's an s.o.b. and I don't like him. And maybe what's going on there is that he's got a red-and-white checkered necktie on. Consciously, I'm saying it's my gut feeling because I don't like the way he looks, but what's happened is that the necktie has triggered the activation of the amygdala through the thalamus, the so-called low road, triggered a fear response in me, which I now consciously interpret as this gut feeling about not liking the guy. But in fact, it's being triggered by external stimuli that I'm not processing consciously."[47]

In his book *Buyology,* branding expert and neuromarketing pioneer Martin Lindstrom points out an example of how Silk Cut, a popular brand of cigarettes in the United Kingdom, in advance of legislation that would ostensibly ban cigarette advertising by forcing the removal of brand logos and messaging, began to position its logo against a background of purple silk in every ad it ran. After the advertising ban came into effect the advertiser simply ran outdoor ads that featured the silk without the logo or any message. Consumers had unconsciously learned the connection so that the logo or the brand and message were no longer needed. Research revealed that virtually all of those surveyed were aware of the brand as a result of seeing the ad. They had transferred their feelings and awareness of the brand to another variable, the purple silk.

Likewise, consumers can be both negatively and positively predisposed to a brand based on their associations with its ads, slogans, logos, mascots, design elements, and brand properties. People may not really know why they love one brand and not another, because conscious thought may have had little to do with the emotional tags that were formed when their preferences were learned. For example, Lindstrom recounts how he helped a leading beverage company create a sound when opening the can that was subtly different from other cans to trigger a unique craving for their brand's drink. The manufacturer redesigned the can to create a differentiating snapping sound, a branded cue of delicious anticipation. They then recorded the sound in a studio and incorporated it into advertising. The manufacturer would play the sound at major concerts and sporting events, seeing an instant uptick in sales for their brand when they did so. Yet when consumers were asked why they suddenly choose that particular beverage over another they would say things like "I haven't the faintest idea, I just fell for it."[48]

What is particularly counterintuitive about memory formation, and important to bear in mind, is that vivid memories are not necessarily accurate memories. They simply correspond with a strong emotion, which often convinces the person that they are recalling the event as it really happened. Research studies that have investigated how emotionally charged memories change over time show that the facts and details of the memories are quite malleable even if the memory itself remains strikingly clear. As LeDoux states, "We know that emotional memories are stored more vividly than other kinds of memories. It used to be thought that they were more accurate, but in fact now we know that they are not more accurate, they're just more vivid and strong in the personal sense. But they can be highly inaccurate."[49]

LeDoux goes on to illustrate how a memory of emotionally charged events can change despite our subjective conviction that we are remembering an experience vividly as it actually happened. He points to research conducted by a group of psychologists that asked witnesses of the NASA Space Shuttle *Challenger* disaster to recall the experience of the disaster immediately after the event had occurred. These witnesses were then surveyed again a year later and their recollections were completely different from their original responses. Several years later after that, their responses again changed completely. As LeDoux indicated, "What we remember is not necessarily what we experienced originally. The accuracy of those memories changes over time, but their strength in terms of your subjective feeling that it was a really powerful experience is there."

This is why market research participants sometimes report with great conviction the origins and circumstances of their own pleasures, preferences, and interests, when the details are not really grounded in actual fact or experience. Our emotions can sometimes deceive us. And marketers can be deceived by those emotions. Very often panelists are surveyed over time, not unlike those in the *Challenger* study, and the accuracy of their memories need to be looked at with a grain or perhaps a chunk of salt. Which is why, as a rule of thumb, it is better to track or observe real behavior rather than opinion.

The possibility of emotional deceit also represents an opportunity for marketers to erase consumers' bad brand memories with strongly positive emotions and experiences. For instance, I learned through talking to cable and satellite subscribers that a television service provider can win back the good graces of a disgruntled customer who had a really poor installation experience by surprising and delighting them with an emotionally charged offer, like a free six months of their premium program package as an apology and gesture of goodwill. Our feelings help us forgive and forget. Good emotions help erase bad memories.

FEELING IS BELIEVING

A fascinating illustration of how this process of associative learning and memory works comes from V. S. Ramachandran. A patient of Ramchandran's, injured in a car accident, slipped into a coma. After several weeks, he regained consciousness but could no longer recognize his mother. On her first visit, the patient exclaimed: "Who is this woman? She looks like my mother but she is an imposter."

This disorder, known as Capgras, can be explained by a structural problem in the brain, according to Ramachandran. When you see someone you know as your mother, the part of the brain called the fusiform gyrus is activated and identifies the face as your mom, and then a signal is sent to the amygdala, which associates the face with emotional memories of "mother." Ramachandran explains that Capgras patients have a severed neural connection between visual recognition and emotional recognition. As a result, the patient recognizes someone that looks like mom but lacks the accompanying feelings that are associated with mother.

According to Ramachandran, because we are so dependent on our emotional reactions to the world around us, the emotions win out over the visual perceptions. The brain rationalizes that the mother must somehow have been replaced with a pretender. The evidence for this explanation lies in an intriguing quirk in the patient's behavior. He was able to easily recognize his mother when she called on the phone and he heard her voice. Yet if she walked into the room, phone in hand, he would reverse his belief and think again that she was an imposter. Our own rationalizations can be quite irrational.

Ramachandran indicates that the reason for this is that the amygdala has different connections to the auditory and visual systems of the brain. Since his connection between his emotions and auditory system remained intact, only hearing her voice convinced the man that it was his mother because that experience was accompanied by familiar feelings.[50]

Ramachandran's findings demonstrate that emotions and sensory perception are intricately connected. In order to make sense of our experiences we need to assign them value through our emotions. After all, our relationship to our mother is among the most emotionally charged. Without the emotional connection of the meaning of mother, the patient's mother lost her precious relevance and identity in the eyes of her own son. Likewise, brands lose relevance when they fail to connect emotionally with people, and without that emotional attachment they can be easily replaced with generic imposters.

THE ANATOMY OF DECISION MAKING

Among the most remarkable contributions to the study of cognition and decision making are those of the renowned neurologist Antonio Damasio, professor at the University of Southern California. Along with Joseph LeDoux, Damasio has helped achieve the long-sought integration of emotion into mainstream cognitive science. Demonstrating that emotions and cognition are inextricably linked, and that our emotional systems are the substrate of much of our ability to reason, these scientists have solidified the theory that decisions are contingent on emotion.

To illustrate this point, Damasio explains the peculiar behavior of one of his patients, Elliot, who had suffered brain damage to a part of the brain known as the ventromedial prefrontal cortex, which is implicated in the risk and benefit analysis of decision making. The ventromedial prefrontal cortex is critical to our ability to relate present events in our life with past emotional associations.

Elliot ostensibly seemed normal, with one glaring exception. He lacked the ability to make decisions, deliberating endlessly in the face of simple, mundane choices such as whether or not to use a black or blue pen.

For example, when deciding which restaurant to eat at, Elliot would painstakingly consider each menu, agonizing over seemingly trivial details like light schemes and seating plans. He would even drive to each location to find out if they were busy. Elliot would obsess over minute facts, logically comparing and contrasting the pros and cons of each choice. If a restaurant was not busy, he would conclude that he could easily get a table, but on the other hand, if there were few patrons that might imply that the food was bad. Because brain damage had severed the connection between his emotions and his rational thinking, Elliot was strangely devoid of feeling and even emotionally numb to his own tragic inability to make decisions.[51]

Damasio's research helped explain this peculiarity through a pivotal research experiment known as the Iowa Gambling Task. This experiment consisted of a psychological test designed to better understand real-world decision making. Subjects could freely choose from four decks of playing cards in an attempt to win money. Two of the decks were bad decks full of high risk cards, while the other two were profitable decks that yielded conservative but consistent payouts and rarely punished players. Participants were able to choose their draws freely from each pile in an effort to determine the most profitable decks and make the most money.

The experimenters asked the participants to report when they could explain why they favored one deck over another. On average it required about 50 cards before a participant began to change their behavior and favor a certain deck, and about 80 cards before they became aware why they favored one deck over another. Rationality is a relatively slow process. But in addition to asking participants to explain their behavior, they also measured their emotional responses by gauging galvanic skin responses, which showed how the electrical properties of skin responded to anxiety and stress through such indicators as perspiration.

The experimenters found that the body got "nervous" after drawing only about ten cards from the losing decks. Even though the subjects were not consciously aware, their bodies developed an accurate sense of fear and anxiety in response to a bad deck well in advance of the rational mind. The subject's feelings were faster and more accurate, having figured it out way before the conscious mind was tipped off to what was happening.

In addition, neurologically impaired patients like Elliot, unable to access their emotions due to damage to their prefrontal cortex, were unable to learn to choose the right cards from the profitable decks. These purely rational patients often went bankrupt because they were incapable of associating negative feelings with the losing decks. Denied the emotional pain of loss and the pleasure of gain, their mind never learned to make the right decisions and respond in the appropriate fashion.[52]

On the basis of these observations, Damasio formulated the landmark somatic marker hypothesis. This model of decision making shows how our decisions often depend upon access to what he calls somatic markers, feelings that are tagged and stored in the body and our unconscious minds. As Damasio states, "It is emotion that allows you to mark things as good, bad, or indifferent literally in the flesh."[53]

These emotional body states become anchored and associated with specific outcomes that shape and guide our decisions. Marketers can learn to trigger these somatic markers by design, by anchoring positive messages repeatedly with specific consistent stimuli through sensory cues of sights, sounds, and even smells. The massively successful "Intel Inside" program that positioned the company's microprocessor as a world-class player synonymous with the computer industry was enabled through marketing cooperation with other computer makers who did much of the advertising on Intel's behalf. Partner advertisers simply incorporated the brief Intel auditory signature and logo at the end of their television spots. The widely familiar Intel tones became powerful affecting sounds, a unique and memorable three-second animated jingle anchoring their logo and the five-tone melody to the positive feelings of reassurance that the best chip powers their computer.[54] Deutsch LA, during the early days of Internet travel sites, introduced a similar two-second sound clip for Expedia, which rang out the lyrics "Expedia . . . dot com" over a brief melody at the end of every spot, unmistakably branding each execution and helping Expedia carve out a lead position in the rapidly emerging online travel industry.

A few years ago, chain hotels began branding their guests' experience with a signature scent. I always notice the same fragrance when I walk through the entrance of the Westin in Reston Heights outside of Washington, DC, on my visits to Volkswagen's headquarters. It automatically gives me a strong, olfactory reminder of my stay. Have you ever noticed how our sense of smell so easily brings about vivid memories? That's because our sense of smell bypasses the thalamus, the brain's sensory switchboard, and goes directly to the memory and emotional centers, which in turn unleash a powerful flood of emotions.[55] Signature scents in marketing if coupled with favorable events can trigger positive emotions, not unlike how the smell of grandma's baked apple pie makes you eagerly anticipate her delicious dessert.

Consistency of branding elements across the five senses is the key to triggering these supercharged branding moments by activating somatic markers, provided your experience with the product is a good one. In the multitude of possibilities, why do we choose Oreo cookies, Kellogg's corn flakes, or Samsung televisions? Because our bodies have taught our minds that these choices make us feel good. If brands are shortcuts for decisions, somatic markers are the mechanism for how these shortcuts are formed, storing them in our bodies as good, bad, or indifferent, retrieving them with our minds and putting the products in our hands.

Because of the work of LeDoux and Damasio, we are beginning to understand that the process of decision-making behavior is led by the heart and followed by the head. As Damasio says, "We are not necessarily thinking machines. We are feeling machines that think."[56] Marketing messages that are most effective strike at our feelings first and foremost with what Damasio calls "emotionally competent stimuli." This does not mean that emotions decide for us, but often weigh in early and heavily into our decisions. In addition, emotions are inextricably interconnected with rationality. The new paradigm suggests that having a sensory experience, such as seeing an advertisement, creates a feeling in the body first, as opposed to a thought. One then becomes conscious of and thinks about those feelings, deciding from there whether or not to take action. Sometimes this process occurs in a recursive loop, where feeling leads to thinking to more feeling to more thinking, etc., before the scale is tipped into a decision and, ultimately, a behavior. In essence, we tend to make decisions emotionally and then justify them rationally.[57] In certain types of retail-focused ads, Deutsch LA has used a philosophy called "brand-tailing," which perfectly fits this two-part process. Based on a belief that a well constructed advertisement can both build the brand and make the sale, it leads with emotion and ends with logical information, such as where and how to buy the product and what it will cost.

Somatic markers are the water level on the iceberg metaphor of the mind, the divide where the vast unconscious becomes conscious. If your advertisement is not stirring a feeling inside the bodies of people, your message is meandering slowly down a country road when it should really be speeding toward your target audience on a superhighway.

PART II
THE SEVEN STEPS TO BEHAVIOR CHANGE

PREFACE

By now I hope that you have grasped the established science behind the belief that the unconscious is the key to behavior. The remainder of this book will focus on putting that understanding into practice: How do the minds of people process information, structure their experience, and form the often-unconscious beliefs and motivations that drive their behavior? How can you reach and change the part of the mind that drives their actions so as to move people to your brand? And what things must happen in order for this change to occur? I include many examples of how marketers have answered these questions as well as several thought-starters to springboard inspiration around your brand. This is not about sneaking messages into minds below the radar of awareness. In fact, a prerequisite to this process is conscious awareness of the brand message. To achieve branding on the deepest, most impactful level, both conscious and unconscious dimensions must combine to produce a physiological transformation in people that can generate immediate results and endure over time.

Here is a brief summary of each step in this process.

STEP ONE—INTERRUPT THE PATTERN

The mind is what the brain does, it is the brain in action, and it works through a process of pattern recognition. If we want to get attention and shift people's behavioral patterns, we need to interrupt their perceptual patterns by doing something interesting and different.

STEP TWO—CREATE COMFORT

Humans gravitate to the known, the safe, and the trusted. Although we are attracted to what is different, we move toward the familiar seeking balance, and rely on predictable patterns not just in our biology but also in our environments.

STEP THREE—LEAD THE IMAGINATION

The prefrontal cortex gives us the unique ability to plan behavior and create new possibilities. It functions like an alternate reality simulator by giving us the capacity to imagine the benefits of a better life and anticipate the consequences of our actions.

STEP FOUR—SHIFT THE FEELING

We do what we do because of how we feel. We assign value to things through our emotions. Because of the way our brains are wired, emotions influence our thinking more than our thinking influences our emotions.

STEP FIVE—SATISFY THE CRITICAL MIND

Consciousness gives us the exclusive ability to rationally reject an idea if it does not make sense based upon our experiences. Often, in order to act, we need to give ourselves logical permission to submit to the emotions and impulses that drive us.

STEP SIX—CHANGE THE ASSOCIATIONS

Our minds and our memories work by association. Repetition and emotion strengthen these neural associations so that they become automatic. If we want to change perceptions of anything, we have to change our associations.

STEP SEVEN—TAKE ACTION

Our brains exist for movement. Things that don't move don't have brains. Physical actions use more of our brain than just imagining a behavior. The more of our brain we use and the more we repeat an action the more ingrained the experience becomes in our unconscious mind. By physically doing something we also engage more of our sensory systems such as tactile (skin) and proprioceptive (internal, such as muscle) feelings; we see it, smell it, possibly taste it, hear it et cetera. This makes the experience deep-rooted in our unconscious, or second nature to us.

4
STEP ONE:
INTERRUPT THE PATTERN

A sudden bold and unexpected question doth many times surprise a man and lay him open.

—*Francis Bacon*, The Essays or
Counsels, Civil and Moral

THE COLD MONTH OF FEBRUARY 2011 WAS UPON US, BUT sports fans everywhere were heating up for what would become the most watched television program in history. Super Bowl XLV featured a match-up of two of the NFL's most title-abundant franchises, the Pittsburgh Steelers and the Green Bay Packers. But like every year, there were really two big games in the making . . . one on the field of play and the other in the field of advertising. Each year, advertisers unshackle their budgets and creative constraints in an effort to "go big or go home" on the world's biggest media stage. Who would capture the title on TV's most expensive and expansive advertising venue? In 2011, neither game would disappoint. The Packers outlasted their opponents despite an impressive comeback to capture the title while advertisers captured a record 111 million television viewers.[1]

Super Bowl ads must be created with a special eye for the context of the big game, considering both the audience and the competition. Since Super Bowl Sunday has become virtually an American holiday, we are competing not only with other great ads but with crowded living rooms full of beer-drinking partygoers and brimming bowls of chips, dips, and salsa. Conventional wisdom has led marketers to up the ante each year with over-the-top humor, high-end productions, and A-list celebrity talent in an effort to stand out and gain attention.

For a few months prior, our creative teams at Deutsch LA had been busy churning out a steady stream of ideas that pushed the boundaries of creativity, addressing the need to feel epic and Super Bowl–worthy. But none of these ideas could unseat the simple charm of a concept that had been on the table early on in the creative development process. As it turned out, this year it was the story of a little boy and a simple, poignant, heartfelt moment that would capture the crown and the imagination of millions worldwide. The commercial featured a pint-sized version of Darth Vader, the Dark Lord of *Star Wars* fame, and quickly became the topic of water-cooler conversation everywhere. In the ad, mini-Darth is seen in a series of unsuccessful attempts to use "the Force" on various household items, each time predictably failing, until he encounters the new 2012 Passat. This time, the car appears to come to life by the power of his little raised hands after his dad secretly starts the engine using the remote start feature on the key fob.

Created to tease the coming of the 2012 Passat, the spot was deliberately leaked onto YouTube a few days in advance in an effort to have it go viral. The strategy paid off in spades. Thanks to the Internet, we can now measure the impact of an ad by the extent to which people voluntarily search and choose to view it, often again and again, the ultimate testament to its appeal. The Force won our Super Bowl before the game even started with an incredible 12.4 million pregame downloads on YouTube and total domination of Super Bowl prebuzz on Twitter.

The ad went on to become not only a powerful marketing effort but also a global cultural phenomenon. At the time of this writing, it has amassed a staggering 54 million views on YouTube and inspired countless accolades, spoofs, imitations, comic strips, movie trailers, sports arena shows, and television news programs. It made a national hero of six-year old Max Page, whose concealed identity had everyone curious to meet the cute boy behind the ominous mask. Adweek selected it as the best commercial of 2011. And in a recent CBS prime-time show, *Clash of the Commercials: USA vs. The World*—a live interactive event broadcast from Las Vegas and hosted by Heidi Klum—online voters chose the ad as the greatest commercial of all time.

The Force struck a nerve and put Volkswagen back into the fore of public consciousness by being ranked as the most memorable ad of all the Super Bowl commercials. Online it became one of the top ten viral ads of all time and among the highest rated ads of all time. The spot won numerous prestigious awards including two Gold Lions at Cannes, a Gold Pencil in the One Show, and a Gold Clio. And even more importantly, it drove significant increases in purchase consideration, upped traffic to the VW.com website by half, and contributed to a hugely successful sales year for the Volkswagen brand. In total it earned a reported 6.8 billion impressions worldwide and more than $100 million in earned media.[2]

But the most intriguing aspect of its success was the effect that the advertisement had upon the minds of viewers. It received the highest "neuro-engagement score" ever in the annual Sands Research Super Bowl Ad Neuro ranking, which measures electrophysiological activity in the brain in response to viewing the commercials that run in the Super Bowl each year. As Dr. Stephen Sands, chair and chief science officer at Sands Research, announced, "Deutsch LA's creative team for Volkswagen for two years in a row has topped our ranking and this year their Darth Vader advertisement elicited such a strong emotional response, it ranks as the highest we have ever tested . . . the positive and negative emotional response flows with the commercial and ends on an extremely positive point." Dr. Sands added that, "By creating an engaging and emotional storyline with strong positive response, viewers were extensively engaged and strongly recalled the spot, and, more importantly, specifically recalled the brand associated with the commercial. Too often that correlation is lost and key branding moments are missed."[3]

A high-density electroencephalogram (EEG) records what areas of the brain are activated from moment to moment while subjects watch the commercial as the storyline depicts a series of expected predictions . . . the Force is powerless on the exercise bicycle, the household pet, the washer and dryer, the doll, the sandwich. But that predictable pattern is finally interrupted. Thanks to the dad's unexpected intervention, the viewers are bemused with the emotional payout of an unsuspecting reward when the delightful mini-Darth becomes surprised and astonished by his own powers. A close analysis of the EEG data shows a very clear prominent spike in engagement and emotion as the dad remotely fires up . . . not only the car, but also the brains of those watching.[4] As Sands also reported, "As the father starts the car from inside the house a peak of engagement ensues in the bilateral parietal lobe (which signals attention) and the frontal lobe (which signals higher cognition). This implies that respondents have continued sustained attention and are processing this event within the storyline." This neuro-engagement is sustained through the all-important display of the brand logo, which immediately follows the pattern interrupt as the engine starts up. As Sands puts it, "The overall engagement to this ad is strong all the way to the end, and we didn't see a significant drop of attention like we do with most ads. The final shot of the logo created a huge right temporal and right frontal and parietal lobe activation. This signifies that respondents were processing the final messaging and brand. Additionally, people were experiencing a positive emotional reaction to it."[5]

One of the reasons the ad became such a force in advertising is that it interrupted another well-known pattern: the image of Darth Vader. The concept of the Dark Lord is simple: the classic antagonist and the epitome of evil. To have an adorable child play this archetype is a complete departure. We took a concept related to darkness and immorality and replaced it with light-hearted innocence. Had the little boy been dressed up like Luke Skywalker, there would have been no interruption, no tension, and much less attention. Several decades earlier, Volkswagen created perhaps the most effective advertising campaign of all time through pattern interruption. It was 1959 when they developed "Think small." *Advertising Age* has ranked it the top ad campaign of the century.[6] While the industry zigged and boasted big, Volkswagen zagged and thought small with charm, wit, and honesty, breaking the convention of conspicuous consumption and transforming our markets and our culture through a refreshing change of pace. Thinking small was actually thinking big.

CONSTRUCTIVE PERCEPTION

Why do some things capture our attention and others go completely unnoticed? Why did mini–Darth Vader become the spotlight of the public eye?

Perception is an active process that is constructed by the brain, not one passively recorded by our senses. In other words, we see with our brain, not just our eyes. Television is our most dominant media because vision is our dominant sense. It is estimated that as much as 85 percent of our perception, learning, and cognition are mediated through our sense of sight,[7] and over one-third of the brain is dedicated to the processing of visual information.[8] But what we see is as much a function of how our brain physically processes that information as it is the physical nature of what we are observing. Nobel Prize–winning psychologist Herbert Simon likened the mind to a pair of scissors in which one blade is the brain and the other is the environment. In order to understand how we perceive and experience the world, we must first recognize the simultaneous interaction between both "blades."[9]

Perception is not a simple linear process, but rather an ongoing back and forth comparison between expectations and incoming sensory data.[10] Our brains create models of the world and compare incoming information to those models. When things that we observe fit these expectations, we don't have to think about them and they become unconscious. That's because our conscious minds work on a need-to-know basis. We can process only a limited amount of information from the environment, so when the world is accurately predicted, we no longer need to pay attention to that information and are freed up to focus our attention elsewhere.[11]

Take for instance the act of learning to drive a car. At first we pay very close attention to everything we are doing, but once we know how to drive the process becomes unconscious. Of course, we are consciously aware of the fact that we are driving a car, but we no longer need to be aware of all the perceptual input and motor coordination required for driving. We become, for the most part, unconscious of the gas pedal beneath our foot, the small adjustments that we continually make in guiding the steering wheel, or the need to switch on the turn signal before changing lanes. Only if something interrupts our pattern with the unexpected, such as the driver in front of us slamming on his brakes, or a dog running out into the middle of the street, do we notice what is happening and consciously react in that moment. Our unconscious mind takes care of most of the driving so that we are able to pay conscious attention to these important interruptions. This example underscores an extremely powerful concept for marketers: awareness of our surroundings occurs only when the things we experience violate our expectations.[12]

It deosn't mttaer in waht oredr all the ltteers in a wrod are. You can stlil raed it wouthit a porbelm bcuseae the huamn mnid wroks by a porecss of ptatern rceigontion. It dtemrines maennig bfoere porecssnig dteails.[13] Amzanig huh?

You are able to read this jumble because your mind works by a process of pattern recognition. Our brains look to organize information into familiar patterns that fit our preconceived or learned notions of the world, seeking connections to things that we already know. That process creates meaning more from the context of a situation than from its specific content. We don't read the actual letters but rather look for the structural patterns. Our brains do this by matching things in the world to patterns or models in our mind. This is what scientists refer to as "a priori knowledge," or in other words, information that already exists in your head. As with the jumbled words, you have already *learned* the patterns in which the letters, words, and sentences commonly occur so the brain automatically decodes and organizes the mess, predicting the intentions behind what has been written.

To illustrate this point of how the brain makes predictions to interpret reality, let's turn our attention to the visual cortex, the part of the brain that processes vision. The visual cortex surprisingly has blind spots, much like the areas you can't see in the rear view mirror of your car. At the back of the retina, where the optic nerve exits the eyeball, there are no photoreceptors at all, making us blind in that region. If the mind didn't make up for this lack, we would have a hole in our visual field. Thankfully, the brain fills in the gap by using information from around the blind spot to infer or predict what *might* be there. We "Photoshop" our reality, manufacturing awareness based on input from the surrounding environment rather than what we actually see. This perceptual filling-in is known as "constructive perception."[14]

In addition to this visual manufacturing to compensate for blind spots, our brain displays its ongoing connection to our reptilian legacy through tiny little jumps called saccades. These occur when our eyes sweep across our field of view, changing focus from one fixed point to another, as when we read. In between these focal points, the information that reaches the brain is blurry, so the visual cortex sees the equivalent of tiny neural "jump cuts." The brain remarkably fills in the gaps of this feed to create a coherent narrative and seamless story from the choppy input.[15]

By filling in the blanks, our brain plays an active role not only in our ability to see but also our ability to generate awareness. In order to capture anyone's attention you need to do more than activate the senses; you need to first actively engage the brain.

THE PAYOUT OF ATTENTION

So how do we begin to embed a new idea about a brand into the minds of people? Because brands are learned behaviors, the first step in the branding process is the same as the first step in the learning process. And when your teacher told you to pay attention, she knew what she was talking about. The best way to learn anything is through focused attention, and nothing focuses our mind better than surprise and novelty.[16] When someone does something different or unexpected, they interrupt our anticipated pattern of perception, which sets off a neurobiological process that commands our notice.

The "Energizer bunny" is one of the longest running and most recognized advertising campaigns in history, a version by ad agency TBWA\Chiat\Day of a campaign developed by DDB Worldwide. According to *Advertising Age*, the bunny is one of the top five advertising icons of all time.[17] The campaign introduced the quintessential power of pattern interruption. You think you are watching a commercial for Sitagin Hemorrhoid Remedy when, out of nowhere, a boisterous little "spokes-bunny" breaks into the commercial, beating his little drum and spinning around uncontrollably. Your momentarily confused brain turns to amused miscalculation as you quickly realize that the ad has nothing to do with hemorrhoids, but is rather a demonstration of the long-lasting power of Energizer batteries.

The human brain is fundamentally attracted to what is different. If it were not, we would never learn. The brain knows to stop and rethink its pattern, so it may react differently to the new experience and better comprehend it. When the bunny disrupts what we think is a hemorrhoid medicine spot or coffee commercial, we switch from autopilot to focused attention. While we make sense of things by comparing them to familiar patterns in our head, we are stopped dead in our tracks when we notice the unfamiliar or lack a connection to a preexisting pattern. That is because we need to understand and adapt to our changing environment in order to survive. As neuroscientist Russell Poldrack explains, "The brain is built to ignore the old and focus on the new. Novelty is probably one of the most powerful signals to determine what we pay attention to in the world. This makes sense from an evolutionary standpoint, since we don't want to spend all of our time and energy noticing the things around us that don't change from day to day."[18]

"Seeking new and unfamiliar experiences is a fundamental behavioral tendency in humans and animals," says Dr. Bianca Wittman of the Institute of Cognitive Neuroscience, University College, London. Wittman conducted an experiment in which volunteers were shown images that they had been familiarized with prior to the experiment. Each image was associated with a unique probability of a reward. The volunteers attempted to choose the ones with the largest payouts. However, when the experimenters introduced new, unfamiliar images, the participants were more likely to take a chance and risk choosing these newer options rather than picking the familiar, and arguably safer, choices.

Using fMRI scanners Wittman and her colleagues discovered greater activation of the ventral striatum, an evolutionary primitive region of the brain that plays a key role in processing reward, suggesting that this process is adaptively beneficial and shared with other animals. "It makes sense to try new options as they may prove advantageous in the long run," says Wittman. For example, introducing new types of food into one's diet may enrich nutrition. Getting a balanced diet of fruit, vegetables, and meat proteins in Pleistocene environments was a good thing for human evolution.

Marketers have learned to exploit this human tendency, such as through the use of limited time offers, those specials that come and go in the food service industries. Wittman's research helps to explain how carefully planned infusions of seasonal varieties can excite people with pleasurable anticipation, like the annual return of Starbucks' pumpkin spice lattes in autumn or the cultlike following for McDonald's McRib sandwich. Unordinary brand line extensions, like Snapple's papaya mango tea, an exotic departure from plain lemon and tea, can also allure us to diversify and add a new product to our carts.

This also helps to explain the appeal of "new and improved" callouts on food labels, or the ongoing redesign of brand logos and packaging even though the product may not have changed. As Wittman further points out, "It also introduces the danger of being sold old wine in a new skin."[19]

Neurobiologists have found that novelty activates a part of the brain called the substantia nigra/ventral tegmental. This area exerts a major influence on learning, as it is closely associated with the hippocampus, the brain's memory center, as well as the amygdala, the center for processing emotional information. Researchers Emrah Düzel and Nico Bunzeck conducted a series of experiments measuring the brain's response to novelty from which they concluded that exposure to new experiences improves memory. When we introduce completely new facts to the mind, it has a better chance of remembering the experience. While novelty acts on a number of different brain systems, it primarily activates the dopamine system. Düzel said, "It is a well-known fact amongst scientists that the mid-brain region regulates our levels of motivation and our ability to predict rewards by releasing dopamine in the frontal and temporal regions of the brain. We have now shown that novelty activates this brain area."[20]

Conventional wisdom has often suggested that constant repetition of the same facts is the best way to learn, but this research challenges those assumptions. Though the brain is receiving additional information through the new facts, it is actually more receptive to the information overall, becoming more focused and more responsive.[21] The success of the Energizer bunny campaign was rooted in the flexibility and campaign-ability of the idea. It was continually refreshed with new commercials and unsuspected interruptions. If Energizer kept running the same spots, our brains would quickly ignore the surprise.

Marketers have become woefully aware of the phrase "media wear-out" in advertising. Running the same television commercials again and again often diminishes their effectiveness. Based upon these observations, slightly changing an ad over time will likely draw increased ability to break through, sometimes without viewers even realizing it. Our brains are unconsciously programmed to scan the environment for contrast and notice change even if those revisions are seemingly below the radar screen of our awareness. This instinctive desire to seek variance is why we enjoy tasks that challenge us to find differences—for example, *People Magazine*'s puzzle called Second Look, in which readers try to find the subtle distinctions between two almost identical pictures. Because of this natural tendency, marketers might be well advised to include variations, additional ads, alternate windows, and varying insights and support points into the same overarching message over time. By deliberately running commercials or ads with a number of slight revisions in copy points or visual elements, and spreading these slightly varied executions over the media flight, marketers will be able to keep viewers engaged longer term. As Dr. Düzel points out, "When we see something new, we see it has a potential for rewarding us in some way. . . . The brain learns that the stimulus, once familiar, has no reward associated with it and so it loses its potential."[22]

That's because our brain learns through the release of dopamine. When we make a prediction and it comes true, we are rewarded with the secretion of dopamine in the brain. Once it is learned, we no longer need the reward of dopamine to encourage our attention. Dopamine neurons get even more excited by surprising rewards, like discovering that those amazing shoes you've always wanted are not only available in your size, but today they're on sale for half off. According to Wolfram Schultz, a neuroscientist at the University of Cambridge, these unpredictable awards can be three to four times more "exciting" to our neurons than awards that are predicted in advance, and can trigger intense emotional responses. The purpose of this surge in dopamine is to draw attention to this new and possibly important information. It is a signal that the brain should take notice and learn what is happening here.[23]

"OH YEAH!" AND "OH SHIT!"

The Old Spice brand completely transformed its old-fashioned image thanks to an infectious effort from ad agency Wieden + Kennedy that was brimming with pattern interrupts. This campaign embedded a much cooler and contemporary brand image in the minds of people by introducing the world to the charismatic hunk of Isaiah Mustafa or "the man your man can smell like." The introductory commercial featured a series of seamless transitional pattern interrupts as Isaiah directs the viewer's attention from unsuspecting scene to scene. He goes from his bathroom, to dropping in on a sailboat, and finally ending up atop a horse. A follow-up spot shows him riding the same horse, but this time the camera pans back to reveal that Isaiah is riding it *backwards* as he proclaims, "Did you know women prefer Old Spice one bajillion times more? Did you know I'm riding this horse . . . backwards?"

The magic behind this amazingly impactful campaign is not just the smooth pitchman of Old Spice body wash, but the equally smooth interruptions. In yet another commercial we see the great-smelling, smooth-talking Isaiah go, in the span of a mere thirty seconds, from standing at an outdoor shower to log rolling in the wilderness, to carrying a gourmet cake, to remodeling his own kitchen with a power saw, to swan diving off a waterfall into a hot tub, and finally . . . as the walls of the hot tub collapse, we are left with him straddling a classically cool motorcycle. Our brains are captivated and delighted . . . again and again and again . . . with the reward of dopamine and the payout of focused attention. With 1.4 billion impressions, this campaign captured more than just attention—it changed behavior with an incredible 32.4 million downloads on YouTube, and a 55 percent sales increase over the three months since it was launched.[24]

But not all pattern interrupts need to be pleasantly surprising to be effective. That's because missed predictions fire another hardwired neural response that biologically commands our attention. This reaction is what neuroscientists technically call the "Oh Shit!" circuit. When we expect something to happen and it does not, a distress signal is released from the anterior cingulate cortex (ACC). The ACC is closely wired to the thalamus, a dual-lobed mass of gray matter beneath the cerebral cortex that plays a critical role in awareness by helping direct conscious attention.[25]

Volkswagen's "Safe happens" campaign from ad agency Crispin Porter + Bogusky chose gravitas over levity to tout the safety of Volkswagen automobiles. Television viewers are brought into the daily mundane interactions between a passenger and a driver, who is behind the wheel of a Volkswagen Jetta. You almost feel like you are riding in the backseat, eavesdropping on a normal everyday conversation, when all of sudden, "Wham!"—or in brain science parlance, "Oh Shit!"—the spot takes a tragic turn when an incredibly realistic car crash takes place. Fortunately, we are relieved to learn no one is hurt. This approach was a departure for a typically fun and friendly brand, but the campaign worked. It became a highly salient message, and one of the most memorable commercials for the brand at the time, communicating safety and firmly anchoring that message to our deepest most reptilian concerns, capturing a great deal of interest, not only in the media but also driving a demonstrable spike in purchase interest and imagery for the brand.[26]

Activation of this distress circuit galvanizes consciousness to bring whatever stimulus is in our environment to the center of our awareness. Our worst predictions, mistakes, and screwups are actually our best tutors. That's because our brains only pay attention to what is around us when our predictions fail, when we experience something that defies our expectations. By paying attention to these mistakes, the brain learns and refines its model of reality. Novelty not only excites us with the promise of reward through the activation of dopamine, but it also teaches us to learn new things when our prognostications fail.[27] It's like the famous adage, "Fool me once, shame on you; fool me again, shame on me."

LIVING IN PATTERNS

We not only perceive the world in patterns, we live our lives in them. Our daily steps often follow the same familiar grooves and well-worn paths. Like streams that eventually turn into rivers, we can't stop the flow of the automatic routines of our daily lives. Among the infinite sea of possible choices in life, we often recreate and repeat the very same activities each and everyday. We sleep on the same side of the bed, wake up at the same time, drink the same coffee, eat the same breakfast, drive the same way to work, surf the same websites, watch the same TV shows, bitch about the same problems, gossip with the same friends about the same recurring dramas, and buy the same brands and products.

Interrupted patterns can provide access to better lives. Mike Sheldon, our CEO at Deutsch LA, often says that "The secret to life is to inject it with new experiences and scare yourself a little." These moments when we take the unexpected and uncomfortable path may startle us. But as we exclaim, "Oh Shit," we also open ourselves to new experiences that can lead us to try new things or better brands. The gateway to personal growth is also the path to brand growth.

Pattern interruption works not only because it excites our sensibilities and teaches us something new, but because it is one of the quickest ways to redirect our behavior: the ultimate goal of almost every marketing effort. But people don't always jump to purchase a new brand. They need to be convinced and romanced over time, not only logically but also more importantly physically and emotionally . . . especially if that purchase is as expensive as a new car.

It began like any other day in Stockholm, Sweden. As early morning commuters entered the Odenplan train station, they walked to either the escalator or the adjacent staircase that would take them to the elevated train platform. On any other day most opted automatically for the path of least resistance, the escalator, but today was different. En route to their train, people came upon a curious demonstration of Volkswagen's "fun theory," developed by the ad agency DDB in Stockholm. The agency had transformed the steps of the staircase into a giant set of piano keys. Would-be escalator riders were interrupted out of their daily routines and prompted to scale the steps, making their own music as they climbed. Their inquisitive minds couldn't resist the allure of the unusually new environment. This branded experience demonstrated that the easiest way to change behavior is to quite literally interrupt one's pattern, and in this instance make it a bit more fun, something people associate with the Volkswagen brand. Sixty-six percent more people than normal chose the stairs over the escalator.[28] Rather than riding the monotonous escalator, they danced and made music a part of their morning commute. By returning people to the fun and innocence of childhood, Volkswagen interrupted their pattern and gave them a truly memorable experience that put smiles on their faces. This event inspired web surfers through a series of award-winning viral videos that expanded the experiential effort for all to see online.

Several years ago I wrote a creative brief to encourage DIRECTV satellite television users to get out of the well-worn grooves of their daily TV-watching habits and watch more pay-per-view programming. After talking to satellite television viewers about their preferences, we discovered that despite over a hundred different channels from which to choose, most people clustered their viewing habits around a narrow subset. When these viewers decided what to watch, a pay-per-view movie was often an impulsive afterthought, not a habitual practice. The main idea of the brief centered around the notion of instant gratification, that right now, while they were watching something old and familiar, there was something new and exciting happening on pay-per-view.

The real brilliance of this effort came from the campaign developed by our creative team, which was based around a set of cleverly conceived pattern interrupts. Viewers were tricked into believing they were watching a classic scene from an iconic film like *Airplane, Karate Kid,* or *Animal House.* Amazingly realistic reenactments of these scenes pleasantly startled the television audience, making them believe the real movie was in progress, but then the protagonist broke character and turned pitchman. In one spot, Leslie Nielsen appears to be piloting the plane in *Airport,* reminding his co-pilot to "Stop calling me Shirley." Just as viewers thought they were watching the actual movie, Nielsen turned to the camera and suggested that they "try a movie you don't know all the words to." It got the attention of customers as well as the trade, getting viewers to consider pay-per-view and snagging a Belding Sweepstakes award, the top creative honors that year in Southern California. Viewers loved being reminded of their favorite films, but they loved the surprise even more, and they also remembered the message, inspired by the suggestions of Nielsen, Mr. Miyagi, and others to try more pay-per-view. This effort morphed into a long-standing, compelling brand campaign that featured many different surprising scenes from culturally relevant movies, convincing cable users to unplug and change things up for the better by switching to DIRECTV.

Much like Isaiah and the increased sales of Old Spice, people follow what begs their attention. And as with the Old Spice commercials and the momentarily perplexing moment when the dad remotely starts the car in the VW ad, one of the key features of pattern interrupts is confusion. When the viewer becomes confused, when predictions fail, there is a burst of dopamine in the brain, followed immediately by the firing of the "Oh Shit" circuit. The conscious mind becomes overloaded with bewilderment and pays close attention. And while the conscious mind is preoccupied, we are less apt to judge, enabling an entry point into a new behavior, such as letting

Old Spice purchasers smell like "the man your man can smell like" and enabling Volkswagen prospects to enjoy the "power of German engineering" in their new Passat.

Confusion not only facilitates behavior change, it is often necessary to the process of learning. We are confused when we first try to learn algebra, or understand a new app on our iPhone, or the first time we hear that the new Lexus can "park itself." Our previous knowledge or perceptions are challenged, forcing us to apply our concentration so we may better understand. In order to get someone to think or to do something differently, or to change their perceptions of a brand, you have to say or do something that may seem a bit foreign at first, even a bit perplexing.

The great poet Robert Frost once said, "The brain is a wonderful organ; it starts working the moment you get up in the morning and does not stop until you get into the office."[29] For so long, business types have been behaving like busyness people, tediously recycling old products and ideas, sticking with the same old approaches even though their customers find attraction in the new and curious. They have been preoccupied by the paralysis of their own analysis, believing that confusion is such a bad thing that they painstakingly screen for it in advertising copy tests and strategic concept evaluations. They end up killing ideas that lead to even the slightest levels of bemusement. What they fail to realize is that some degree of confusion is the first step to behavior change.

FIRST STEP, NOT MISSTEP

But marketers must do more than just interrupt. Their efforts must also make people receptive to and interested in doing business with them. During the Internet boom in the late 1990s, Outpost.com interrupted people's patterns on television by firing gerbils out of a cannon at a wall! The ad got them plenty of attention but not a sustainable business model. Unfortunately for Outpost, folks were still not sure about buying things online, and without winning the consumer's trust through advertising, how could a commercial which ostensibly abused animals make them feel comfortable about sending their hard-earned money through the Ethernet? Today, if you type Outpost.com into your browser, it will interrupt your pattern again by redirecting you to Fry's Electronics, a company that is known to be a reliable source of discount electronics, never having shot a single gerbil at anything.

Several years back, Quiznos restaurants employed another ill-fated pattern interrupt through the use of rodent-like creatures that sparked plenty of water cooler conversation but questionable interest in their product. This commercial featured small, furry, ratlike characters levitating aside Quiznos sandwiches, one wearing a bowler hat singing his praises to the refrain of "We love the subs!" while another in a pirate hat strummed along on an acoustic guitar. The goal was to entice viewers to buy their submarine sandwiches, and though those little guys were very funny, not all attention is good attention. Rats and food just don't mix. In fact, the last time I checked, the mere thought of rats next to food is repulsive to most people. As one blogger put it, "They do not inspire me to buy Quiznos, they inspire me to throw up." We need to do more than just interrupt patterns; we need to connect products with invitingly appropriate associations that move people in the direction of wanting to buy the product.

We frequently are disturbed by stimuli that disrupt but fail to engage us further. When you surf the Internet, you have probably experienced those pop-up ads that prevent you from being able to read the article you are really interested in. Some of them even have that built-in motion graphic that does little to entice but draws your attention away from the real reason you visited the site. Or maybe you have been forced to sit through a commercial that you didn't want to see on television, let alone on the web. But in order to get to the cool video in the headline, you have to annoyingly wait through the commercial or give up altogether and close out the screen.

When I go to my local gas station, I am now forced to complete one more step of my transaction, accepting or denying an offered car wash. I am warned that if I accidentally push the wrong button there are no refunds! That's a lot of choices set against increasing gas prices, and those annoying video screens on top of the pumps hawk advertisements at a volume set loud enough to compete with the local traffic. No wonder I can never remember what they're selling. Attempting to force compliance through unwelcome intrusions is a losing strategy. It makes life more difficult when brands are supposed to be shortcuts to make life easier. It makes us feel bad when brands are supposed to make us feel good.

BUYING AND SELLING EMOTIONS

We need to remind ourselves that we are all in the business of buying and selling good feelings. Whether it's a teenager who offers to mow the lawn on Sunday to convince his parents to let him stay out late on Saturday or an advertiser convincing men to shower with Old Spice body wash . . . we are all peddlers of dopamine. That's right, good marketers are selling the best drugs in the world, drugs that are produced by the exquisite pharmacies of the brains: the molecules of our own feelings. And, when it comes to pattern interruptions, the more you surprise and the bigger the reward, the better the buzz.

And that's why great pattern interrupts like the "Energizer bunny," "The Force," and "The man your man should smell like" work so well. They are like hitting the jackpot on the one-armed bandit at the Hard Rock in Vegas: They just feel good. And it can be just as good a feeling for the marketer who creates it as for the consumer who experiences it. I recall the excitement that spread throughout the halls of Deutsch and Volkswagen as downloads of "The Force" ticked steadily upward day after day and heartfelt support and appreciation poured in from the trade, the media, and, most importantly, the everyday fans of the brand. After all, Volkswagen is the "people's car." We all want to share in the high, the rush of good feeling, and that's really what happens when a marketer generates a viral buzz. We are not just selling a product; we are producing a positive and life-affirming feeling for the millions of people who are engaged by our efforts.

Ads that appropriately use pattern interrupts are like magic. They misdirect our senses with the smoke and mirrors of our own beliefs and pay us back with satisfyingly unexpected outcomes that make us feel simpatico with our world. They produce natural reactions that happen without effort or thought, that bond people together over the shared experience. Like a hilarious joke whose punch line you didn't see coming, the pleasure from the experience is not just a sales tactic, but a gift from marketer to consumer.

When pattern interrupts are used strategically, they can pay out huge dividends. One of most intriguing examples of the empowerment is the queen of shock herself: Lady Gaga. In 2010 she topped Forbes Celebrity 100, even unseating Oprah Winfrey from her number one spot. When Lady Gaga stepped on stage at the Video Music Awards to receive her Video of the Year award from pop legend Cher, she was wearing a dress made of out of raw meat! She boldly announced to the crowd, "I never thought I would be asking Cher to hold my meat purse."[30] Lady Gaga did more than capture the attention of our reptilian brain, she upstaged even Cher, one of the leading fashion pattern interrupters. As she told Anderson Cooper on *60 Minutes,* "As part of my mastering of the art of fame, part of it is getting people to pay attention to what you want them to pay attention to, and not pay attention to the things you don't want them to." As a result, she has amassed $90 million from a monster tour, 32 million Facebook fans, and 10 million fans who follow her on Twitter, all of whom helped her sell a million downloads of her latest hit "Born this Way" in five short days.[31]

If pattern interrupts are well executed, striking the right associations and triggering the right emotions, marketers can leverage some of the most fundamental inclinations of humans, startling awareness and piquing curiosity. By creating a memory that is retained in people's minds, successful marketing can begin to drive them to choose a new product. But even more importantly, it will introduce and open them to the process of change.

THOUGHT-STARTERS ON USING PATTERN INTERRUPTS

Embed pattern interrupts. Include these devices throughout marketing communications across all media. In order to effectively employ pattern interrupts in advertising, you don't need to go over the top or shoot for shock value. Advertisers painstakingly obsess over the production of advertisements, editing and fine-tuning commercials to get to that one elusive final cut. Cognitive science tells us that we don't notice the world around us when it's reliably predicted away, when what we are experiencing in the moment matches our intuitive predictions. Once we know the drill, the gig is up. We stop paying attention. So how do we change the drill?

Consider shooting several versions of the same spots with slight twists in the background, plots, characters, product features, etc. Advertisers often generate multiple cuts anyway as a result of the editing process. Run these throughout the media flight instead of leaving them on the editing room floor. The same holds true for digital, print, outdoor, and experiential ads. Slight twists of the unexpected go a long way over time.

Break with industry standards. To change your business, you have to change your business. Try something completely different and even counterintuitive in your day-to-day business operations. For example, Zappos decided to throw out the book on how they ran their call centers. Rather than follow the prevailing industry norm of working off well-developed, highly researched, time-tested if-then sequential algorithms, they did something remarkably unanticipated. They told their customer service representatives to throw out the script and do whatever it took to help the customer. The direction: Solve the problem in any way you see fit, as long as it gets solved. The result: Zappos now consistently ranks as one of the best companies in the United States for customer service, ahead of BMW and Apple and on par with Ritz-Carlton.[32]

Don't default to the expected solution. When I worked at ad agency Messner Vetere Berger McNamee Schmetterer/Euro RSCG (now Euro RSCG New York) in the late '90s and early 2000s, chairman and CEO Bob Schmetterer told a fascinating story about an Argentinian ad agency that had a client that needed a big ad campaign to drive traffic to their new riverfront development. The real estate complex was located off the beaten path in a remote part of town. Rather than investing the $4 million budget in advertising, the agency came back and recommended building a bridge instead. Even though the client was expecting an ad campaign, he approved the brazen idea and the spectacular footbridge became a cultural landmark emblematic of the new Buenos Aires, generating more publicity than advertising ever could have and physically delivering thousands of customers to their shops, restaurants, and businesses.[33]

Surprise people in emotionally meaningful ways. Several years ago our team at Deutsch LA pitched and won the CiCi's Pizza account. The brand positioning that I came up with revolved around the extraordinary lengths that CiCi's employees went through to treat their customers special, as compared to the service apathy so prevalent in typical fast-food restaurants. The insight for this strategy was illustrated to me firsthand when the then-CEO invited me to have lunch with him at one of the local restaurants in Texas. As I walked through the door a couple of employees warmly and emphatically called out: "Hi! Welcome to CiCi's!" I looked behind me for someone more important than myself, and when I found I was alone, I shrugged my shoulders as if to say, "Are you talking to me?" Treating people with uncommon care, respect, and kindness is likely one of the primary reasons CiCi's has become one of the highest performing brands in the nation.[34]

This philosophy extended far beyond a gimmicky salutation by well-trained employees. It was at the core of the company's manifesto of business operations. What made it even more unforeseen was the fact that they were offering an "all you can eat pizza buffet" for a mere $3.99 at the time. There is no overhead cost associated with a heartfelt "hello" or "thank you." The pleasantly unusual first impression turned curious diners into loyal customers. After all, when people do right by us, we are hardwired to return the favor.

Rethink traditional copy testing research. We have created an industry of ad development for copy testing that is designed to beat the system, rather than connect with and move people to action. Some agencies are paid on the basis of how well their ads test, not how well they perform in the real world. And though fortunes are spent on them, traditional copy test measures are often perilously inadequate and don't reliably predict in-market behavior. We need to stop asking respondents to repeat the main idea from the brief back to us and think we have some how done our job. Consumers are people, not parrots. They have a far more complex relationship with an ad's message than just to memorize and regurgitate its catchphrase. When a research study tested Volkswagen's "The Force" in a traditional setting, many said the main idea was about "fun to drive" or "surprisingly powerful," which was not the ad's intended takeaway.[35] Neuromarketing has revealed that the ad had an inordinately tremendous capacity for engaging our neurology and spiking emotion at a critical moment, which was a far more engaging experience than just remembering and repeating the content or copy points.

The next time you test ads consider ways to measure unconscious emotional response. If you conduct focus groups, do something completely unorthodox, forbid note taking, and check laptops at the door. Pay attention to the faces, bodies, and physical reactions of people, and not just the screens and keyboards of your laptop computer. Try to see the bigger story unfolding in the group, and don't take the individual verbatim commentary on face value without this larger social context. Remember the true insight lies in the feelings generated, not just the words expressed.

5
STEP TWO:
CREATE COMFORT

Every man, wherever he goes, is encompassed by a cloud of comforting convictions, which move with him like flies on a summer day.

—*Bertrand Russell*

THE CEO OF GENERAL MOTORS DID SOMETHING THAT IN BUSIness circles would ordinarily never have even raised an eyebrow. In 2008 Rick Wagoner, then-leader of one of the world's top ten largest corporations, stepped onto the tarmac and boarded his company's $36 million luxury aircraft. His company at the time was the biggest automaker in the world, a dominance sustained for several decades since 1932. Flying on the corporate jet was business as usual, affording Wagoner the ability to more flexibly and efficiently attend routine meetings across far-flung business operations. But on that November day, Wagoner's journey was anything but ordinary in these extraordinary times for both GM and the American buying public.[1] The end of the first decade of the twenty-first century found the United States reeling from the worst economic downturn since the Great Depression, and business as usual had quickly changed to business under fire.[2]

On that morning, Wagoner was on his way to Washington to testify before the House Financial Services Committee in his bid to save the beleaguered automaker from bankruptcy. He told members of Congress that his company was precariously burning through cash and requested $10–12 billion in "bail out" loans.[3] All of the CEOs from the Big Three—GM, Ford, and Chrysler—who collectively sought $25 billion in government loans made the same mistake. All flew in their separate corporate jets departing out of Detroit. The estimated cost of one of these round trip flights from Detroit to Washington was about $20,000. In comparison, a first-class seat on Northwest Airlines was available online for $837. Those routine plane trips, which combined carried about a $60,000 price tag, inadvertently became the flint that sparked public outrage, a conflagration fueled by the media that spread like wildfire from Capitol Hill to the far corners of the American landscape.[4]

Wagoner told the Senate Banking Committee, "We want to continue the vital role we've played for Americans for the past 100 years, but we can't do it alone," yet committee members had little interest in historical musings or self-aggrandizement. They needed to know what GM was doing right then to fix their financial woes and, if given a second chance, how they planned to do things differently to become a viable company again in the future.[5] Wagoner resolutely maintained that cost reduction changes were already in place. "We're all slashing back," he explained, further promising, "We're going to be dramatically leaner."[6]

Moments later Rep. Gary Ackerman fired back, pointing to the glaring and troubling inconsistency of Wagoner's plea for more public funds in spite of continued excessive private spending. He called it a "delicious irony" and "a little bit suspicious," offering the evocative metaphor, "It's almost like seeing a guy show up at a soup kitchen in a high hat and tuxedo."

Ackerman reasoned, "Couldn't you all have downgraded to first class or jet-pooled to get here? It would have at least sent the message that you do get it."[7] Later in the hearing, Rep. Brad Sherman openly tested the management of the Big Three by posing a challenge and, perhaps, a chance at redemption. He asked if any of the CEOs planned to sell their private corporate jets? There was a long pause of dead air and then crickets. When not a single hand was raised, the embittered Sherman remained unmoved: "I don't know how I go back to my constituents and say, 'The auto industry has changed.'"[8]

This incident was merely the straw that broke the camel's back, a poignant reminder to strapped and stressed Americans of a much bigger problem in play. The Big Three were being judged with heightened skepticism because of the climate of general distrust that is often created, and regularly undermines economies, during times of recession. Trust was the central theme of Adam Smith's vision for progress of humankind and the driver that fuels individual energy, creativity, and market growth. When consumer confidence is shaken and trust compromised, markets contract because individuals withdraw. Regaining confidence is the key to turning things around.[9]

Much like Marie Antoinette's alleged suggestion to the breadless, starving French populace to "let them eat cake," Wagoner's use of the private plane reinforced people's belief that General Motors was out of touch with the reality of the times and the values of Americans who once so proudly drove their vehicles. More significant was how blind the execs were to the great depths of that divide, a breach that began decades earlier when American carmakers failed to anticipate and compete with the cost structure and quality of the Asian imports that ultimately usurped the American car market. GM, once the symbol of US prosperity, was now hobbled with debt and dysfunction and fettered by bureaucracy. The quintessential American company, once beloved by many, was now the object of derision and disdain.

Wagoner's blunder certainly interrupted the pattern of everyone's attention, but it also sparked a media frenzy. It tripped an alarm deep inside the public psyche, the cultural equivalent of triggering the aggressive or fearful fight-or-flight response in the brain's amygdala. The problem was GM was no longer in rapport with Americans or car buyers. The fact that people simply no longer had confidence in the carmaker's ability to repay their bailout highlights a basic human and business truth: Before you can even begin to push your business model on to consumers, you first need to understand their model of reality. As Stephen Covey puts it, "Seek first to understand, then to be understood."[10]

Consumers anthropomorphize brands as people, viewing their representatives (whether it is a greeter at Wal-Mart or the CEO of a Fortune 100 corporation) as the face of the brand. The word "corporate" comes from the Latin root *corporatus,* which means made into a body, hence the legal term "body corporate" refers to a corporation. The best way to build rapport with people or companies is to share in their beliefs and behaviors. When we don't mesh with someone, when he or she rubs us the wrong way, or when we don't aspire to the same values and passions, we routinely dismiss that person, just as we reject brands that are out of sync with our own lives.

While pattern interrupts, the first step to behavior change, alert our attention, they also narrow and direct our focus, preparing us for possible threats. But the next step on the path to sales closure requires opening the prospect's mind to new possibilities, a mental state that only comes with an easing of tensions and a building of trust. Before you get your consumers really excited about your product or brand, you need to first reduce their apprehension to make them receptive to your pitch. In other words, you need to connect with them in a harmonious, empathetic, authoritative, and believable manner, which leads to a level of comfort and rapport in your overture.

According to a study led by Dr. Michel Tuan Pham at Columbia University, shoppers who are more relaxed are more likely to ascribe higher values to a product, which also lends to a willingness to pay more. The researchers showed subjects videos known to relax or excite people and then asked those subjects to place values on certain products, even using an eBay-style auction to allow them to place bids on everyday items such as car tires, paper shredders, and tennis rackets. They found that the relaxed participants would pay about 15 percent more than those less relaxed. The researchers concluded that one of the key elements to accomplish this—in terms of evolutionary psychology—is the reduction of threat levels. Humans have evolved for many millennia to first and foremost avoid harm, which is why our skittish nature can make us very fickle consumers.

When a shopper is in a state of heightened arousal and stress, he or she is more likely to focus on the rational, concrete components of the sales pitch—details like cost, product specifications, hard facts, and potential limitations. When shoppers are more relaxed, and any outstanding threats subside, they are more apt to open their minds to abstract thinking, enabling them to envision possible benefits, such as how the product might accomplish their future goals, as well as the more cultural and emotional implications of the purchase.[11] In their state of agitation, the House Financial Services Committee simply could not conceptualize the hypothetical possibilities of a better future for GM. Their stress had them fixated on the implications of the flights, even if the cost of a single trip on a private jet was a fraction of a multibillion-dollar bailout.[12]

MANNING UP

Months after that ill-fated trip to Capitol Hill, General Motors management told Deutsch LA, one of their advertising agencies, the highly confidential news that they were anticipating bankruptcy. They asked for our assistance in making the announcement, hoping that we might be able to help them get Americans back on their side by convincing the public that GM would be viable again if given a second chance. The effort had to announce Chapter 11 bankruptcy filing, convince people that the company was truly changing for the better, and sell cars in an incredibly anemic car market, one of the lowest in the industry's history. The goal was to help GM emerge quickly from bankruptcy with a revitalized focus on profitability and fewer, but stronger and leaner, core brands.

Mike Sheldon, leader of our agency in LA, was deeply attuned to the task at hand. He grew up in a Detroit suburb and was the son of a GM executive. Mike pulled the team into his office, closed the door, and told us: "We are under a microscope. The work we are about to create will be dissected like private jets. This will be the single most scrutinized and criticized effort you will ever work on in your career." We were to be judged by the same millions of Americans who had already cast judgment on GM, writing them off. We were being asked to take what many would perceive as more public money and turn it into an advertising campaign promoting yet more private interests. Would this self-promotion fall into the same perceptual bucket as excessive spending? Would the public respond by saying, "Make better cars, not ads"? Should GM even be advertising right now? Was there a better way to communicate their plight and plan?

In order to answer these looming questions and write the creative brief for the assignment, I decided to do focus groups to talk to car shoppers across the United States instead of conducting quantitative surveys. I can always get to the bottom of an issue faster and more accurately by observing respondents in person because I can view their unconscious reactions and their emotions, and not just what they report. I provide more weight to emotional responses and body language, and if there is incongruence between word and deed, I can challenge the response and dig deeper, probing the core areas of my seven-step process. Over and over again I heard panelists tell me that they simply couldn't care less about GM's fate. They scolded and blamed upper management for "resting on their laurels" and "not being able to build cars that people wanted." But their intense emotions belied their words. If they really didn't care about GM, why were they so worked up and so pissed off? There's an old adage, "The opposite of love is not hate, it is indifference," and these people were anything but indifferent.

Beneath the surface GM represented something that was both much wider in scope and deeply personal: "the American dream." This sentiment had been best expressed by the lyrics of the former jingle of its flagship brand: "Baseball, hotdogs, apple pie, and Chevrolet." We also couldn't let a linchpin of the US economy go under. As one panelist suggested, "GM is to the US economy what Kevin Bacon is to the acting community." There were six degrees of separation between the American automotive industry and every other aspect of our national economy. If GM went belly up, the ripple effect meant a potential crippling blow to both our fragile economy and our nation's psyche. But a communication approach that reminded them of this fact was destined to backfire. It would be perceived as a threat and an attempt at manipulation. Using fear tactics among an already frightened audience would only fuel their antipathy. The sticking point was comfort. GM had already grabbed the attention of the public. The next step was to assuage their alarm, placating their animosity so that they could be responsive and listen to what GM had to say.

What we discovered was that GM's plight was really an unconscious symbol for the plight of all Americans. GM's decline was emblematic of national decline, a painful reminder that America's collective star had fallen in an increasingly competitive global marketplace. The ironic truth was that beneath the vitriol people really cared deeply about GM. The real reason why people were so upset with GM was that they felt let down—GM's looming demise deep down engendered a feeling of vulnerability. They were worried about their own fate and that of their children in a country whose supremacy and prosperity was crumbling before their eyes.

Among all the ideas I explored in the initial set of focus groups, there was one approach that really gained traction. Eric Hirshberg, our then-president and chief creative officer, had written a brief speech, which I read aloud to the panelists, highlighting the themes of transparency, responsibility, and action. The idea was to have Wagoner come clean and man-up by addressing the public from the headquarters at the Renaissance Center in Detroit, acknowledging GM's shortcomings and mistakes, and declaring the rebirth of GM in a very open, honest, and public fashion. The speech really touched a nerve with just about everyone in the focus groups. But unlike the corporate jet saga, this time the vibe was quite comforting. As I read it, the participants' arms uncrossed, their brow furrows dissipated, and slight but authentic smiles emerged in acknowledgment. The shift in the room was palpable, not unlike observing quarreling good friends finally finding a pivotal moment of common ground.

The power of the speech was not so much the facts or the language, but the way it was written, and more importantly how it began. It did something that few marketers will ever consider doing: It began with a statement of wrongdoing. This led to a huge breakthrough moment. Despite their malevolent wishes and angry protests, most Americans were silently hoping to be led out of this mess by GM, the object of their scorn. People simply needed to hear GM admit to their mistakes, much like a friend who waits to hear another say, "I'm sorry, I screwed up." The American public was so incensed because it was easier to hide behind the conscious defenses of their indignation and anger than to expose their real fear and inner insecurities. Anger and fear are essentially two sides of the same coin, and are even centered around the same part of the brain, the amygdala.

Encouraged by that epiphany, I entered the back room on the other side of the two-way mirror to check for questions. I told my colleague Tom Else, the leader of the GM account team, that there was a "nugget of gold" in that speech. Ironically, while I had been calming the nerves of panelists in the focus room through the eloquent speech, Tom was getting all riled up in the back room. He could no longer contain his agitation, exclaiming loudly with arms flailing, "Are you out of your fucking mind! We can't have Wagoner give that speech!" Tom was right. The speech was wrong. But not all wrong. It couldn't come from Wagoner. Context often determines the meaning of a communication, and Wagoner was the wrong envelope to deliver this message. He was collateral damage of a war waged by the media and no longer a credible authority. And since there were no plans at that point to replace him as CEO, it simply wouldn't fly. It would be better to deflect the focus away from troubled management and use a television announcement as the conduit for those same ideas. Hirshberg had brilliantly found a window back into the hearts of people, and it was the tone of that voice that finally made the medicine go down smoothly. A dose of contrition and an ounce of humility would convince Americans that GM had indeed "got it" and was on the path to recovery.

A sixty-second spot began by admitting up front, "Let's be completely honest, no company wants to go through this," and that "there was a time when our cost structure could compete worldwide . . . not anymore." The ad showed a series of "down but not out" imagery, a runner racing with determination encumbered somewhat by a specially designed prosthetic leg, a hockey player knocked down to the ice, a tattered and ripped American flag flapping helplessly in a storm. It was punctuated with a nod to gritty defiance by cutting to a giant bronze statue of famed boxer Joe Louis's fist, which stands in downtown Detroit. These images served as rich metaphors that connected deeply with our intuitive unconscious.

The ad was not just an emotional message but also a rational outline of a business plan of action that made it believable: fewer brands and models, greater efficiency, greener cars, and new technologies. It concluded on an upbeat note proactively proclaiming: "This is not about going out of business. This is about getting down to business. Because the only chapter we're focused on is Chapter 1." In the end, the ad suggested that Chapter 11 was not the death knell of GM but rather a much-needed catalyst for the rebirth of the leaner, stronger, and better GM, and by implication, a better America. GM had finally stepped to the plate and said, "I got this!"

"Chapter 1," as the spot was called, ran in heavy rotation beginning on June 1, 2009, the day that GM filed for bankruptcy. It helped lay down the foundation for the recovery of a new company and was praised in the press for being straightforward. It began to reverse the tide against GM as they came out of bankruptcy in a record-breaking 40 days. The campaign dubbed "reinvention" helped sell cars when the bottom had dropped out of the market, moving business metrics upward during the launch and the months that followed. It won a David Ogilvy Gold Award for the automotive industry, the industry's top achievement for breakthrough research insight that creates a powerful, profitable campaign.[13]

All too often marketers puff out their chests, making even bolder and bigger claims in the face of adversity, only to create greater social distance. When someone tells us how great they are, we just see their flaws. We see through the veil of their insecurities and their hidden agendas. Sometimes when we lead with the self-deprecation of our foibles, our status ascends as our audience intuits confidence because our minds process information through inference. This same counterintuitive, self-effacing approach has helped classic advertisers discover advantage in disadvantage. Avis rental cars said, "We try harder" because "we are number 2, not number 1," in an ad series deemed among the top ten campaigns of all time. Likewise, Listerine proclaimed, "The taste you love to hate," which helped it to lead the mouthwash category, a position it still enjoys today. And a classic 1966 Volkswagen Beetle print ad, created with the honesty, charm, and wit characterized by ad legend Bill Bernbach, boldly stated that

"Ugly is only skin deep." The brand and the car led the creative revolution in marketing and advertising and sold a ton of Beetles. It also transformed the American automotive industry long before the Asian imports succeeded. It might seem ironic, but so too is the mind.

BULLSHIT ALARMS

Nature and nurture have instilled programs within our minds that seek out the deeper meaning behind every message, taking nothing at face value. This is especially true for marketing messages that, experience has taught us, seek first to profit and influence. The unsuspected trap Wagoner and the Big Three leaders flew into was that their actions were not aligned with their words. All too often marketers say one thing and do another. They view communications plans as separate from business operations. This antiquated view flies in the face of the current age of information and transparency in which consumers are empowered to level the playing the field by publicly calling "bullshit"—a reality all marketers need to heed or prepare to endure the consequences. Harmonious connection to people and brands is often determined by the extent to which there is alignment of their words, appearance, behavior, and deeds. When companies are out of sync with their own promises and the sensibilities of consumers, people instinctively develop a feeling of distrust that reflexively undermines corporate intentions. As Richard Dawkins says, "We are evolved to second-guess the behaviors of others by becoming brilliant intuitive psychologists."[14]

Our brains do this by unconsciously scanning for contrast and inconsistencies in the information being interpreted. This process equips consumers with bullshit radars that communicate the perils of deception and the treachery of cheaters through the feelings generated by their low-road unconscious circuitry. When things don't add up, or something just doesn't feel right, it is because the brain is simultaneously parallel processing multiple channels of sensory information. When there is a mismatch of signals being sent, neurochemicals of stress like cortisol are released, warning us to hold back and be wary. It's not unlike making eye contact with a stranger on the street who looks normal enough and acknowledges you pleasantly, yet something feels inexplicably askew. Sure enough, the person approaches you and asks: "Can I borrow a dollar?" This also happens when a salesman tells you that someone else is interested in buying the car you are checking out, but he'll make you a deal if you buy it today. Inauthentic advertising and salesmanship are like telling someone how much you care while simultaneously averting your gaze and fidgeting nervously. Incongruities generate the chemicals of our anxious, cautious emotions.

But we are not only programmed to detect deception; we are also made to challenge the affront. Humans often instinctively respond to attempts of being cheated with aggression, a strategy in game theory known as tit for tat, or the English expression for "equivalent retaliation." This human strategy evolved to ensure stability, fairness, and prosperity in hunter-gatherer societies.[15] Tit for tat, much like reciprocal altruism, reflects our inclination to not only reward nice people but also punish bad ones. We have evolved to possess both an acute sense of feeling wronged and also a drive to articulate that threat in the form of public outrage. Individual grievances become collective sanctions as we raise red flags to others, not unlike the warning call of a bird signaling to the flock in the presence of a predator. So strong is this instinct that we do so at our own peril, provoking and challenging big business behemoths much like the brave bird who draws attention to the hawk only to expose itself to predation. It may seem ironic that some of our noblest and most selfless moral intentions come from the depths of our most primitive and unthinking parts of the brain.[16]

Today social media provides ample opportunity to amplify this effect, exposing wrongdoers or singing the praises of do-gooders.[17] For instance, Trip Advisor has revolutionized the hotel industry, Yelp has forever changed the way in which we dine, and Amazon.com reviews and recommendations have transformed the landscape of the publishing industry. According to Forrester, an independent research company that provides advice to global leaders in business and technology, there are approximately 500 billion word-of-mouth impressions created every day in social media—online word of mouth now rivals advertising. The management consulting firm McKinsey and Company estimates that two-thirds of the US economy is now driven by word of mouth.[18]

In this new paradigm of transparency, marketers can no longer simply buy trust through advertising, and companies can no longer view marketing as a veneer across their business model, the face to the public. They will need to earn it through better products and services. If the aim of marketing is to connect to the sensibilities of today's consumers, business must begin to treat communication efforts as central, not peripheral or incremental, to business processes. Today many marketers still view the term "integration" as only making their communications efforts "look and feel" as if they are coming from one place . . . and one voice. But increasingly, it's less about what you say and more about what others say about you, and more importantly, what you do. Any good psychologist will tell you the most effective way to change someone else's behavior is to change your own. Integration should not just be about how marketing appears but also about how businesses act.

THE TRUST HORMONE

There may be a lot of truth to John Lennon's observation that "All you need is love," which in many ways parallels the adage "Without trust there is nothing." And science is proving both. Researchers have identified the physiological basis for establishing trust, a neurotransmitter known as oxytocin, also known as the "love drug." Excitement over the neurotransmitter began in the 1990s when researchers noted its calming effect on breast-feeding women.[19] Oxytocin is best known as the biochemical facilitator of familial bonding behavior between mothers and infants as well as pair bonding in mates. It is most easily generated by physical contact, spiking during activities such as breast-feeding, hugging, cuddling, and sexual intercourse.[20] But in recent years the focus has shifted toward its effects on all of us, as males and females alike produce the hormone. It turns out we don't just consciously choose to trust someone. Trust is a feeling generated at deeper levels, often in reaction to our physical environment but also induced by our internal thoughts and imagination.

The latest research shows that the neurochemical is also the catalyst for successful economic exchanges. Dr. Paul Zak of Claremont Graduate University, one of the founders of the emerging field of neuroeconomics, which combines economics with neuroscience, biology, and psychology, calls oxytocin the "social glue" that binds people and societies and the "economic lubricant" that enables a host of transactions on which markets depend.[21] His pioneering work has earned him the nickname "Dr. Love." Suggesting that oxytocin is the chemical behind morality and reciprocal altruism, Zak explains, "We discovered that this molecule in the brain called oxytocin is released when someone trusts us and induces us to reciprocate trust."

In many ways today's markets and digital economies are at odds with the ways in which trust is generated. Exchanges are based upon financial transactions, not upon the emotional and physical bonds between people, and virtual realities often remove physical interaction from the equation altogether. There is a dearth of the unity, security, and personal connection that has bonded people together throughout the history of evolution among tightly knit bands of people. As evolutionary psychologist John Tooby states, "In hunter-gatherer societies . . . there is a real feeling of closeness, but in market societies though the absolute welfare goes way up . . . it creates a deep insecurity; do these people really care about me or not?"[22] In hunter-gatherer societies implicit caring, not explicit financial exchange, was the basis for altruistic transactions. Evolutionary psychologist Leda Cosmides adds, "Explicit exchange is a sign of social distance . . . every time I go to Starbucks and get a mocha I'm engaged in explicit exchange . . . every time I do that, I'm getting a signal of social distance . . . that these people do not care about my welfare, that I'm not uniquely valued."[23]

Zak believes trust is the key factor that determines whether or not a society is working well, creating lower crime, better education, and greater economic development. In a 2011 interview, he explained to me how Norway—the nation with the highest levels of trust—has more stable governments and higher income levels. "Social capital" begets "economic capital" as the positive interactions of its citizenry enable greater and more robust transactions and larger markets. He believes that Norway's high levels of trust are because many of its citizens share common ancestry and surnames. You are more likely to trust your relatives and similar others, just as we did back in hunter-gatherer times when tribes were often comprised of close kin. Treating others as you would your own family is not just good for humanity; it's good for business and the economy.[24]

Swiss and American scientists have demonstrated that by increasing oxytocin levels, you can increase investment behavior. Using a nasal spray containing the neurotransmitter, they found that a group of investors were much more willing to trust a stranger posing as a financial adviser. The group that got a few squirts of the oxytocin nasal spray offered twice as much money as the group that only received a placebo. Those who received the dose felt more secure that their investment would pay off even though there were no guarantees of profit, demonstrating that the hormone oxytocin triggers the brain's "trust circuits."[25] It diminishes the levels of the stress hormone cortisol, which activates the fight-or-flight response, making us feel more secure and reducing anxiety.[26]

And according to Zak's research, the hormone can even increase advertising effectiveness. Zak discovered that oxytocin also raises empathy toward issues in television ads. In another study, participants were given sniffs of oxytocin and shown public service announcements regarding global warming, smoking, alcohol, and reckless driving. They were then given the opportunity to contribute some of the money they earned for participating in the research study. Those that received oxytocin gave 56 percent more money to the advertised causes than those who received a placebo. As Zak says, "Our results show why puppies and babies are in toilet paper commercials."[27]

And according to Thomas Crook, PhD, CEO of Cognitive Research Corporation in Florida, and a former researcher with the National Institutes for Mental Health, our thoughts can trigger increases in levels of the hormone. Crook explains that familiar thoughts and comforting sensations like the smells of your mom's signature cookies, the dawn choir of chirping birds, or the sound of your favorite music can trigger positive memories that release oxytocin. In a research study from the University of North Carolina at Chapel Hill, happily married women quickly released a dose of the hormone just by daydreaming about their husbands while they were apart.[28] Similarly, Zak observed that using social media can result in a double-digit increase in oxytocin levels. One research participant exhibited an astounding 150 percent increase while online at his girlfriend's Facebook page and another subject increased oxytocin levels simply by tweeting to his social network—both demonstrating that the brain does not differentiate among real or imagined or virtual friends.[29]

In fact the "love drug" may be at the heart of the success of the much-lauded Southwest effect in the airline industry, whose ticker on the New York Stock Exchange is LUV. The well-documented economic impact of that effect—which reduces costs for travelers across the board and increases air traffic to cities serviced by the airline—has engendered goodwill among its customers for years and may in part be fueled by employee and customer bonding and oxytocin. In 2009 Southwest Airlines was the largest airline in the world based on the number of passengers that fly the airline each year,[30] and in 2011 it was not only America's leading low-cost carrier but was also rated America's favorite airline by Consumer Reports.[31]

Joe Harris, a labor lawyer for Southwest, explains that the company's harmonious employee relations are no accident. "At Southwest, our employees come first; our customers come second; and our stockholders come third," he said. "The rationale is pretty simple. If we treat our employees right, they're going to treat our customers right. If our customers are treated right, they will come back and our stockholders will benefit."[32] As Southwest's CEO Gary Kelly explains: "Southwest is a company of people, not just planes. We hire great people who have a passion for serving others, and we give them the freedom to be themselves and to take care of our customers. We treat our employees like family and our customers like guests in our home. Our guiding principle is, above all else, the Golden Rule." It's no surprise that "Do unto others as you would have others do unto you" is also what evolutionary psychologists call reciprocal altruism, the enduring cornerstone of humanity since the dawn of man.

To accomplish bonding with customers, Southwest uses its fundamental understanding of the value of physical social interactions. They have brilliantly turned a captive audience of travelers into an opportunity to demonstrate how much they care about them. One customer wrote to Southwest to thank the flight attendant who helped her and her fiancé on their way to California to get married. The flight attendant assisted them with their carry-on luggage, which included the wedding dress; he then gave them a free cocktail and, to top it off, as the flight was preparing to land, he got on the public address system and asked all passengers to close their window shades to provide a candlelight ambience before he sang to the young couple. The customer wrote, "I want to sincerely thank this flight attendant for going above and beyond his job description and for adding a special touch to a trip we'll always remember!"[33] With greatly narrowing windows of physical interaction with customers, companies would be better served to identify touch points and to surprise and delight their clients rather than upselling or ignoring them. Southwest turned their captive audience of travelers into a brand-building opportunity. Similarly, other interactions such as requesting to speak to a customer service agent can also be turned into a branding moment, not just an annoying sales call.

TRUST IN THE DIGITAL AGE

Consumers are increasingly cautious of privacy issues online, fearful of placing their information in the wrong hands. By their very nature, digital business models collect terabytes of personal data that can be used to the company's advantage to better target their sales efforts and lure advertisers. In addition, these models remove physical contact and proximity to people, the most powerful means of engendering trustworthiness. On the flip side, the virtual realm opens up the opportunities to increase rapport and gain respect by understanding and responding to people's needs, beliefs, and behaviors—a key prerequisite to comfort building. What these models lose in their physical proximity to people, they can potentially gain in customer knowledge and empathic anticipation. The future of online businesses rests in this delicate balance of navigating the competing interests of privacy and personal attention.

For instance, Amazon.com is among the world's leaders in sharing information with advertisers. Yet Amazon's use of that information—drawing from the receipts of its more than 59 million active customers—has demonstrated that well-crafted personalization and service can overcome privacy fears.[34] In fact, Amazon.com, according to a research study reported in 2010 by Millward Brown, ranks as the most trusted brand in America. This study also concluded that the long-term success of a brand depends upon trust plus recommendation, confirming that brands excelling along these dimensions enjoy a brand-customer bond ten times in excess of the average and are nearly seven times more likely to be purchased, exhibiting a high likelihood of near-term growth in market share.[35]

Unlike traditional marketers that invest primarily in high-level branding efforts through advertising, Amazon has built its trust from the bottom up by focusing on better products, pricing, and customer service. As Amazon CEO Jeff Bezos says, "Advertising is the price you pay for having an unremarkable product or service."[36] In an interview with *Wired*'s Chris Anderson, Bezos explained, "We did a 15-month-long test of TV advertising in two markets—Portland and Minneapolis—to see how much it drove our sales. And it worked, but not as much as the kind of price elasticity we knew we could get from taking those ad dollars and giving them back to consumers. So we put all that money into lower product prices and free shipping. That has significantly accelerated the growth of our business." Bezos believes that "more and more money will go into making a great customer experience, and less will go into shouting about the service." When asked if traditional marketers need be alarmed, Bezos remarks, "I'm not saying that advertising is going away. But the balance is shifting. If today the successful recipe is to put 70 percent of your energy into shouting about your service and 30 percent into making it great, over the next 20 years I think that's going to invert."[37]

FAMILIARITY BREEDS AFFECTION

This is not to say that big ad budgets and strong distribution levels don't build trust and sales. The essence of branding is to create comfort, which stems directly from familiarity. It has been proven that leading a category on share of voice or distribution is a time-tested strategy for becoming the default choice in a herd-mentality market. One of the many paradoxes of the human mind is that although we are attracted to the novelty of pattern interrupts, we move toward the complacency of the established and familiar. The number one drive in human behavior and biology is homeostasis, or the seeking of the same stable, balanced, predictable state.[38] Although we are excited by what is new and different, we also seek certainty and stability in our lives, deriving pleasure in the comfort of the known. We learn to love and trust what we are accustomed to, not just in terms of the people and environments we gravitate toward, but in the brands, products, and services we choose to buy.

Psychologist Robert Zajonc, of Stanford University, demonstrated that familiarity breeds affection, a process he labeled the "mere exposure effect." Zajonc's seminal experiment in 1968 showed participants a randomly chosen series of shapes in rapid succession, making it impossible for the group to consciously discern how often each shape was shown. What he found was that when asked which shapes they found most pleasing, subjects would reliably choose those that they had been exposed to most often, even though they had no conscious awareness of how often they had seen the shapes or which they'd seen more often.[39]

Numerous studies have demonstrated that this preference for familiar things can apply to important economic decisions, from the investments and donations you make to the occupations you choose, to the places you live and the brands you like to buy. An Oppenheimer study suggests that the easier a company's name was to pronounce, the more likely a potential customer was to associate it with a sense of comfort and safety, driving up stock selection and prices.[40] When Quincy, Illinois, was damaged by floods in 1993, the town received a charitable amount of assistance from people in Quincy, Massachusetts.[41] And even the familiarity of one's own name can have a peculiar influence on our decision making. People named Dennis are more likely to become dentists, Louises are more likely to move to Louisiana, and Marshas tend to prefer Mars bars instead of a Snickers bar.[42] Since we gravitate to the familiar, when possible it's always best to address your customer by name—as in direct mailers and email. Or when choosing a product name, it may be helpful to choose a term that already has meaning and familiarity with the segment of consumers you are trying to reach.[43]

ONENESS WITH BRAND

Much as incongruities and differences push us away from some people, corresponding agreements with others can synchronize and bond us. That's because our social brains were not designed to work in isolation but rather in a back and forth looping process with the minds of other individuals, unconsciously inclining us to transcend the boundaries of our own being. The conscious mind thinks "I." The unconscious feels "we." This ability to synchronize with other humans in an effort to empathize is innate and automatic. Psychologist Andrew Meltzoff, an expert on learning and child development, demonstrated this when he wagged his tongue at a baby just 42 minutes old and she wagged her tongue back.

Not surprisingly, many of us love to sing together at concerts, cheer in unison, do the wave with 80,000 other sports fans, pack ourselves mat to mat in yoga studios, pedal side by side in spinning class, dance at clubs with complete strangers, and join the club that brands provide. We are hardwired to synchronize with others through this low-road unconscious neurological process in which our mirror neurons imitate others so that we can share in the experience.[44] We are constantly having deep dialogues with the world around us. These intuitive two-way conversations extend beyond the superfluous surface level of our idle, conscious chatter. When a mother embraces and bonds with her infant child, she demonstrates such unconditional love and devotion that not a single word needs to be spoken.

It sounds kind of spiritual, but the feeling is really seated in the biology of our brain. In his book *I Am a Strange Loop,* cognitive scientist Douglas Hofstadter describes the intensity of his connection to his recently deceased wife upon staring at her picture:

> I looked at her face and looked so deeply that I felt I was behind her eyes and all at once I found myself saying, as tears flowed, "That's Me. That's Me!" And those simple words brought back many thoughts that I had had before, about the fusion of our souls into one higher-level entity, about the fact that at the core of both our souls lay our identical hopes and dreams for our children, about the notion that those hopes were not separate or distinct hopes but were just one hope, one clear thing that defined us both, that wielded us into a unit, the kind of unit I had but dimly imagined before being married and having children. I realized that though Carol had died, that core piece of her had not died at all, but that it had lived on very determinedly in my brain.[45]

Jeffrey Blish, chief strategy officer at Deutsch LA, who has the intuitive ability to distill vast information eloquently and succinctly, says "Truth has few words, absolute truth none." This connection of people and brands is part of a much deeper identification. To achieve this connection, marketers need to tap into the part of the brain that seeks to merge with others. Just as people unconsciously seek a deep connection with people, brands become modern surrogates for this desire of connection. Great brands act as people that see the world as we see it, bonding us at the core of our being, as if to say, "That's me!" or "You got me!" If you want further evidence of this just look at the incredible loyalty to brands that radiate the shared passions of their audience. Apple asked people to "think different" and "challenge the status quo" which ironically led herds of their customers to wait together for hours outside Apple stores just to be the first to buy their products. Nike tapped into our inner sense of self-loathing and desire for achievement by telling us to "Just do it!"—its logo transcending sports to encompass our life goals and aspirations as human beings. Harley-Davidson offered people the rebellious freedom to escape the confinement of the daily grind, prompting owners to view the brand with religious fervor, as well as to bond with fellow riders as if they were their own brothers. People don't just buy products; they buy into values. When these beliefs and aspirations closely mirror their own, companies can achieve brand fans for life.

MICHELANGELO EFFECT

A ripe metaphor for marketers comes from the work of the great Italian artist Michelangelo, who understood the intuitive power of releasing beauty from within. He said, "Every block of stone has a statue inside it and it is the task of the sculptor to discover it."[46] As Michelangelo demonstrated through his lifetime of enduring art, it is less about changing the nature of the physical object and more about revealing the deeper beauty that resides inside the subject. The ultimate example of this belief is his famous statue of David, sculpted out of a ruined block of marble which had been rejected by others. And in the striking Captives series, the figures emerge from the stone as if the sculptor had released them from imprisonment.[47]

Marketing is like art. We must find the person inside who fits the brand and release their inner, repressed desires. We need to "sculpt" people by identifying who they really are inside, not just who they wish to become. And to do so on their terms, not ours. This empowering insight cuts to the core of the inner self and not just the persona, driving great, enduring, successful branding efforts like L'Oréal's proclamation, "Because I'm worth it," and the U.S. Army's rousing call to "Be all you can be." The marketer's role is to recognize and affirm individuals' true ideals while facilitating their goal of authenticity.

This human insight was at the core of Call of Duty's "There's a soldier in all of us" ad campaign. Activision interrupted the tried and true pattern of video game launches, forgoing depictions of actual game play, instead featuring ordinary people as protagonists and heroes in their own militant fantasies. In one spot we don't see combatting soldiers but rather plainclothes citizens, everyone from a high-heeled businesswoman to a short-order cook, taking command of the battlefield with great skill and courage. In another spot, average newbie Jonah Hill is teamed up with experienced veteran Sam Worthington as Jonah is transformed from goofy noob to self-assured badass. These efforts expanded the franchise from fanatical gamers to all walks of life, putting everyday people on their path to greatness and gaming mastery and Call of Duty on track to the two biggest launches in entertainment history.[48]

Likewise Nike salutes everyday athletes and offers inner inspiration, launching the "Find Your Greatness" campaign in 2012 to coincide with the summer Olympics. The centerpiece was a commercial—breaking first on digital channels and social media and then on television in 25 countries—that showed everyday athletes across the globe striving to excel at their sport on their own terms. In another commercial, a jogger seen approaching from the distance is gradually revealed to be not an elite athlete but an overweight twelve-year-old boy determinedly struggling alone down a country road. The voiceover refutes the idea that "greatness is a gift reserved for a chosen few," and instead affirms that "we're all capable of it." The campaign is supported by a global Twitter-promoted hashtag, #findgreatness, to help spark conversation around how athletes everywhere can find their own defining moments in sport, and a digital ecosystem that enables over 8.5 million global members to gauge their performance, share their success stories, and motivate themselves and others to do more to achieve their goals.

By establishing deep empathy, Nike's "Find Your Greatness" campaign quickly led the Viral Chart, capturing the spirit of the competition as well as 4.5 million views during the first week of the London games. It beat out its competitor Adidas, whose "Take the Stage" campaign accumulated 2.9 million views during that same week. What makes this particularly impressive is that Nike lacked the benefit of sponsorship, since Adidas had exclusive marketing rights within the UK as an Olympic partner, having spent £100 million on

its Olympic marketing in the previous four years. During the campaigns, a large-scale online survey indicated that 37 percent of US
consumers identified Nike as an Olympic sponsor as compared to
only 24 percent for Adidas, the real sponsor.[49]

Brand relationships are like personal relationships: after a while
you really do start to look like each other. The power and pervasive-
ness of this process of brain looping and body mirroring is illustrated
by a remarkable example. Couples who live happily together in a
continual state of emotional alignment come to actually resemble
each other, resulting from the parallel sculpting of facial muscles over
years of conditioning, reinforced by their shared emotions and similar expressions. They actually mold the same ridges and form similar
wrinkles, furrows, and folds as they smile or frown in empathetic
accordance. Studies have revealed that the happier couples are, the
greater their facial similarity.[50]

But in reality many consumers feel that something is missing in
their daily lives. They feel underappreciated and often imprisoned
by the routine of their mundane lives, leading them to unconsciously
seek the greater emotional connection that they feel is missing. Brand
allegiances have become the modern expressions and choices that
appeal to this hidden desire for connections. Consumers see brands
they love as reflections of the secret strengths they hope to nurture
and fully realize.

This art metaphor of finding inner beauty and desires serves well
to guide not only our relationship to others but also our relationship
to brands. The questions marketers need to ask are, How can we
bring out the ideal self in our customers? and How can we go beyond
a transactional state of explicit financial exchange to a related state
of implicit emotional exchange and self-realization? Amazon.com
has the goal of becoming the most customer-centric company in history. Their business model can be viewed not only as saving time and
money, but also as one that anticipates the needs of their customers,
much in the way friends in deep rapport finish each other's sentences.
The benefit to consumers is as much about discovery of an idealized
version of themselves as it is about low prices and convenient service. Amazon gives people tools to create their ideal experience and

their ideal self, such as the "Amazon Betterizer" that lets customers fine-tune preferences by "liking" products and then matching their tastes. The role of marketing is not converting customers or conquering competitive owners, but rather sculpting and shaping dynamic relationships by tapping into the inner desires and secret strengths of people's optimal selves. It's not about changing who they are, but rather recognizing who they are.

THE REAL ME

In 2004 Dove launched the highly successful *Campaign for Real Beauty* using real women, not models, to advertise its firming cream. The campaign featured average women in an effort to offset the stereotypically thin and impossibly flawless models conventionally used to advertise cosmetics. In 2006 the campaign won the Grand Effie award, taking top honors for advertising effectiveness that year. As Ty Montague, who chaired the Grand Effie judging panel, commented, "The Dove campaign was . . . rooted in a powerful human and cultural insight: that beauty has heretofore been defined by the media and is actually defined much differently by real women."[51] Dove tapped into the inner beauty within every woman, and it paid big dividends, making women feel not only good about themselves but also really good about Dove.

To add to the campaign, Dove released a Real Beauty viral video, regarded as one of the top ten best social media efforts. The piece demonstrated through time-lapse videography how an ordinary girl can be transformed into a supermodel through the falsifying magic of hairstyling, makeup, and photo retouching. The video tapped into all women's insecurities and feelings of inadequacy; it helped them feel better about themselves by showing them how impossibly beautiful models are, in fact, distortions and not reality.[52]

Back in the 1990s, at the ad agency JWT New York, I was responsible for account planning for what was then Warner Lambert. Included in their roster were a handful of category-leading brands, such as the pregnancy test kit E.P.T, for which JWT had created a fantastic award-winning campaign. The premise was simple, powerful, impactful, and a seminal example of the true power of "reality advertising." In the ads, genuine couples trying to get pregnant shared the captivating moment of their discovery on camera for all to see. Unscripted live results of real-life pregnancy tests earned the brand an Addy award, but more importantly the campaign helped position E.P.T. as the category leader, securing claim to the benefit of trust where trust is everything. To this day E.P.T. remains the market leader in home pregnancy test kits.[53]

I believe delivering unscripted, authentic, honest and emotionally charged subject matter to consumers especially through web videos is one of the most ripe areas and opportunities for marketers in the digital age.

MIND MELDING

Marketers often speak of the need to make their messages resonate with consumers. There is now neurological evidence that effective communication actually physically resounds in the brain of the receiver, echoing the thoughts and sentiments of the communicator by inducing and shaping neurological responses. A remarkable study, led by Princeton University's Greg Stephens, determined through fMRI brain scans that in both the communicator and listener, similar regions of the brain fired when engaged in unrehearsed, real-life story telling, leading the researchers to conclude that brain cells do synchronize during successful communication. As the study says, "The findings shown here indicate that during successful communication, speakers' and listeners' brains exhibit joint, temporally coupled, response patterns. Such neural coupling substantially diminishes in the absence of communication, such as when listening to an unintelligible foreign language. Moreover, more extensive speaker-listener neural couplings result in more successful communication." The deeper the conversation, the more deeply our minds meld. In some instances, the listener's brain patterns actually anticipate where the story is going, in deep rapport with the storyteller.[54]

Sometimes rapport is as simple as closely imitating your customers. Research by a Dutch psychologist showed that waitresses who mirrored their customers yielded 140 percent larger tips. "Mimicry creates bonds between people—it induces a sense of 'we-ness,'" says Rick van Baaren of the University of Nijmegen.[55] The findings lend credibility to the notion that people are more comfortable with those who share their behaviors, and that they are often unable to consciously notice when they are being imitated. Without their awareness, those customers that had been mimicked believed that they had better service.[56] By being in sync with someone, you implicitly demonstrate that you understand and agree with him or her. For service representatives this may mean it's a good idea to repeat and paraphrase your customers' statements to demonstrate that you really heard them and are truly listening.

It may sound trite but it is too often ignored, if you really want to open a dialogue that creates incredibly loyal customers . . . understand them first, treat them as you would people for whom you genuinely care, and mirror their beliefs and behavior. We have a huge sign that hangs on a wall of Deutsch LA that reads "Care the Most." It is a piece of art created by our former co-CEO and chief creative officer, Eric Hirshberg, and it was his encapsulation of our working philosophy. Words to live by—in business and in life. For marketers who have gone astray, this is perhaps better stated as "Give a shit, don't be full of it."

THOUGHT-STARTERS ON CREATING COMFORT

Keep it real. The age of access and transparency is upon us. Now everyone has access to information about your business and access to an audience to talk about your product. Because of this, truth and trust are today's table stakes. Marketers need to be more authentic and honest in behavior and communications across all media. This doesn't mean advertising needs to be realistic in a literal sense, but it must ring true. We know the Energizer bunny doesn't really go forever, but we still can believe its batteries last the longest.

Trust in the digital age is becoming more difficult to earn as more marketers jump into the fray of social media, seeking to control and contrive the conversation in their favor. Company representatives may pollute the blogosphere, posing as consumers in support of brands or practicing "like-gating" by offering access to certain content only if prospects "like" their brand, in an attempt to generate more Facebook fans, or even setting up web-advertorials that pretend to be authentic news sites, complete with artificial commentary. But efforts to this end can backfire as people see through the deceptions and are preprogrammed to retaliate or warn their friends.

According to a survey by the public relations firm Edelman, there has been a decline in trust in recent years for word of mouth. The number of those who perceive their peers or friends as credible sources about companies declined by almost half, from 45 percent in 2008 to 25 percent in 2010.[57] Conversely, trust in CEOs, who have been trotted out to comfort concerned consumers, has increased. For example, GM's new leader, Ed Whitacre, oversaw the company's biggest year-over-year increase, from 17 percent in 2009 to 26 percent in 2010. Companies can't simply hide behind well-crafted social media campaigns. They need to use this technology for greater transparency from within.[58]

Be responsive. As the digital age obviates the need for live interactions, gaining trust becomes more of a challenge. Person-to-person interactions carry benefits (such as facial expressions and gestures) that facilitate the manner in which humans typically generate trust. Have you ever made a joke in an email that didn't go over well because the recipient couldn't discern your banter or sarcasm (even with the addition of your sadly inadequate smiley face)?

Judy Olson, a professor of information and computer sciences, has been researching the essentials of building trust online. Her findings are steeped in a fundamental truth in psychology: People quickly pass judgment when given incomplete information, or when it appears that competence or reputation is lacking. They construct whole profiles from limited information about someone else's personality. Psychologists have found that when we make a mistake, we are more prone to blame it on situational circumstances, and when someone else makes a mistake, we are more apt to blame their personality, quickly ascribing value judgments such as uncaring, irresponsible, or selfish.[59]

In the absence of trust indicators like voice intonation, emotional expression, and body language in the text-based messages that predominate online, Olson has found that research participants default to speed of response as a key marker of trustworthiness. Marketers who act quickly are more trusted, even if the fast response informs consumers that they're simply looking into the matter at hand and will get back to them soon. For example, when filmmaker Kevin Smith sent a series of agitated tweets to his 1.6 million followers after being kicked off a Southwest Airlines flight for being "too fat," Southwest jumped quickly onto the thread, helping to deescalate the spread of criticism and diminish the anger of an influential consumer, tweeting several responses such as "I've read the tweets all night from @thatkevinsmith—He'll be getting a call at home from our Customer Relations VP tonight." And "@thatkevinsmith—Again, I'm very sorry for the experience you had tonight. Please let me know if there is anything else I can do."[60]

Another way to gain trust over the Internet is to use video, which provides the opportunity for more empathic communication by adding gesture and inflection. Domino's CEO Patrick Doyle demonstrated that when he went before the camera to promptly apologize and display his sense of frustration, urgency, and accountability in responding to an infamous YouTube prank in which an employee uploaded a video showing another employee spraying snot on food, sticking cheese up his nose, and passing gas on a slice of salami before placing it on a sandwich he was assembling for delivery. Immediately seeing and hearing the sincerity of Doyle's pleas helped consumers gauge his trustworthiness and offer Domino's forgiveness.[61]

Make them laugh. Science is also explaining the prevalence of humor in advertising as a tool to bond consumers to brands. According to the neuroscientist Robert Provine, laughter is not really primarily about humor but rather social relationships, as it tends to disappear when there is no audience. It is a signal we send to other people that synchronizes the brains of speaker and listener toward greater emotional attunement, the hallmark of successful communication. The evidence suggests that laughter is an innate, preprogrammed, cross-cultural behavior that is triggered unconsciously, which is why it is so hard to fake real laughter.[62]

In essence, laughter is a lot like human bonding communication. It is akin to saying, "I like you," or "I want you to like me." Evolutionary psychologist Robin Dunbar says that belly laughing may have worked like "grooming at a distance" for early ancestors, allowing them to maintain bonds within larger groups than their primate peers could.[63] Laughter also functions to release tension and oxytocin, firing the trust circuits to help us attract mates or seek approval from those of higher status, which explains why partners in love laugh so often, and why everyone laughs when the boss intimates the slightest hint of a joke.[64] On top of all that, laughter is contagious, causing others to share in the connection automatically and unconsciously.[65] This also explains why television shows have been using canned laughter for over a half a century, unwittingly bonding viewers to the show and convincing them that the show is actually entertaining.[66]

So when marketers scoff at ad people who try to insert their silly little jokes into commercials, bear in mind the power of triggering laughter, a force that bonds consumers to brands through the mediating variable of advertising. Funny ads are more likable, and ad likability has been identified as one of the single best predictors of advertising success according to the Advertising Research Foundation (ARF) Copy Research Validity Project.[67]

Reduce frustration. Marketers need to discover ways to employ technology to their advantage in identifying and responding to the purchase barriers of heightened anxiety and negative emotions. For instance, some call centers now use voice stress monitoring to analyze the acoustic indicators of stress (voice pitch and intensity) so that stressed-out callers can quickly be routed to (hopefully) understanding agents. If you really want to build real trust, don't reserve access to real humans as a luxury for the select few.[68]

Incidentally, some English-speaking call centers in India rename their agents with English names, provoking distrust instead of instilling harmony. The science suggests the incongruity of this practice may exacerbate suspicion if the caller believes that Sanjay is not really Roger. When in doubt, err on the side of transparency and honesty.

Google demonstrates the power of respecting consumers by recognizing that the reason people launch Google is to get the job done quickly and efficiently. They have focused their energies on building the best search engine, and through the use of white space that lets you and the playfully inviting logo breathe easy, they chose not to clutter the landing page like other web portals.

Google is now looking at ways to actively increase that empathy by identifying behavioral hints that suggest irritation arising from search difficulty. They discovered that in addition to sighing and biting their nails, users' key identifiers of stress when searching for information include "typing their inquiry as a natural language question, spending a long time staring at a results page, or completely changing their approach to the task." Google believes that such triggers, when used together, can be used to build a model that one day will make it possible for computers to detect real-time frustration.[69]

Create relaxation at the point of sale. Because stress and anxiety reduce oxytocin, which promotes trust and receptivity, heightened states of arousal can actually inhibit purchase behavior, which is why marketers are better advised not to stir consumers into a buying frenzy when they are reaching for their wallet.[70] For example, high-end car dealerships take great strides to make the dealer experience feel comfortable and relaxing, creating living-room-like waiting rooms with plush couches and luxury amenities to facilitate a low-key sales process. When Infiniti cars were first launched, the showrooms included "contemplation zones," so that buyers could take a moment to pause, greatly reducing the effect of the high-pressure sales tactics often associated with car dealerships. Similarly, retailers may want to think twice about letting shoppers watch television as they wait, since television content is ripe with excitatory triggers like news sensationalism and movie violence.[71]

When selecting music for retail environments, decision makers should choose music that is familiar and soothing, enhancing the calming effect so that customers' attentions are redirected to future benefits and not to short-term costs. Researchers have found that slow music can increase sales by as much as 38 percent by pacing shoppers to languidly stroll through aisles rather than rush out of the store empty-handed.[72] Psychologists have even found that certain colors like red, orange, and yellow encourage excitement while other colors like blue, green, and violet tend to relax, opening up our minds and our purse strings.[73]

Be consistent. We gravitate to the familiar, which is why the more a company varies their branding elements, from advertising to points of purchase, the more social distance they will create with customers. Marketers need to behave more consistently by tying together campaign elements into one clearly identifiable brand appearance. While not a new idea, it remains a sentiment that needs to extend across all business practices and is still a time-tested strategy for building rapport through consistent recognition.

The fact of the matter remains: We live our lives in patterns and we find meaning in pattern recognition. The more routine, identical, and scalable your business practices are, the more recognizable the pattern and the more you magnify the effect of that familiarity. And when advertising your brand, choose a tightly knit campaign, not a series of ad-hoc shiny objects that your agency sells you. Remember: You will tire of the work long before consumers will. As the Australian psychologist and social researcher Hugh Mackay puts it: "Although we love the idea of choice—our culture almost worships it—we seek refuge in the familiar and the comfortable."[74]

Add a twist to the familiar. Because we are programmed to pay attention to what is different but we move toward the familiar, adding a twist to a familiar idea is a great way to gain attention and receptivity. This is why we often enjoy hearing the remix version of a popular song and like seeing a good ad parody, or why there is so much copycat advertising. But, much as it is with the remix or the ad, make sure that the sequel is at least as good or better, or it will likely backfire. No one likes a rip-off artist or a cheater.

6
STEP THREE: LEAD THE IMAGINATION

I dream my painting, and then I paint my dream.

—*Vincent van Gogh*

IN 1955 SHIRLEY POLYCOFF JOINED AD GIANT FOOTE, CONE
& Belding to work on the newly acquired Clairol account, becoming
the lone woman writer at the agency in a male-dominated industry.
Driven by her spunky determination and intuitive understanding of
the female market, and despite all the historical disadvantages of being a woman, Polycoff had an advantage in her field, which almost
exclusively targeted women, who were the traditional purchasing
agents of the times. Her assignment was for Clairol's hair color line.
Her job was to "make it respectable," removing the stigma that had
long tainted the idea of dying one's hair. Perhaps she understood this
because of her own experience.

When Polycoff reached her teens, she became distraught as her
blond hair, what she viewed as her only physical distinction from
her attractive raven-haired sisters, began to darken. This prompted
her to do what only women who were considered "fast" back then
would do. She went to a local hairdresser and asked to have it light-
ened so that the front would match the back. Little did she know that
this small act of defiance would inspire her to become a role model
for several generations of women.

In 1956 Polycoff penned the titillating ad slogan, "Does she . . . or doesn't she?" a campaign that would forever shift the fashion sensibilities of American women.[1] At first, obtuse executives at *Life* magazine refused to run the suggestive print ad, concerned over what could be perceived as its smutty connotations. Polykoff challenged them, suggesting they survey the women around their office to see if they found any offense in the statement. She knew what most advertisers failed to see, and still fail to consider: the inner workings of the human mind. She knew that no decent lady in the conservative 1950s would ever admit to the off-color overtones of the risqué line. She was right. The women polled reported no such offense, keeping the unstated implications to the confines of their own imaginations. So the magazine's executives decided to run the ad and, according to Polycoff, "Everybody got rich."

Almost overnight the slogan would become a national catchphrase, helping to transform hair coloring from an exotic, low-class aberrance to a cultural norm, accepted and flaunted by many. The incidence of hair coloring skyrocketed from 7 percent to about half of all American women within a decade. And sales of Clairol soared, going from $25 million to $200 million, accounting for more than half the total of hair color sales, a market share dominance that endures today with industry sales in excess of $1 billion.[2]

Polycoff's feminine intuition paid huge dividends in the face of male-minded, overly rational resistance because of her deep and intrinsic understanding of the art of persuasion. Before anyone considers doing something out in the real world, they often first do so inside the private domain of their own mind. The imagination drives how we perceive something, particularly when faced with such a rebelliously suggestive phrase as "Does she . . . or doesn't she?"

It would take more than thirty years before another advertising slogan would lead the imagination and change behavior on such a grand scale. This would come in the form of an eight-letter phrase that would go on to become one of the most lauded and influential campaigns in advertising history.[3] Nike's "Just do it" suggestively stimulated people to take action across the globe while simultaneously elevating the brand to become the world's largest sporting goods manufacturer. The campaign that spawned the phrase gave rise to the Nike decade, boosting Nike's share of the domestic sport-shoe business from 18 percent to 43 percent, from $877 million in worldwide sales to $9.2 billion in the ten years between 1988 and 1998.[4]

Like "Does she . . . or doesn't she?" the effectiveness of "Just do it" was due to its ability to lead the imagination by being artfully vague. Its creator, Dan Wieden, co-founder of Nike's ad agency Wieden + Kennedy in Portland, Oregon, had come up with the phrase in the middle of the night after remembering the final words of convicted killer Gary Gilmore, who upon his execution said, "Let's do it."[5] From that small and dark recollection, Wieden conceived and inspired an entire movement. The open-ended suggestion went on to convince everyone from the fair-weather walker to the world-class winner that they could push through their own uncertainties and accomplish whatever goal they might hold. Nike reported receiving letters from people who confided that the phrase had driven them to do everything from leave an abusive husband to accomplish a heroic rescue from a burning building.[6] Had the slogan instructed people to "Just get off your ass and go jogging," it would have been summarily rejected. By leaving the "it" to people's imagination, the phrase inspired their dreams and opened their wallets.

Runner's World publisher George Hirsch summarized the strength of the line to move people: "The Nike 'Just do it' slogan gains new power for us all. This is really advertising that comes from the heart and goes straight to the heart and the gut."[7]

Great copywriters like Wieden and Polycoff, whose poetic lines stimulated action for so many, know something that escapes the average individual. They intuitively understand the psyche in a way that has long eluded scientists, allowing them to be guided by their unconscious hunches and not deductive rigors. Wieden and Polykoff had intuited the rules of the persuasion game before science could. Freud conceded many decades ago: "Everywhere I go I find a poet has been there before me. Poets are masters of us ordinary men, in knowledge of the mind, because they drink at streams which we have not yet made accessible to science."[8]

Freud yearned to learn what scientists now know. Today, neuroscience is providing access to the viscerally perceptive streams of the poets and persuaders, explaining their gifts through two inexorable cognitive truths of humanity. First, the brain doesn't always clearly differentiate between something real and something imagined.[9] Our imagination and our perception of the real world are closely linked since both functions engage the same neural circuitry. Numerous scientific studies confirm that visualization and mental imagery enhances actual physical performance,[10] demonstrating the very real benefits of mental rehearsal. From playing sports, to succeeding in business, to buying the car of your dreams,[11] behavior change therapists have learned that guided imagery of future goals is often greatly enhanced through the process of mental rehearsal. If you can get someone to imagine something vividly enough, you are well on your way to making the suggestion real.

Advertising that fires up our imagination in the direction of our intended goals acts as an exercise in this form of mental rehearsal. The simple process of imagining makes us more likely to buy because we have gone through the motions quite literally in our own minds. Practice does indeed make perfect.

Second, allowing people to go inside their own minds, and to use their imaginations, transforms the message from a universal one to a uniquely personal concept, prompting individuals to perceive the message as their own idea and not an attempt at external manipulation. Much in the same way that we often believe that "the book is better than the movie," when we create our own narrative, replete with characters, scenery, and images of our creation, we identify more strongly with the story and what is being said. The more people feel and relate to the experience on a personal level, the greater their commitment to buy the brand. This is the essence of intrinsic motivation and the opposite of external manipulation. We do it because we want to do it, not because someone else told us.

Imagination is the primary device of all great persuaders and inspirational leaders. Martin Luther King Jr., the most prolific proponent of the Civil Rights movement, brilliantly employed this prime directive of influence and, in turn, changed the course of an entire nation. Through his famous "I have a dream" speech, King rallied Americans for change: socially, legally, politically, and culturally. Those words would become the most memorable and productive moment in his pursuit to end segregation and prohibit discrimination. By encouraging all people to look within themselves, he allowed them to find a place of common vision and a hope for a better future.

The goal of the marketing communication should be to transport people to a destination of their own making, which in turn should lead them to the destination of the brand itself, an approach exemplified by the classic and effective ad for the moisturizing bath foam Calgon. A distressed and harried mom exclaims, "Calgon, take me away," while floating in her bathtub—inside a metaphorical bubble to her unknown destination of choice. The imagination takes the viewer away, while presumably the desire for that outcome takes her to a grocery store to buy some Calgon.

MOVING PICTURES

Imagination is the process of forming mental images. Great writers succeed not just because of the words, but also because of the pictures and feelings attached to the text. This is why images can often be more powerful than words. They are the language of the unconscious, highlighting the truth to the adage "a picture is worth a thousand words." If you want proof of this human truth look no further than the campaign that propelled the Apple iPod to become the world's top-selling MP3 player, an effort driven by the brilliant art direction of the ad agency TBWA\Chiat\Day in Los Angeles. In October 2003 Apple introduced their outdoor "Silhouettes" campaign to Los Angeles, following it with a national television and print effort. The imagery of the ads was strikingly simple yet convincingly animated: black silhouettes of people who were sharply contrasted by white iPods and colorful, bold backgrounds. The silhouetted characters were shown listening and dancing to their favorite music. The only word in the ad was the product name "iPod" next to the Apple logo. Despite analysts' predictions of only $400 million, the "Silhouettes" campaign helped Apple achieve an incredible $1.2

billion in net sales during the first quarter of 2005 alone, accounting for nearly 90 percent of category share,[12] and winning the Grand Effie award in 2005.

By supplanting real people with the darkened silhouettes, prospects were empowered to project themselves and their identity into the experience, giving them the opportunity to find their own meaning and relevance. When the mind has the chance to fill in the blank, it does so in uniquely stimulating and evocative ways, taking with it a personalized message that allows the individual's personality to shine through. Apple has built a global movement around this concept, creating an identity that is at once its own and that of everyone who owns their products.

The power of concealed and interpretive identity helps explains the overwhelming viral success of our own efforts at Deutsch LA with Volkswagen's "The Force" television commercial. The Darth Vader mask added an element of mystery and intrigue so that viewers could envision their own mini-Darth, projecting and personalizing their own story through their children and family. Had the spot revealed who the little boy actually was, this ability would have been lost. Deutsch has an agency philosophy that we all adhere to known as, "Human spoken here." This belief states, "All great stories are built around human truths, no matter what channel they live on. The best songs, the best movies, the best ads let you see yourself in them somehow."[13]

Digital technology offers new, imaginative ways to connect personally and powerfully with potential customers in traditional ways like direct marketing. A great example of this comes from a Toronto Porsche dealer who went around some of the Canadian city's most affluent neighborhoods with a shiny white 911 sports car, a digital camera, and a mobile printer. Taking photographs of the brand new vehicle parked in the driveways of these upscale homes, the dealer printed out custom ads and dropped them into the mail slots. The campaign featured the provocative headline: "It's closer than you think." The result was an astonishing 32 percent response rate, which means about a third of these prospects called to schedule a test drive, a staggering improvement over the very low single digit response rates typically deemed successful in traditional direct mail efforts.[14]

WORLDLY BLENDS

Archaeological evidence suggests that our imaginative abilities evolved about fifty thousand years ago during the Upper Paleolithic era. For the first time in human history, a remarkable set of human singularities emerged, becoming routine parts of our stone-age lives. They showed up in the forms of religion, science, art, language, fashion, music, dance, and advancements in tool use. Humans were exhibiting the skills to be imaginative in everything they encountered, and this unprecedented cognitive capacity has become a defining characteristic of modern humans ever since.[15]

Imagination gives us the ability to combine dissimilar concepts. The most evolved form of this mental operation is called "double scope blending," what cognitive scientist Mark Turner refers to as the "engine of human imagination." Turner explains, "It operates largely behind the scenes. Almost invisibly to consciousness, it choreographs vast networks of conceptual meaning, yielding cognitive products, which, at the conscious level, appear simple."[16]

Double scope blending gives us the ability to combine two distinct conceptual worlds into one combined reality. This confers our uniquely human capacity to see ourselves taking on a better life, and it allows us to imagine that such a life might be aided by the benefits of a new brand. As the writer Steven Pressfield eloquently states: "Most of us have two lives. The life we live and the unlived life within us."[17] In today's market economies, people buy brands because they're buying into what they wished their lives would become. Imagination is the vehicle that makes it possible for us to understand what that might be like, allowing us to blend two separate realities, not just for purposes of fantasy or amusement but for real change for the better. It is an evolutionarily adaptive process that helps us to succeed in the challenges we encounter in our lives. As Turner puts it, "These blended conceptions are put together for the important purposes such as making real choices."[18] We evolved to be imaginative not only to invent new things but also to help us make better decisions. If marketers don't tap into our imaginations, they are not taking advantage of the fundamental process by which we make brand choices.

LEVERAGING THE WATER LINE

Imagination occurs at the watermark of our metaphorical iceberg, the confluence of the external world and our internal state, the blending of conscious and unconscious. It is very much a necessary part of our everyday existence. As neuroscientist Chris Frith says, "Our perception of the world is a fantasy that coincides with reality."[19]

Imagination is a place of two-way communication between what we are aware of and what lies below the surface. Here the conscious mind is able to eavesdrop on the deeper remote associations of the mind in an effort to actualize new connections unlocking creative solutions to life's challenges. Conscious thoughts are sent to the unconscious seat of motivation, communicating the words, feelings, or images that we encounter in our daily lives, such as seeing a pair of shoes online, talking with a friend about a ski resort, or watching an ad for the latest dish detergent. These thoughts and ideas insinuate themselves in the immense intelligence of the unconscious mind, which often seeks to realize these suggestions into action. The unconscious communicates back to us in the form of dreams and daydreams, intuitions, hunches, new ideas, and plans, telling us, "Maybe I should buy those shoes" . . . vacation in the Caribbean Islands, or purchase that detergent. There is a neurobiological truth to the spiritual saying "thoughts are things." Unconscious thoughts become matter when we materialize those thoughts into actions, which can thereby lead us to brand purchases. What we manifest in the physical world often starts out in our minds as nonmaterial intentions. The goal of the marketer is to instill a sense of collective consciousness that turns into the power of mass intention. Coined by the French sociologist Émile Durkheim, collective consciousness reflects the unifying force of shared beliefs and attitudes within a society.[20] The more people share the same dreams, fantasies, desires, favorable beliefs and attitudes toward your brand, the more likely they will buy it.

When products and services are designed to engage man's unique capacity for imagination, companies can benefit from one of the most influential of human truths. That's why we love movies, books, television, theater, spectator sports, and video games. They let us observe, imagine, and create new worlds. When Electronic Arts created the Sims, a life simulation game that empowered people to live vicariously through another character's life, they tapped into a deep longing of the human imagination. The Sims went on to become the top-selling PC game in history in 2003 with worldwide sales in excess of 6.3 million copies.[21] In 2009 with the introduction of Sims 3, the game again topped the worldwide list as the top-selling PC game, making it the most successful launch of a game in the 27-year history of Electronic Arts, and the sixth time in the decade that the Sims led the annual PC chart.[22]

Our interests in our dream world are even displacing our interests in the real world. This is strongly evident in the widespread increase of fantasy sports leagues. Fantasy sports have existed in obscurity for decades, but with the rise of digital connectivity, their enthusiasts have grown exponentially. According to polls, the industry doubled between 2003 and 2008, from 15 million fantasy players to nearly 30 million. The information in these surveys suggests that many participants in fantasy leagues have an even greater interest in and affinity with the performances of their imaginary teams than in that of their "real" favorite team in the National Football League. If imagination can shift such a powerful allegiance as that of a sports fan, imagine what it could do to the field of marketing.[23]

THE STRENGTH OF STORIES

When you tell a brand's story, you are laying the foundation for successful communication, because story telling is at the essence of how humans relate to one another. When George Lucas created the screenplay for *Star Wars,* he leveraged this truth in the very first words of the script, writing: "A long time ago, in a galaxy far, far away." When we hear a story coming, the depths of our minds open to receive whatever communication is about to be transmitted. That's because story telling is key to how we think, decide, and behave. As Mark Turner says, "Narrative imagining—story—is the fundamental instrument of thought. Rational capacities depend on it. It is our chief means of looking into the future, of predicting, of planning, and of explaining. . . . Most of experience, our knowledge, and our thinking is organized as stories."[24]

Our penchant for story telling emerges from the two-part process of decision making. Since our brain is designed to lead with emotion first and logic second, our nature inclines us to tell stories, giving meaning to what our bodies are sensing and feeling at any given moment. In essence, our minds are designed to make up stories about how our bodies are feeling. Our quick and intuitive unconscious mind is automatically reacting to the environment while the conscious mind is fabricating those interactions into logical narratives. It is busy making sense of the experience that is unfolding as we constantly try to understand the world around us. Story telling is not only how we do that but also how we communicate those ideas to others.

As hunter-gatherers, we spent hundreds of thousands of years sitting around the fire telling stories. It is how we related to one another. Unfortunately, many of the ways in which we now do business and communicate are disconnecting us from our story-telling origins. Immersed in our spreadsheets, sales charts, target projections, and Powerpoint presentations, we are removing ourselves from the natural patterns of effective communication. We need to know how to better communicate with our colleagues as well as with our customers. So much of what we do in marketing today depends on our ability to sell a product in such a way that prospects and customers will remember what the brand stands for and why they should care about it. You can't tell a brand story effectively in a linear, logical Powerpoint presentation, complete with graphs that look more like convoluted eye charts. As the writer Daniel Pink says in his book *A Whole New Mind,* "Stories are easier to remember because in many ways stories are how we remember." Because of this we need to make story telling part and parcel of all of our business efforts, internally and externally.

When Mark Hunter joined Deutsch LA as our chief creative officer, he stood on a stage before 400 colleagues eager to meet him for the first time. He didn't qualify himself. He told a story. Mark recounted his trip to Brussels to present a Euro Effie award. There was one little hitch. He wasn't just a presenter. He was the co-host of the big, black-tie gala event with a popular Belgian TV personality, and was briskly handed a script "the size of a screenplay with onstage interviews with Flemish and German ad-land bigwigs with names impossible to pronounce." But Mark went on, thinking, "You only get ridiculous opportunities like this a few times in life," only to experience yet another glitch, "the one in a million chance that the bloody teleprompter went blank." But rather than panic, he quipped, "Technology, eh! At least I'm hosting a show, not landing a plane for you!" The screen finally came back up and off he went.

Through his telling tale, Mark had already demonstrated his communication expertise. He instantly established rapport with his new agency as we all empathized with the feeling of being onstage before strangers. He demonstrated authority. He had, after all, been chosen to host a prominent industry event awarding ad effectiveness. He displayed competency, unflappably handling adversity and coming through in the clutch. Did he do this all by design? Of course not, he was just telling a charming story, a skill that great creative leaders intuitively share.

Warren Buffet is not only one of the most influential business leaders and one of the richest men in the world; he is also a master storyteller. When he was once asked what his worst investment was, his response was evocative and ironic. He tells the story of his first large investment, which involved the purchase of his namesake holding company, Berkshire Hathaway. Buffet said, "We went into a terrible business because it was cheap. It's what I refer to as the 'used cigar butt' approach to investing. You see this cigar butt down there, it's soggy and terrible, but there's one puff left, and it's free. That's what Berkshire was when we bought it—it was selling below working capital—but it was a terrible, terrible mistake." While many business leaders will bore you with easily forgotten financial facts, Buffet doesn't just tell stories, he sells stories. Creating a sound bite not easily forgotten but easily passed on to others, he provided a multisensory metaphorical handle that you can see, feel, and even taste, invoking deeper imagery and richer associational territory.[25]

Story telling is the cost of entry in today's increasingly cluttered branding marketplace; when done right, it helps to spread information and embed messages. For example, one of the enduring attributes of Volkswagen in America is the belief that they're built to last—perhaps due to the many old Beetles and microbuses still on the road today, or just to the simple fact that German vehicles feel more solid. To bring this insight to life in another one of the Volkswagen commercials created at Deutsch, we showed viewers a child's birthday party in the backyard of a suburban home. There is no dialogue except for the angry grunts of a determined child as he repeatedly takes a whack at a colorful piñata shaped like an automobile. All to no avail and much to his chagrin, the hanging papier-mâché SUV remains intact while partygoers look on in deadpan disbelief. The piñata-as-metaphor simply hangs there, swaying and spinning, and then slowing to reveal the VW logo. The voiceover announces: "Built like a Volkswagen." The father grabs the bat and tries his hand in frustration . . . whack after futile whack. This story and the metaphor of an indestructible piñata said more about the brand's durability and design than any banal message about "sturdy B-pillar construction" or "laser seam welding." It was the type of ad that people talked about because it was a charming story and not just a set of facts.

By the end of 2011, Volkswagen had achieved record sales in the US on four of its models including the Tiguan, the vehicle featured in the piñata television commercial.[26] Volkswagen is on track for their ambitious longer term plan to triple sales in America, assisted by the power of story telling and the magic of metaphor. In 2012, Volkswagen was selected as the CLIO Awards 2012 global advertiser of the year honoring the brand whose global work achieves creative leadership and demonstrates a commitment to innovation in advertising, proof that creative excellence and ad effectiveness are not mutually exclusive. As Luca de Meo, the Global Director of Marketing of Volkswagen Group puts it, "All of the Volkswagen Group advertising for the past year worked to build on the brand's heritage of telling human stories in a simple and powerful way, and we're glad that people are connecting with the ads."[27]

THE POWER OF SYMBOLS

Symbols are abstract cultural representations of reality. Unlike signs, which are precise and direct, symbols defy literal definition and require emotional interpretation. According to psychoanalyst Carl Jung, a symbol doesn't have any definition. Instead, it has multiple levels of interpretative nuances that let people discover subjective transcendent meanings and insights. Great brands are symbols, not signs. They must stand for something more than the product itself. As Jung put it, "The sign is always less than the concept it represents, while a symbol always stands for something more than its obvious and immediate meaning."[28]

Cultures have long used symbols to change the way the world thinks, guiding movements and even altering the course of mankind. Not surprisingly, the most powerful symbols of all are those that embody religious significance, such as the Christian cross, the star of David, or the Muslim star and crescent. These emblems reflect missions that drive people at the highest level of identity and spirit. Humans began using symbols to express their identity about 100,000 years ago. Our ancestors used symbolic adornments such as jewelry, which is believed to represent their affiliation with groups or their social status within groups.[29]

Today, brands have become the new symbolic ornamentations of social identity and religion-like affiliation. As Mike Sheldon, CEO of Deutsch LA, says, "We look at brands as clubs or, in a way, religions. If you look at some of the most powerful brands in this country—Volkswagen, Nike, Apple—they're something that people gravitate toward that transcends product and transcends pricing." Sheldon's sentiment has anecdotal support from a team of British neuroscientists that scanned the brain of an Apple fanatic and found that the brand was activating the same regions of the brain that religious imagery stimulates in people of religious faith.[30] Martin Lindstrom corroborated this finding when his research discovered that when people viewed images associated with strong brands like Apple's iPod, Guinness, Ferrari, and Harley-Davidson, their brains exhibited the exact same patterns of responses as they did when viewing religious images.[31]

When a brand borrows equity from other symbols, it is bootstrapping that product to the cultural movement already represented by that emblem. Victorinox, the maker of the Swiss Army knife, is far more recognized by its logo than by its brand name. The logo is unconscious branding at its finest, conferring benefits from its favorable associations with other well-known symbols: the Christian cross, the Swiss flag, and the shield, along with their respective connections to spirit, craftsmanship, and protection. With these rich associations, the logo itself does much of the heavy lifting in the brand's marketing efforts. Company leader Carl Elsener says that traditionally, "Victorinox was not so much 'about the marketing,' and 'all about the product,' manufacturing and providing the best knives possible." This is a luxury you can afford when you have a powerful brand symbol.[32]

Known primarily for its pocketknives, Victorinox's business was drastically impacted by the tragic events of September 11, 2001. Almost overnight the brand declined 30 percent in sales revenue as airlines forbade knives on planes. But Victorinox would find resilience and strength in its brand as it continued to extend beyond its core knife business to include watches, travel gear, fashion, and fragrance. A previously product- and manufacturing-focused company quickly became brand- and image-focused. In 2009 these new product lines, still displaying the resonant image of the Victorinox logo, represented up to 60 percent of company sales revenue, a huge success in brand diversification and line extension by any stretch of the imagination. And, it accomplished this growth without denigrating the core business, continuing to export knives to over 100 countries on all five continents, commanding an enormous 80 percent market share outside Switzerland, and, as of 2011, producing 34,000 pocket-knives per day.[33] When your brand is a powerful symbol, it can be effectively leveraged and extended because it is solidly grounded in the unconscious.

THOUGHT-STARTERS ON LEADING THE IMAGINATION

Be as clear on your own mission as you are on that of your customers' mission. Marketers often think the answer lies in the words of the customer when, truth be told, only you truly hold the keys to your own castle. When you are very clear and specific on a meaningful corporate vision and strategic purpose, and when your beliefs and values are in alignment and match the sensibilities of your audience and product, people will follow you and your brands.

Promise a better life, not just a better product. Henry David Thoreau said, "The mass of men lead lives of quiet desperation." Remember that deep down, people are consistently yearning for someone to lead them to a better existence. If your campaign simply talks about your product and fails to inspire people about life's possibilities, then you will fail to connect to the deeper places of motivation within the prospects' psyches.

Use metaphors to inspire creativity. Metaphors are ideal to inspire creativity in marketing and advertising team members. Summarize your brand challenge as a metaphor and not a set of verbal constraints. Metaphors encourage the overlapping of ideas, which are the engines of imagination. Neuroscientist V. S. Ramachandran believes that metaphorical thinking and creative thinking are linked, because creative people are eight times more likely to have a peculiar condition called synesthesia, which is characterized by the cross-wiring of the brain's sensory perceptions.[34] Synesthetes might perceive numbers as colors or tastes as geometric shapes, for example, the number one is red, or sugar feels round. To some extent, we all share some overlapping of senses evidenced by such phrases as "loud tie" or "sharp cheese."

Employ stories to uncover and communicate. Use story telling not only in your brand communications but also as a tool to gather information in qualitative market research. For instance, marketing consultant Dr. G. Clotaire Rapaille asks people to tell stories about words or concepts to get at what he calls "culture codes." These are common, unconscious associations, borrowed from Carl Jung's concepts of archetypes and a collective unconscious. This approach uncovers deeply embedded motivators for advertising. For instance, Rapaille found that the cultural code for SUV is "domination," which is why the Hummer at one point became such a popular brand, representing domination of the road and suggesting a sense of status and safety in the reptilian brain. As Rapaille is quick to point out, "The reptile always wins."

Feel free to dream. We live in a culture that discourages dreams, fantasy, and daydreams as well as the information that comes from them. If you are a lucid dreamer, you know how real and rich these experiences can be. Even through the filter of the conscious mind, recalled dreams can often help people receive practical insights and workable intuitions. When you are trying to solve business problems, work on trying not to think so much. Find a way to get distance from the problem by shifting your focus elsewhere or inward. And always keep a pad and pen next to your bed as you sleep.

Remember, audio is the "theatre of the mind." Radio advertising has become the bastard stepchild of the marketing world. But because it requires internal interpretation, its well-told narratives are by their very nature often the strongest persuaders. Reconsider the story-telling power of this medium and begin considering the imaginative uses of online digital audio, which can tell a story and fire up the senses, as well as motivate people to imagine owning or using whatever product is being sold.

7
STEP FOUR:
SHIFT THE FEELING

Any emotion, if it is sincere, is involuntary.

—*Mark Twain*

WHEN I WAS GROWING UP, MY PARENTS WOULD SOMETIMES take us on Sundays to St. Cecilia's Church in the New York City suburb of Englewood, New Jersey. Built in 1866, St. Cecilia has an imposing air and a storied legacy. Home to the first coaching job of the legendary Vince Lombardi, it became noteworthy after his successful eight-year stint as the football coach of St. Cecilia High School, which included two consecutive undefeated seasons in 1943 and 1944, well before Lombardi became the most revered leader in the history of the National Football League.[1] Lombardi consistently racked up championships, including winning the first two Super Bowls. But what he was truly famous for were his inspiring locker-room speeches and his amazing ability to win despite having the odds stacked against him. It would be no surprise if Vince had learned much of his motivational skills in the church where he got his start. A devout Catholic, he had studied to become a priest before turning his attention to football. I know that for me, those early ecclesiastical teachings would be instrumental to my instruction in the art of influence.

Lombardi once said, "If you can't get emotional about what you believe in your heart, then you're in the wrong business." While our imagination creates the vision of our intentions, our emotions move us in the direction of making them real. Like great evangelists, coaches, or inspiring business leaders, Lombardi bridged the ethereal and secular worlds with his uncanny ability to lead winning teams on the field. He said, "Leadership is based on a spiritual quality; the power to inspire, the power to inspire others to follow."[2]

But what does it mean to inspire? We use the word all the time in marketing and advertising, especially when we are briefing creative teams to come up with the communications intended to generate product sales. To inspire has carried several meanings over the centuries: to blow on or breathe into, to infuse with thought or feeling, and to guide or arouse by divine or supernatural influence. Perhaps without consciously realizing it, many in the marketing industry are already taking a page from the St. Cecilia playbook and from one of the great models of human persuasion: religion.

THE SCIENCE OF RELIGION

Just as we can learn a great deal about people today by studying the origins of early humans, much can be gained by exploring the past success of humanity's institutions. The historical establishment of the Catholic Church is an example of how organizations can shift feelings to change beliefs and behaviors and to attract and retain loyal followers.

The Catholic Church is one of the world's oldest, most organized institutions, and by far the largest religious group within Christendom. Christianity remains the "best-selling" religion with nearly 2.2 billion "customers" worldwide.[3] Catholicism ranks as the dominant "brand" with about a 50 percent share in a very crowded segment.[4]

The term "catholic" means "universal" or "of interest to all." So it's no wonder that the Catholic Church would be the biggest corporation in the United States based upon their real estate and business holdings, exceeding that of AT&T, Standard Oil, and US Steel combined.[5] By Catholicism's name alone, the religion has identified itself as an absolute, available to all people. As Steven Pinker says, "According to surveys by ethnographers, religion is a human universal. In all human cultures, people believe that the soul lives on after death, that ritual can change the physical world and divine the truth."[6] Paul Bloom, a psychologist at Yale University, says, "There's now a lot of evidence that some of the foundations for our religious beliefs are hard-wired."[7] And, as the neuroscientist Andrew Newberg indicates, "When we think of religious and spiritual beliefs and practices, we see a tremendous similarity across practices and across traditions." Newberg says there are universal features of the human brain involved in religious practice: the frontal lobe, which focuses our attention in prayer and meditation; the limbic system, which creates feelings like awe and joy; and the parietal lobe, which is the seat of our sensory information.[8] Newberg points out that the circuits of the parietal lobe also detect where the body begins and ends, but when we are participating in prayer and meditation, this circuitry can be silenced, creating a powerful feeling of oneness with the universe and with God.[9]

The forces that drove the widespread acceptance of religion are likely the output of both nature and nurture. When questioned about the notion of preprogramming, Oxford University's Richard Dawkins said, "I am thoroughly happy with believing that children are predisposed to believe in invisible gods—I always was. But I also find that indoctrination hypothesis plausible. The two influences could, and I suspect do, reinforce one another."[10]

THREE COMMON INGREDIENTS TO
BELIEF AND BEHAVIOR CHANGE

The past success of the Catholic Church stems from not only a natural inclination to religion but also a very clearly defined and emotionally charged mission: to save humanity from sin and glorify God forever by spreading the gospel of Jesus. Catholic indoctrination also has a clearly defined process of how to accomplish that goal, a perfect case of unconscious branding and a prime example of a "hypnotic modality." Hypnosis is a form of focused attention that is very similar to meditation and prayer. It creates access to the unconscious mind, engendering feelings of openness and oneness with the universe. This happens all the time, not just when we are on our knees or in the lotus position, but even when we are engrossed in reading a good book or sitting in a darkened theater watching the latest movie. According to George John Kappas, the director of HMI College of Hypnotherapy, "A hypnotic modality is anything that attempts to control or modify behavior by affecting our belief system." Therefore, effective efforts at religion, teaching, and even marketing and advertising are by definition hypnotic modalities. The goal of every communication, whether one is being offered the eternal salvation of God or the benefit of using a stronger and more absorbent paper towel, is the acceptance of a suggestion.

Kappas says there are three key ingredients to every hypnotic modality. The first is *authority*. The subject must perceive the presenter as an authority figure in order to begin considering accepting the message. To start, the presenter must establish control of the environment through one-upmanship, a social dynamic whereby the presenter is perceived to hold a position of power, control, and higher status. A common technique to establish authority involves the use of special clothes. For instance, doctors wear white lab coats, law officers wear blue uniforms, and military personnel don progressively more decorated uniforms as their accomplishments and status ascend. These special clothes suggest authority. So much so that when actor Peter Bergman, who played Dr. Cliff Warner on the soap opera *All My Children,* starred in a commercial for Vicks Formula 44 and espoused, "I'm not a doctor, but I play one on TV," many viewers took his words as a credible endorsement. Since they had often seen Bergman in a white lab coat, in their eyes he had license to become a real medical authority.

Catholic Church law insists that the priest wear "suitable clerical clothing, according to the norms issued by the Episcopal Conference and according to legitimate local customs."[11] The list starts with the alb, an ankle-length white linen vestment with sleeves, and ends with the zucchcetto, or skullcap. The list is a veritable dictionary of cloths, crosses, pom-poms, tassels, and cloaks.

The priests are not only adorned in incredibly elaborate clothing, but they also stand before worshippers on elevated stages behind great podiums with distinguished titles and accomplished credentials. The word "reverend" means "worthy of respect" and everyone knows you must always obey your "father." The congregation is required to display deference to the clergy, subserviently kneeling in prayer. Clearly, the churchgoers are neither in control nor are they the authority in this situation. Have you ever felt authoritative when you were on your knees? For marketers, techniques that establish authority include awards, industry accolades, and the ever-present claims of best-selling or category leadership.

The second key ingredient is *doctrine/paradigm/translogic.* One or more of these must be present in order to establish the credibility of the messenger. In terms of importance, doctrine ranks higher than paradigm, which in turn ranks higher than translogic, but all three can play a pertinent role in the effective communication of an idea. Doctrine—the highest form of rational proof—is the one that religions leverage most. It represents the written proof of whatever theory is being communicated, suggesting that it has been inspired by a higher authority even than the presenter. In the case of religion, this would be the word of God as transmitted through the Bible. In marketing, illustrations of doctrine can be expert third-party tests and product reviews done by consumer advocacy groups like *Consumer Reports,* trade press information, expert bloggers, or even the news media in general.

Paradigm is a model of how something works, such as visual representations, verbal proof points, numerical charts, and graphs. Examples of paradigms in advertising range from common product demos to facts and figures supporting competitive claims to method of action explanations such as Listerine's "kills germs by millions on contact."

Translogic is last and represents temporary logic. Like the number 44 in the cold medicine Vicks Formula 44, or the trademarked Retsyn in Certs breath mints, when a number or technical sounding

ingredient is offered, the product takes on a more proven, creden-
tialed, perhaps scientific aura, suspending the prospect's resistance
and prompting people to contemplate the brand's merit.

The third and most important ingredient is *overload of feeling*.
We need to be overwhelmed with sensational feelings to gain access
to the reactive, unconscious part of the mind. When the conscious
mind is preoccupied with information input from the environment,
we lose our ability to critically filter the message. We thereby default to the unconscious, which faithfully responds to these emotions
in the form of visceral and physical reactions. We don't choose our
emotions. They often choose for us. If you don't create this deeper
level of experience, the message will be dealt with only logically. It
will fail to effect the belief system of the subject and thus have little
or no effect on behavior. In advertising, the most important thing is
to get the receiver to feel the experience and perceive the message as
real, which can happen by generating tears, smiles, laughter, chills,
or goose bumps.

This critical ingredient, overload of feeling, is what distinguishes
the Catholic Church from its competitors. During Catholic mass,
there is a deluge of emotional and sensory stimulation that moves
people toward the goals and visions of the captivating mission of the
church. Let's deconstruct how the church maximizes the impact on
each of the five senses. There is the inundation of entrancing visuals:
the full spectrum of colorful light emanating from the stained glass
windows, the abundant flickering candles, the intricately elaborate
and ornate architecture, and the beautiful artwork. There are ample
and pervasive sounds: the colossal bell summoning the congregation
to mass, the deep bellow of the organ, the many melodic voices of the
choir, the singing of worshippers in unison, the rhythmic chanting of
hymns, and the hypnotic cadence of the priest's patter. There are the
tactile and kinesthetic experiences: the repetitive rituals as you shift
your body from sitting on the hard, wood seats to standing at attention, to kneeling, to the ceremonial holding of hands. There is the feel
of the leather-bound bibles or textured vinyl covers. And the rever-
beration of the organ throughout the building coalesces the auditory
with the kinesthetic. There is the distinct experience of receiving the

consecrated elements of the Holy Communion: the taste of the bread and the flavor of the wine, both symbolic of the body and blood of Christ. And there is the olfactory, the smell of the billowing wafts of smoke from the thurible as it swings back and forth, emanating incense throughout the chapel.

It is impossible not to experience this ceremony without succumbing to the feeling of sensory overload, which, of course, is no accident since this is the crucial ingredient to change beliefs. This very real experience overwhelms the limits of the conscious mind, producing the enraptured state that denies the brain access to rational resistance, opening our unconscious and emotional mind to new suggestions, new beliefs, and new behaviors—actually suspending our ability to function voluntarily.

BRAND AS THE NEW RELIGION

As the late Roy Disney said in his shareholder speech of 2004,

> The Walt Disney Company is more than just a business. It is an authentic American icon—which is to say that over the years it has come to stand for something real and meaningful and worthwhile to millions of people of all ages and backgrounds around the world. This is not something you can describe easily on a balance sheet, but it is tangible enough. Indeed, it is the foundation on which everything we have accomplished as a company—both artistically and financially—is based. I believe our mission has always been to be bringers of joy. . . . We do this through great story telling, by giving our guests a few hours in another world where their cares can be momentarily put aside, by creating memories that will remain with them forever.[12]

A critical step in the evolutionary process of becoming human was expressing ways to externalize consciousness and represent our thoughts in the physical world, going beyond the realm of our imagination to make fantasy a reality. The paradox of branding is that the goal is to stand for something that transcends the physical product yet roots that experience in very tangible, powerfully moving ways, just as religion has done. The Disney brand is one of the most powerful in the world, and the reason why a trip to Disneyland is so cherished is that it turns our fantasies into realities through a cornucopia of escape, emotion, and sensory delight.

Costco, which many may think of as a value-driven rational brand, succeeds where others don't because they turn shopping trips into real life adventures, or what Senior Vice President of Costco Jeff Long calls "treasure hunts." While most competitors have been struggling to break even or stay in business, Costco remains the number one wholesale buying club in the country, posting a massive 25 percent increase in quarterly profits, topping even retail giants like Target and Home Depot. In comparison, its biggest rival, Sam's Club, announced the closing of ten stores in early 2010. One of Costco's secrets of success is to "let them get lost." The Costco stores induce a trancelike sensory overload, overwhelming customers with the immense square footage of the retail environment, aisles upon aisles of brand variety and bulk product offerings. Costco strategically places popular fresh items in the back of the store and intentionally doesn't put signs up to show where the products are, forcing shoppers to wander the store instead. This turns the mundane task of product purchase into an exciting expedition of discovery and delight.[13]

THE MIND-BODY DIFFERENCE

Everything we do in life we do because of how it makes us feel. While we often perceive emotion and feeling as synonymous, behavioral neurobiologist Antonio Damasio draws an important distinction when he observes that emotional processing is really comprised of two steps. Emotions are complex neural and chemical responses that start off unconsciously, becoming conscious feeling states only when sensed by the body. Damasio explained it this way in an interview with *New York Times* columnist David Brooks: "Emotion, by definition, to begin with is nonconscious . . . we learn about it through feeling. It's when we feel the emotion that we know we have it. Feeling is like the sea level of the water." Damasio adds: "Emotion is really about action. It is a collection of automated actions."[14]

The implications of this are clear. If marketers are not generating emotions and feelings, we are not taking advantage of the very things that drive behavior. Branding is more than stimulating an intellectual process of imaginative thought. It is about experiencing those thoughts as emotionally charged feelings that lead to real actions. Feelings are turned into waking thoughts, which then become intentions, and finally, purchase. The goal of every marketing program should be to infuse products with emotions so strong that customers become loyal not just to the brands but to the brand missions, instilling devotion and uniting people and marketers with common causes and shared values.

What makes Catholicism different from many other Christian faiths is a belief in the physical and not just the mental. The Catholic Church teaches salvation by works, meaning you have to actually do something to gain salvation. The observance of the Sacraments, rituals like baptism, in which a child is blessed with water, and communion, in which churchgoers ingest the bread and the wine (which is offered at every mass, unlike other churches that practice this sporadically) are tangible ways to demonstrate the physical presence of Christ. These are outward signs of inward grace that take us beyond our head to our heart and body.

Successful brands every day act similarly—that is, go beyond our head—which supports the observation that "brands are the new religion." Two separate studies, done by business and marketing professors at Tel Aviv, Duke, and New York Universities, found that nonreligious people in the United States rely on brands to a much greater degree than do religious people. This suggests that brands may play a similar role as religion, providing people with a measure of self-worth and everyday tangible ways to create meaning, identity, and a sense of belonging to something greater than themselves.[15]

BRANDING FEELINGS

Marketers are in the business of selling states of emotion, not products or services. Feelings exist not for our amusement or to make us happy, but rather to guide us in living successful lives, to move us away from harmful choices and toward better fortunes. As Damasio says, "An emotion consists of a very well orchestrated set of alterations in the body. Its purpose is to make life more survivable by taking care of a danger or taking advantage of an opportunity."[16] Like religion, brands play off our hopes and fears, our joy and our suffering. Yet despite the amount of evidence and conversation in advertising and marketing about the importance and effectiveness of emotion on sales, there is still a prevailing industry belief that rational efforts alone are more effective and do the so-called heavy lifting for the brand. Cognitive science strongly refutes this position, as do the architects of successful brands. Scott Bedbury, who is credited with building strong brands like Nike and Starbucks, says, "A great brand taps into emotions. Emotions drive most, if not all, of our decisions. A brand reaches out with a powerful connecting experience. It's an emotional connecting point that transcends the product."[17]

Research suggests that even hard-nosed retail brands like Walmart benefit tremendously by emotionally bonding their consumers instead of speaking to their rational, value-conscious sides. In fact, being a satisfied customer is not enough these days. The mere suggestion of satisfaction intimates a state of complacency and a simple calculation of value = quality + price. If you really want loyal followers, and not just customers, your company must go above, beyond, and over the top, like Disney, Costco, or even Catholicism. It's not about selling a convenient product at a good price; it's about establishing unconscious, emotional ties. There is evidence that retail brands like Walmart, Best Buy, Gap, and Macy's perform much better when they can establish such connections with their customers. A market research study of retail chains indicated that while only about one in five shoppers in the United States felt they had an emotional connection to a retailer, the ones that did were much more valuable as customers, brand advocates, and evangelists. Emotionally connected customers were highly desirable compared to those who indicated that they were merely "familiar" or "satisfied" with the retailer. These emotionally bonded customers were four times as likely to shop at their preferred retailer and

50 percent more likely to recommend the brand. They were also four times as likely to follow their brand on Twitter and Facebook, and ten times more likely to shop at their retailers' site on a mobile device.[18]

MAKING DOLLARS, NOT SENSE

Emotions exist to guide behavior, but there are times when they don't always make sense. If you still need further convincing that we don't purchase logically, look no further than our dual brand purchases of teeth whitener and mouthwash. Why in the world would anyone brush with toothpaste clinically proven to whiten teeth and then rinse with a brightly colored green mouthwash containing blue dye #1 and yellow dye #5? Try as you might, you would be hard pressed to find a major brand of mouthwash that doesn't contain artificial dyes in shades that would be most unflattering to the teeth. But through past repetition of other colored products, our unconscious minds have learned to associate the color green with the feeling of clean, fresh, and minty. So much so that now every time we see the color green, it comes with a powerful emotional affect, overriding any concerns about why we are buying whitening toothpaste.

Likewise, why do we love the smell of a new car so much? The scent symbolizes the pride of ownership that elevates our ego with a feeling of specialness and importance. But this fresh, new odor is actually a potpourri of poison and toxic gases. An independent green organization announced that much of the material in most car interiors contains chemicals known to pose major health risks—chemicals linked to birth defects, premature births, impaired learning, and liver toxicity among other serious public health threats. Even when the new scent fades over time, we voluntarily extend our daily exposure to additional chemical cocktails by purchasing fake new-car scents. According to a fragrance industry spokesman, these so-called air fresheners contain chemical compounds such as aldehydes, esters, and ketones.[19]

We are not rational creatures; we are emotional beings. And sometimes those emotions can lead us to questionable decisions and irrational behaviors, even if their evolutionary purpose is to keep us from harm's way.

USEFULLY WRONG

If our biology has predisposed us to religious thought, there has to be a lot more to it than just people making up stories about the existence of God. Because religion is highly emotionally charged, it can appear nonsensical in nature in that its practice is not driven by rationality. But emotions remain purpose-driven actions that serve important evolutionary goals. Rather than simply undermining religion, we are best served to explore and understand its usefulness. Whether in the world of marketing or religion, we need to remind ourselves that how we determine value in our lives doesn't always have to make logical sense. Indeed, it is through our emotions that we assign such value in the first place.

And certainly, religion has had its fair share of detractors questioning its rationality. As George Carlin once said: "Religion has actually convinced people that there's an invisible man living in the sky who watches everything you do, every minute of every day. And the invisible man has a special list of ten things he does not want you to do. And if you do any of these ten things, he has a special place, full of fire and smoke and burning and torture and anguish, where he will send you to live and suffer and burn and choke and scream and cry forever and ever 'til the end of time! . . . But He loves you."[20] And in the comic novel by Peter De Vries, the Reverend Mackerel says, "It is the final proof of God's omnipotence that he need not exist in order to save us."[21]

We are irrational by nature, but many strategies, including religious worship, evolved for rational reasons, because they work and because they can deliver real, important benefits. Even though religious truth has been challenged by the evolutionary sciences, we can still use those same evolutionary sciences to explain the existence and proliferation of religion and its utility to humanity. Some scientists argue that shared religious beliefs spread widely because they helped our ancestors survive, prompting the formation of tightly knit groups that improved cooperation for hunting, foraging, and protection. Whether or not God exists may be a moot point. Many agree that the question itself is simply beyond the scope of scientific inquiry.[22]

And sometimes the truth of the matter is that truth doesn't really matter. What's important are the results and the outcomes. As the evolutionary psychologist Robert Kurzban explained to me in a 2011 interview: "I think that one way to think about it is that being right is not necessarily the best thing for any given organism, particularly for a social organism. Being right is usually pretty good. But there's lots of times when being wrong is more important than being right. So a really simple example is: Suppose I hear a stick cracking behind me and I'm walking in the woods. I can't quite tell if it's a bear or the wind. I'd probably rather err on the side for thinking it's a bear. I'm probably going to be wrong, but I'm usefully wrong."[23]

Science itself is built on models and not necessarily absolute truths. In 2011 scientists said they had discovered subatomic particles that travel faster than light.[24] The bedrock of physics is derived from Einstein's Theory of Relativity and the observation that energy equals mass times the speed of light squared. This is based on the fundamental principle that nothing can go faster than the speed of light. But this law has now fallen into question, potentially unraveling everything we know about physics, and everything that has helped explain the behavior of the physical world for the past century. If Einstein's theory turns out to be wrong, is it not fair to say it was usefully wrong?

Steve Jobs was known to bend the facts, a tendency Apple software designer Bud Tribble labeled the "reality distortion field," a phrase he adopted from an episode of *Star Trek*. Some believed this was just a clever way to say that he tended to lie. But maybe Jobs simply realized that our realities are largely shaped by our minds. Jobs could convince anyone of practically anything, however far-fetched, because he would mold reality to the purpose at hand. He had the charisma to inspire his team to do the seemingly impossible and change the course of the computer industry with a fraction of the resources of his competitors. Apple programmer Bill Atkinson believed that Jobs would deceive himself so that he could better convince others to believe his vision. Self-deceit has an evolutionary advantage as it makes for extremely confident leaders and, in this instance, dramatic progress in technology, great new products, and incredible brand growth.[25]

USEFUL MODELS

The main distinction between the endeavors of religion and those of marketing is that businesses focus mostly on the facts, the conscious, and the logical, and religions focus their efforts on the ethereal, the unconscious, and the emotional. Humans are about nine-tenths emotional and one-tenth logical, so business targets not only miss their mark, they do so by a long shot. Ironically for logically minded business practitioners, their math simply doesn't add up. As Daniel Pink observed in his best-selling book, *Drive: The Surprising Truth About What Motivates Us,* "The goals of management are usually described in words like efficiency, advantage, value, superiority, focus and differentiation. Important as these objectives are, they lack the power to rouse human hearts. Business leaders must find ways to infuse mundane business activities with deeper soul stirring ideals. Humanize what they say and you may humanize what they do."[26]

Translating insights about the abstract unconscious mind into more concrete and conscious terms is not without its challenges. But one model from Robert Dilts, a leading consultant in the field of business leadership, has proven to be very useful. Dilts' clients have included Apple Computer, World Bank, Hewlett-Packard, Ernst & Young, Lucasfilm Ltd., and more. From his esteemed work, he has developed a behavioral hierarchy that he calls the "neurological levels," inspired by the work of anthropologist Gregory Bateson and his "logical levels of learning" construct. This prioritized framework, by demonstrating how the mind relates to the world around us and the relative influence of that relationship on changing our behavior, can help marketers better focus their message on the dimensions that are most impactful.[27]

At the highest and the most impactful neurological level is *spirituality.* This level focuses on the vision of the bigger picture, our connection and contribution to something greater than self, and our feeling of interconnectedness and unconditional devotion to a higher cause. Spirituality reflects the bigger soul-searching question at the heart of religious philosophy, Why are we here?

One of the great advertising examples of the motivating power of spirit comes in the famed De Beers campaign "A diamond is forever," which was named the number one slogan of the century by *Advertising Age*. Launched in 1938, the approach fuels one of the most successful and longest-running marketing campaigns in history, helping position the brand as the leading diamond company to this day.[28]

"A diamond is forever" is a deceptively simple sentiment that captures the essence of unconscious branding. Since all humans seek a greater sense of connection and enduring purpose, the campaign speaks powerfully to the very real but very ethereal essence of spirit as embodied in the lasting bond between people in love. And it is not just the message. Diamonds themselves are both metaphorical and tangible embodiments of the everlasting, with the age of some stones estimated at 4.25 billion years old.[29]

The next level is *identity*. This level encompasses our personal mission, our sense of self in relationship to others and our personality and inner purpose. It challenges us to think and act and reflects the question, Who am I? For example, it is through the perpetual meaning of our identity that great brands like Dr Pepper are truly empowered. It wasn't simply the unique flavor of the product that made the beverage so popular and adored. It was the promise of a distinct, enduring personality, the "always one-of-a-kind original" that makes you different. This evocation of identity was best encapsulated by their famed tagline, "I'm a Pepper."

The next neurological level comprises *values and beliefs*. These are perceptions that we hold to be true about the world and the things that are significant and relevant to us—including our desires and motivations. They answer the question, What is important to me? These include attitudes about the product and one's lifestyle, from a desire for "whiter whites and brighter brights" when choosing a detergent, or the desire to be a better mom by choosing Jif peanut butter.

Below that is the level of *behavior,* or What do I do? These include shopping habits and purchasing behaviors, the types of media with which you engage, and activities that you do professionally or in your spare time.

And on the lowest level are the external dimensions of behavior, or the *environment* in which we live. These are reflected in the questions Where? and When? Think of this as the various places and times you encounter the brand or its messages, such as in your living room where you see the actual television commercials, or the point-of-purchase, buy one get one free promotions, or the eye-catching package designs that you find on the shelves of your local supermarket.

As you go up the hierarchy, the levels become more psychologically encompassing and therefore more impactful. The higher you go, the impact on behavior will become more abstract and unconscious, but it will also be more influential in changing actions. Conversely, the lower you are on the hierarchy, the more tangible and conscious the behavioral result but the lesser the influence on changing behavior. In addition, a change at the higher levels automatically influences and reorganizes the levels below it. If you want to change someone's behavior at a specific level, it is best to focus your efforts on the level or levels above it. Einstein's belief that "no problem can be solved from the same level of consciousness that created it" is central to this model.[30]

For instance, if you change the perception of a brand at the levels of spirit and identity, it automatically shifts the levels below, altering the audiences' values, beliefs, behaviors, and environment. The devotion to Harley-Davidson and Apple is a dedication to the brands that is spiritual in nature and a reflection of who you are as a person. When you buy these powerful brands, you automatically become part of a better club and a bigger mission. Brand purchasers are empowered with a sense of belonging to a higher cause and an aspirational and exclusive group. And once you see yourself as a Hog owner or a Mac guy, it affects many other things about you, including what you believe, what is important to you, the people you relate to, where you hang out, and what you do.

The problem is marketers spend most of their effort and resources on the lower rungs of the hierarchy, the what, where, and when of consumer behavior. They focus on what consumers say in market research, what the product does, and what words or images to use in the ad explaining its benefits. They then spend their time and effort determining where and when to run those messages in media plans.

Marketers need to shift their focus toward the sources of real power and feelings, concentrating their efforts up top where unconscious branding occurs most, on the higher cause, the vision, mission, and meaning to people and humanity. That is how they can instill the sense of purpose and personal identity in the prospect that will command loyalty and dedication to the brand. In other words, in order for the brand to be most effective, it needs to reflect who we are and why are we here.

Not only is this model helpful for developing marketing messages, it is also an extremely valuable tool for maximizing business operations. Dilts contends that the key to a healthy psyche and a healthy organization is to align your objectives from the top down, starting with a clear goal of why you are doing what you are doing and the logical tactics to support that vision.[31]

In Simon Sinek's book *Start with Why,* he makes an insightful, eloquent and inspiring case that, "People don't buy what you do, they buy why you do it." Focusing on the product and the bottom line alone is bad for business. Yet the bottom line has always been the main reason most people do business. This approach is not only wrongheaded, it can be tremendously damaging to economies and human lives. Sinek and I worked together at Euro RSCG in New York when one of our clients, the then-CEO Bernie Ebbers of WorldCom, acquired MCI, the telecommunications giant. Ironically, MCI was a powerful brand that had previously succeeded through a clear sense of mission: "To free consumers and business people from the constraints and costs of the monopoly that AT&T had on the telecommunications market." MCI, a healthy and storied brand, would fall victim to the financial pressures and tactics of Ebbers's WorldCom, whose only clear vision was increasing shareholder value at all costs. Senior executives at WorldCom did whatever it took to inflate revenue, even if it meant breaking the law and orchestrating one of the biggest frauds in the nation's history, which ended in a 25-year prison sentence for Ebbers and left the company in ruins.

Whether to help to align corporate initiatives or to provide fodder for marketing communications, the more you begin with a clear focus on how to shift prospects' feelings, the more likely you are to succeed. I have the privilege of being responsible for developing brand strategy for Volkswagen in the US as their agency partner. The company is among the few great brands borne out of a very clear and emotionally charged mission. The name Volkswagen in German means "people's car," and this company began as a vision and belief that everyone should have access to automotive transportation. This clear sense of purpose has made it one of the most powerful brands and one of the largest auto companies in the world. Working with our clients, we have developed a new mission that has the brand on track for remarkable growth in America: the belief that "Everyone deserves a better car." This universal expression threads the needle of empathy, emotion, and higher purpose for all car buyers—a belief that the feeling of owning and driving a German-engineered vehicle should not be reserved for the privileged few. By the end of 2011, this strategy had helped drive the brand to the best market share stateside in 30 years with a 26 percent annual increase in sales,[32] and Volkswagen was on its way to becoming the fastest growing car company in America as reported in 2012.[33] This is not just a message we send to prospective customers but rather a way to do business, creating an impetus for everyone who manufactures, markets, or sells the brand to get out of bed each day with a bigger and more important task than just moving sheet metal. The essence of the brand is a feeling, even if the tangible experience of the premium vehicle is what makes it superior.

THOUGHT-STARTERS ON SHIFTING FEELINGS

Rouse hearts, not heads. If your meetings feel more like math classes or accounting lectures, you need to infuse more meaning, emotion, and inspiration into your business. As Steve Jobs once said: "The only way to do great work is to love what you do. If you haven't found it yet, keep looking. Don't settle. As with all matters of the heart, you'll know when you find it."[34] If you don't love what you do, change your mission or quit your day job. If your vision statement reads more like a business goal of dominance than a higher cause of purpose, take a page from the religion playbook and find one that inspires people and their devotion.

You need to make the higher vision the centerpiece not only of your marketing but of all your operations. According to Harvard-trained brain experts Jeff Brown and Mark Fenske, we remember better and encode more strongly when (1) We are in a highly emotional state; (2) The message has significant meaning; (3) It's really unusual; and (4) We are paying close attention.[35]

Increase your emotional acuity. Emotions, not words, are the universal language of humans. Don't ask people to explain how they are feeling; observe it firsthand. Psychologist Paul Ekman's pioneering work on emotions has demonstrated that facial expressions are biologically determined and universal across cultures. He has developed a system that trains people to reveal and recognize subtle unconscious "micro expressions" that would often have otherwise gone unnoticed. If you are going to become a more empathetic marketer, you need to first become a more empathetic person.

Leverage multiple senses. Inspire and excite all of the senses in your marketing efforts. If you are not leveraging the five senses across the range of marketing experiences, you are not leveraging the full range of human experience. Make sure that your message is expressed in multidimensional ways that fire up the senses. We can better recall and appreciate the taste of bacon when we hear, see, and smell it sizzling on a hot grill—and the same goes for any other product on the market.

Are there hidden opportunities in your current brand experiences? For instance, BMW transformed the annoying buzzing sound you hear when your seat belt is unfastened into an opulent melodic note similar to the classy strum of a harp instead of the clamor of a cheap alarm clock. Instead of "Buzz!" you hear "Bling!" befitting of luxury and the premium nature of the brand.

Employ ritual. Rituals are some of the most powerful ways to brand because they often involve multiple sensory experiences and repetitive acts, driving information into the unconscious mind. For instance, Apple has turned the process of unboxing your new product into a ritual not unlike opening gifts. When I last purchased my iPhone, the salesperson handed the box to me with the words "do the honors." See if your brand already has a ritual. Like the two-part pouring process of Guinness, these rites can inspire a highly successful campaign or slogans like the beer's "Good things come to those who wait." If you don't have a ritual, try to create one out of an authentic experience that is natural to the brand.

Bridge digital with experiential marketing. Given the power of the physical, digital marketing feels dangerously at odds with these essential real-life experiences. Experiential marketing, such as brand-sponsored events, is an underused yet impactful way to inform people about a brand. Leverage digital media with experiential marketing by tying these efforts together, such as using social media like Facebook to recruit and invite target prospects in easy cost-efficient ways. And, whenever you have events, make sure to create and use digital memories of them by posting and sharing them online afterwards.

Smile more often. Because emotions are contagious, processed unconsciously, and without our conscious control, the best way to spread emotion is to go there first. In one study, even brief exposure to images of smiling or frowning faces, shown so quickly that subjects were not consciously aware of them, affected the amount of money test subjects were willing to pay for a drink. When shown happy expressions, thirsty participants were willing to pay about twice as much for the drink as compared to those that saw angry expressions. Conscious feeling was not influenced. The subjects didn't report feeling more positive or negative after viewing these images. The researches called this phenomenon "unconscious emotion" since participants were neither aware of the stimulus nor the shift in emotion.[36]

The implications for marketers suggest that we are always picking up unconsciously on the emotions of those around us, so we need to be careful about what suggestions we are sending others. For instance, while not a new idea, training retail employees to smile makes good business sense. The more positive the emotions we send, the more positive the results we will get back.

8
STEP FIVE: SATISFY THE CRITICAL MIND

As a man thinketh, so is he.

—*James Allen*

THOUGH THE UNCONSCIOUS MIND IS OFTEN DESCRIBED AS the sacred gift of wisdom's past, it is our conscious mind that gives us the ability and insight to shape our futures. By giving us the arcane sense of self-awareness—that uniquely human capacity of not only knowing but also knowing that you know—this mysterious mental process has long captivated philosophers, theologians, and scientists. Though consciousness might escape us each night as we fade into sleep, we awaken faithfully with it each morning, using it to grab hold of life's reins, making decisions and directing behaviors. Over time it has given us the unprecedented ability to establish and transform cultures, wielding a hand in our own evolution. Though the unconscious mind might dream of tall castles in the sky or flying high like a bird above the world's atmosphere, it is the conscious mind that actually turns those dreams into the engineering that builds skyscrapers and the science that flies us to the moon. It is consciousness that creates art, contemplates our own existence, and plans the purchase of a new product or service.

But how does this amazing process come to be? Simple. It is through our feelings that we are able to step into the enigmatic world of consciousness. Feelings enable humans to become aware of their emotions, those automatic programmed behavioral responses to environmental cues. As a result, much of conscious thinking is actually just a series of reflections and interpretations about how we are feeling. As Antonio Damasio suggested in his "somatic marker hypothesis," which established a revolutionary model for understanding decision making, environmental stimuli trigger unconscious emotions that lead to conscious feelings, resulting in the mental exploration of the challenges and opportunities presented to us. By evolving the faculties for conscious contemplation, humans were able to transcend their innate programmed behaviors and rationally design solutions to contemporary problems not covered by evolutionary development.[1]

Consciousness has also given rise to higher thought processes such as imagination, speculation, and structured thought and language, which allowed our ancestors to develop strategies and better coordination in social settings to ensure survival. Through language we were able not only to communicate with others but also to speak to our selves. Essentially this is consciousness—the "self-talk" in our head that often judges the potential outcomes of our choices. By weighing the advantages and disadvantages, this internal committee helps us decide whether or not to purchase a product and which one to buy. Today the contemporary challenges we face include how to navigate and manage the ever-increasing array of brand choices we encounter daily. Making the right brand investments and consumption choices is the new evolutionary imperative for survival and success in today's industrialized market economies.

The conscious mind enables a broad spectrum of intellectual thought. From abstract reasoning to concrete analysis, it empowers our attraction to lofty ideas and ideals as well as precise facts and figures. It can either align us with the brand vision of a computer that changes the world or can impel us to investigate the nutritional facts on a jar of peanut butter that promises better health. Still, our intellect is ironically driven by the motivational pleasures of our most basic instincts. As Read Montague says, "Evolution has essentially bootstrapped our penchant for intellectual concepts to the same reward circuits that govern our animal appetites. The guy who's on hunger strike for some political cause is still relying on his midbrain dopamine neurons, just like a monkey getting a sweet treat."[2] In essence, higher thought uses the same neural currency of the feel-good responses of primary rewards such as food and sex, helping us to assess the relative rewards and risks between options. As Montague explains, "You don't have to dig very far before it all comes back to your loins." In other words, the higher meaning we ascribe to a given mission or cause can be so gratifying that it subordinates even our own biological interests, largely because it taps into the same pleasurable feelings that drive our primary appetites.[3] This is why when people align themselves with the higher beliefs of a brand, those beliefs can create an overriding loyalty—a loyalty so strong that customers are willing to overlook occasional product and service shortcomings due to the pleasures generated by the overall allegiance to the brand's mission.

NOT RATIONAL OR EMOTIONAL, BUT BOTH

One of the biggest enduring debates in marketing is whether to employ a rational or emotional approach in advertising—a pointless argument from the stance of cognitive science. While the evidence suggests that overwhelmingly it is emotions that drive behavior, it is misguided to believe that thinking and feeling are somehow mutually exclusive. Emotion and logic are intertwined. Rational decision making requires emotional input to function properly.[4] And facts and numbers can just as easily excite our sensibilities through eye-opening proof points, such as a 400-horsepower engine, a 750-gigabyte hard drive, or a five-carat diamond. Statistical signature characteristics of quality and superiority trip the circuits of anticipatory pleasures for prospective buyers. This is especially true when the fact is unexpected and the product attainable.

For example, knowing how much per bottle that glass of the Romanée-Conti costs (the French Burgundy known for fetching over $1,500) will likely heighten the anticipation and enjoyment for wine drinkers. In one study, scientists at Caltech and Stanford told subjects they would be comparing Cabernet Sauvignons at various price points when in fact the researchers gave the participants the same wine and varied only the price. The subjects consistently believed the higher priced wine tasted better. Later, brain scans revealed that there was greater activation in a pleasure center of the brain when the participants in the study believed they were drinking more expensive wine, even though the wines were identical.[5]

By using tried and true product-focused competitive advertising, many companies have created enduring marketplace momentum in their brand's favor. Perhaps the most prolific and beloved example of this is Apple's "Get a Mac" campaign (also known as "Mac versus PC"). This was essentially a series of side-by-side factual product-based comparisons, using the amusing odd pair of anthropomorphic brand ambassadors. They entertained us with their barbs and banter, but the content of the ads focused on hard-hitting claims of competitive superiority, including claims that PCs ran slower because they came preloaded with often-useless trial software. Most marketers usually consider demonstrations of their products' advantages versus those of the competition as the domain of hard-sell rational tactics and not that of the emotionally evocative. But Apple's effort effectively appealed to both our emotional and our rational sensibilities.

Another immensely popular and effective campaign featured one of the UK's best-loved television animals, the Andrex puppy. These heavy-lifting, touchy-feely spots did more than just tug at the heartstrings. Since its introduction in 1972, the puppy has been featured in nearly 120 commercials, an approach that has helped Andrex to a commanding market leadership for more than 40 years.[6] Many experts are quick to attribute the success of these advertisements to the emotional appeal of the cuddly pup, but the campaign originated out of a basic product demonstration of the hard facts: soft, strong, and long. When the adorable Labrador gets tangled in a roll of Andrex toilet tissue, menacingly unraveling it throughout the house and yard, a voice-over rationally affirms, "In fact, it gives you more paper on every roll than almost any other tissue."

Are these triumphs of emotions or logic? It is invariably both, and delineating the relative effect of each in specific circumstances is difficult if not impossible from the stance of cognitive science. These two brain systems are confoundedly interdependent and inextricably linked. The frontal lobe, the part of the brain that plans behavior, is deeply connected to the emotional regions below. Every day we are inundated with conflicting facts, figures, and emotional entreaties as marketers vie for our attention and affection touting their brand as the best option. A neural process of "executive control" helps us to resolve these conflicts. We do this through our anterior cingulate cortex (ACC), an area near the top of the brain's frontal lobe and along the walls that divide the left and right hemispheres, which is believed to mediate between fact-based reasoning and emotional responses like anticipation, love, and fear.

"For a long time we've been interested in how the brain figures out how to integrate cognitive information about the world with our emotions, how we feel about something," says Joshua Brown, a research associate in psychology at Washington University in St. Louis. "For many reasons, people think the ACC might be the brain structure responsible for converging these different signals. It seems to be an area that's involved in deciding what information gets prioritized in the decision-making process. It seems able to link motivational and affect information—things like goodness or badness—and to use this information to bring about changes in cognition, to alter how we think about things." Brown believes that the ACC may function to anticipate the potential of making mistakes and help us to avoid them altogether.[7]

While neurobiologists have demonstrated that unconscious emotions have primary influence on thought, certainly our thinking can similarly impact our emotions. Cognitive behavioral therapy has amassed plenty of evidence that changing rational thinking can reshape and change our emotions and behaviors. Our lives are not merely the products of unconscious emotions and instincts but also the sum total of all of our thoughts as we react to those inputs and impulses. We can't always choose what happens to us, or the emotions that result, but we can consciously reframe the meaning of those events and feelings. Albert Ellis, one of the most influential psychologists in history, developed "rational emotive behavioral therapy," which is a type of cognitive therapy that emphasizes how one can replace irrational thinking patterns with thoughts that are reasonable, empowering patients with positive emotions and productive behaviors. Neuroscientist Joseph LeDoux has uncovered that whenever we recall a strong emotional memory and think about it differently than before, it actually gets chemically recorded in the brain in a completely new way. Introspection can actually modify how our memory is imprinted in the brain, developing a neural basis to lasting changes in thought and behavior.[8]

But marketers continue to not only reinforce this artificial divide of emotion versus logic but also take sides. Proof of how muddy these waters can get comes from the results of an ongoing study by TiVo Inc., the maker of digital video recorders. The findings from this research have been used to support the argument that rational ads work best. The study examined television commercial viewing habits of 20,000 households to determine what ads are fast-forwarded least. Among the least skipped ads were those that put the product front and center. These so-called harder sell and direct response ads communicated in a straightforward and fact-based manner. And according to the study, viewers watched and listened. But in looking at the study more closely, their results might have had to do with more than just the facts. One report indicated that two of the top-performing so-called rational ads were a commercial from Bowflex home gym and a commercial for Hooters restaurant. Is it possible that the infamous well-endowed Hooters girls and the chiseled bodies of the Bowflex models are somehow purely rational commercials? It might be more logical to conclude that viewers hesitated to skip these spots because of the passions in their loins rather than the logic in their heads.[9]

SEXY PRODUCTS AND STRAIGHT ADS

Though James Dyson is now known by millions as the man who made vacuum cleaners sexy, his pitch was anything but. Dyson's ads were as straight as Joe Friday's "Just the facts, ma'am" style of criminal investigation. As *New Yorker* magazine reported in 2010, "Dyson is in the paradoxical position of being the chief marketer of an anti-marketing philosophy, and the name behind a brand that pretends to have nothing to do with branding." An inventor and industrial designer, Dyson founded his company on twin product pillars, equal parts engineering and design. Dyson didn't employ glitzy branding or fancy ad campaigns. The allure of the brand came from the product itself, as he turned an everyday household appliance into a fashion statement. Made of beautiful polycarbonate plastic with flecked aluminum and a pleasing glossy bright-colored sheen reminiscent of a Jeff Koons sculpture, they were sold even by clothing impresario and prolific fashion designer Paul Smith in his London store.[10]

But Dyson made millions because he also offered visible proof that his product worked, by letting people actually see the dirt they sucked up with his pioneering see-through, bagless vacuum cleaner. His advertising was as effective as his product because he told a simple, sensible brand story aimed squarely at a key marketplace weakness: "Bags and filters lose suction." As the brand spokesman in an early ad, Dyson succinctly summed it up: "A few thousand prototypes later, I had it. No bags. No clogged up filters. And the first vacuum that doesn't lose suction." Dyson never waivered from the facts about how his best-selling vacuum came to be. From the hard-working end product of 5,127 prototypes to a clear product demonstration, from patented Cyclone technology that moves the air inside the vacuum at 924 miles per hour to a smart-sounding, technologically advanced name, G-Force Dual Cyclone, Dyson knew the least sexiest aspects of his vacuum would sell the sexiness of its design. The end result is a remarkable perception that the vacuum cleaner is worth every penny of its premium price. Dyson now owns a brand image that is head and shoulders above the competition.[11]

Today Dyson is a billionaire and one of the wealthiest people in Britain. His products continue to steal market share from everyone; they have earned the brand a 40 percent leadership share of British sales as well as market leadership in the US, Canada, Australia, France, Belgium, Spain, Switzerland, Ireland, and New Zealand. Even during a recession in 2010, the company reported that it had doubled operating profits in the past 12 months to £190 million thanks to new products that are equal parts fashion and utility. Dyson has moved past vacuums and into such products as an unusually cool-looking and easy-to-clean bladeless fan and a high-tech hand dryer that obviates the need for paper towels.[12]

THE LAZY BRAIN

One of the classic brands I planned strategies for in the 1990s was Trident gum. Trident had established its unique ownership of an oral hygiene niche, based on one data point from a survey conducted among practicing dentists: "4 out of 5 dentists surveyed recommend sugarless gum to their patients who chew gum." Through a single simple statistic, Trident usurped a highly relevant position in the chewing gum category. Importantly, the claim addressed barriers to usage by leveraging the credentials and endorsement of medical authorities who challenged the prevailing widespread belief that chewing gum is bad for teeth and socially undesirable.

JWT, Trident's then-agency of record, developed a campaign called "Chew on this," a thought-provoking effort that earned the brand a 1994 Effie award for marketing effectiveness. The "Chew on this" platform communicated a few key facts simply but effectively to support the claim that Trident "helps fight cavities." In one spot the voice-over announces, "Chew on this: nearly seven out of ten of us usually don't brush after lunch . . . now chew on this: great tasting Trident actually helps fight cavities when you chew it after meals." To expand on this message, our creative team at JWT developed a pool-out spot based upon another couple of statistics, further encouraging greater usage frequency in an ad we labeled "Average American." In this commercial a voice-over announced: "Chew on this. The average American eats five times a day and only brushes twice. Chewing Trident after eating can help you fight cavities five times a day." The success of Trident's "Chew on this" advertising was rooted in the simple, relevant facts that were consistent with the brand's oral hygiene heritage. The ads weren't sexy, but they still excited the sensibilities of gum chewers, inspiring a significant sales increase through the power of easy math.

Nobel Prize–winning psychologist and behavioral economics founder Daniel Kahneman observes that compared to our intuitive, unconscious systems, the cognitive system that supports conscious rational problem solving is lazy. Deliberate critical analysis is slow and tiresome, requiring a demanding cognitive effort that uses up energy in the form of glucose. Because of this, we structure our daily lives to economize our thoughts, leaning on intellectual tools like math and logic especially when we are feeling overwhelmed and lethargic. In addition, when we lack energy, we lack the ability to critically filter information. Kahneman says: "There is evidence that people are more likely to be influenced by empty persuasive messages such as commercials when they are tired and depleted."[13]

And when given just the right amount of easily understood facts or figures, it helps people to overcome resistance by reducing discernment to marketing lures. One of the reasons this occurs is that when the mind is busy consciously processing information, it loses the capacity to critically filter additional information. The facts and figures occupy our limited waking thoughts and we momentarily let down our guard. To understand this effect, Stanford University professor Baba Shiv conducted an experiment in which experimental subjects were provided with two options: a tempting chocolate cake or a healthful fruit salad. During one experiment, the group was asked to remember a two-digit number while deliberating between the sweets, and in another, they were asked to memorize a seven-digit number. Previous studies have shown the limitations of working memory at approximately seven units of information. By pushing the limits of conscious thought, they reduced their subjects' ability to consciously resist their unconscious physical impulses. The brakes of restraint could not be as easily applied because their cognitive effort had been redirected toward the task of remembering the number. Those required to remember only two digits had the available cognitive capacity that made them more likely to resist the temptation of the chocolate cake and instead choose the fruit salad, the healthier, more rational option.[14]

CONSISTENCY AND COHERENCE, NOT QUANTITY OR QUALITY

Often too much information can backfire. When marketers attempt to cram a lot of information into a short ad, the results can be self-defeating. Less is in fact more. That is because the conscious mind will leap to conclusions, forming a coherent narrative based upon partial information. This strong tendency to draw conclusions from incomplete information is a cognitive rule that Kahneman calls "What you see is all there is." Kahneman argues that consistency and coherence, not quantity or quality of information, are the keys to forming opinions.

As he explains, "The confidence that people experience is determined by the coherence of the story they manage to construct from available information. It is the consistency of the information that matters for a good story, not its completeness. Indeed you will often find that knowing little makes it easier to fit everything you know into a coherent pattern." In other words, if the story increases in complexity and length, it runs the risk of reduced coherence, inadvertently undermining the effectiveness of the communication. Kahneman observes that evoking consistent associations and providing cognitive ease for processing information are essential for causing us to accept a statement as true, adding that "much of the time the coherent story we put together is close enough to reality to support reasonable action."[15]

Marketers need to provide a logically connected argument that customers can easily understand and pass on to others to justify their actions in buying a brand. As Kahneman describes it, "Neither the quantity nor the quality of the evidence counts for much in subjective confidence. The confidence depends on the quality of the story they can tell." We need to arm prospects not with a laundry list of facts or a complex in-depth product analysis but with the right narrative. It is not through the tedious tale, but rather through the simple story made up of uniformly fluent facts that are repeated consistently and can be accepted as true, that the mind settles on a coherent pattern that suppresses doubt.

For example, Dyson's marketing campaign has always been grounded in the same consistent story, the immutable account that began one day when Dyson became frustrated when he was cleaning his house and his vacuum cleaner lost suction. Inside every box of Dyson vacuum cleaners is a little brochure that tells this brand story.

It explains how Dyson discovered an obvious design flaw as he tore apart his vacuum cleaner's bag, finding that it had become blocked with dust and dirt, and setting him off on his committed journey to design and build a better vacuum; how he overcame adversity when the odds were stacked against him; and how he failed more than 1,500 times before getting it right, launching the product that was first doubted and ignored by competitors and later admired and imitated.[16]

The implication for marketers: Coherence, not content, is king. Our minds are designed to seek patterns, and when something feels askew, we take notice and become guarded. That's because humans have evolved to avoid harm and today we approach brands with instinctive trepidation. Our higher circuits are designed to imagine every possible scenario of what might go wrong to help us plan how to protect ourselves from danger. Losses are typically weighed about twice as much as are gains.[17] When faced with conflicting associations and a convoluted rationale, we retreat, cutting our losses and decreasing our risks. Shoving the kitchen sink into a thirty-second ad or cluttering retail shelves with obfuscating brand extensions backfires because cognitive ease and fluency of communication are critical to persuasion.[18] Simple, uncluttered, clear-cut stories and environments work best because of their ability to soothe and assuage our slothful, critical, and often suspicious minds.

Instead of making it easier and simpler, most marketers have made it more difficult. Today we are mired in a plethora of new products each touting a tenuous raison d'être in an attempt to secure yet another irrelevant niche. For example, the average drugstore sells 350 different kinds of toothpaste and 55 floss alternatives.[19] We are faced with an increasingly cluttered and fragmented media environment of conflicting messages. Studies in North America have shown that on average we see 3,000 ads per day.[20] It's no wonder that eight out of ten new products fail. This quicksand of content freezes shoppers in indecision, forcing them into paralysis by analysis, as their ability to process multiple streams of information becomes cluttered and unintelligible. Brand and marketing message proliferation overloads consumers and undermines the very purpose of brands as shortcuts to easier choices and better lives, creating a lose-lose situation for marketers and consumers alike. Psychologist Barry Schwartz argues in his book *The Paradox of Choice* that too much choice not only erodes our psychological well-being and happiness, it can also demotivate us in making purchase decisions. Our mind is programmed to fixate on potential shortcomings, the glass that is half empty. Instead of reveling in the variety, we tend to assemble an idealistic composite of the forgone choices and focus our attention on a wider range of slightly inferior offerings. In one study, shoppers were more likely to purchase jam when they were offered free samples of six different jams as opposed to being offered samples of twenty-four. In another study, experimental subjects were asked how they would react if the price of a desirable Sony appliance was dramatically reduced and displayed in a shop window. The offer was met with foreseeable enthusiasm. But when a second, similarly marked-down appliance was placed next to it, enthusiasm waned and sales dropped as hypothetical customers became frozen in indecision.[21]

GIVING PERMISSION

The panelist sat in front of me, with his arms crossed and face steadfast. "Not gonna happen . . . no way," he retorted, explaining in no uncertain terms that he would never buy a German vehicle. These were the Asian-brand buyers, the die-hard Toyota and Honda loyalists who wore their self-righteous pragmatism like a crown. They preferred the low end of the car lineup, the compact sedans, the more utilitarian and affordable the better. Quality was defined on their terms, and for them it meant getting from points A to B . . . period. They had an emotional attachment to their logical sensibilities, creating missions out of their rationalizations. This sense of purpose made them feel a bit smarter, even a bit better than others, a belief that bordered on hubris and self-righteous indignation. They scoffed at those flaunting the conspicuous consumption of so-called luxury badges.

But something unforeseen happened as the focus group was hijacked and ushered into the adjacent showroom to view the all-new Jetta prototype. They had been instructed not to discuss their thoughts with others until they had a chance to regroup in the focus room. Instead, I watched as their heads nodded and their eyes narrowed and widened as they vacillated between inquisitive investigation and contemplative consideration. Later, they went back to the table in front of the two-way mirror and were asked the million-dollar question: "How much do you think it will cost?" They aimed high, somewhere in the $20,000-plus range. When they were told that the starting price was about $16,000, the collective back pedal commenced. The vibe in the room shifted as if the winds had blown in a completely new set of panelists who were now excited about the prospect of a German designed–vehicle proudly adorning their driveways. Instead of rationalizing why they would never consider Volkswagen, they began asking buying questions. "No way" became "When is it coming out?"

This episode reminded me of a sophisticated, well-dressed woman I once interviewed at a major North American auto show. I was pulling people out of the crowd to videotape their reactions to the all-new Lexus LS 460 that shimmered as it rotated behind the velvet ropes on a large circular stage. She had been checking out the adjacent Mercedes-Benz exhibit and was perhaps drawn by the crowd and camera crew surrounding the new full-size luxury sedan. Inviting her inside the car, I discovered that Lexus wasn't realistically in her consideration set. "What do you drive now?" I asked. She replied, "I have a Bentley." She smiled coyly as if trying not to boast while at the same time tacitly acknowledging the elite status that so few were qualified to hold. But when I told her that this luxurious, 400-horsepower Lexus would come in a hybrid version, retailing for more than a hundred thousand dollars, she began singing a whole new tune. Her resistance turned to enthusiasm—she simply "had to have one."

In both of these examples, brand rejecters turned on a dime into brand advocates because of key pivotal facts: for the Jetta, it was the lower retail cost suggestive of value, and for the Lexus, it was its availability in a hybrid and the higher retail price suggestive of quality and status. Satisfying the needs of prospective buyers for rational justification made this unlikely U-turn in the purchase funnel possible. In each instance the logical facts were not working in isolation, devoid of feelings. Quite the opposite. They actually excited the emotions of prospective car buyers by signaling the attainability of something they had long desired. The Volkswagen Jetta rejecters who became interested had an unrealized, latent desire to own a better class of vehicle. Their unconscious defense mechanism that drove their utilitarian pride was no longer necessary when they learned that they were, for the first time, able to affordably join the ranks of the elite. Likewise, the Bentley owner had a very real emotional desire in sharing the social status of the green movement that the Toyota Prius had made so famous, and Lexus was the first brand that allowed her to take pride in this cachet while still on her more exorbitant terms.

Returning again to our Trident gum example, an important reason the Trident "Chew on this" campaign was effective is that it gave people a reason to chew gum, overriding social pressures and personal resistance to do something previously stigmatized. It allowed people to act on their physical impulses without guilt or hesitancy by giving them justification for their behavior. I recall surprising an acquaintance of mine, who frowned upon gum chewing, with the revelatory fact that chewing Trident actually helped to fight cavities. A couple of weeks later I ran into her and was surprised to catch her in the act of chewing a stick of Trident bubblegum. I said in a good-natured accusatory tone, "I thought you didn't chew gum." She bantered back, "I'm not chewing gum. I'm fighting cavities."

NOT RATIONAL BUT RATIONALIZERS

The behavioral economist Dan Ariely, in his book *Predictably Irrational,* has convincingly popularized the idea that systematic hidden and irrational forces guide decision making and behavior. It turns out classic economic theory had it all wrong. The free choices of individuals are not always what is best because we often decide irrationally. What standard economic theory fails to take into account are the roles of the unconscious and our emotions in the assignation of value in decision making. Similarly, classical marketing theory is also wrong in the belief that all that is needed is a unique sales proposition that positions the brand apart from the competition as the more logical choice. A logical proposition works only if there are emotions behind it to drive brand momentum. Only then will brand prospects seek out their own rational reasons to do something about it. We are not rational creatures. We are rationalizers.

And when our emotional desires begin to shift toward a prospective brand, we subsequently seek to align our reasons to be consistent with that intention. Our rational mind is always looking for evidence to support our dominant beliefs . . . the stronger the emotion, the stronger the belief, and the greater the tendency to seek out supporting evidence. This confirmatory bias is why we often overlook the flaws of the ones we love, even if that loved one is a brand. We focus our attention on the positive qualities of the brand while ignoring the deficiencies. This predilection is what prevents Republicans and Democrats from finding common ground in the same set of facts, and why it is impossible to win an argument with someone on an emotionally charged issue like abortion or the existence of God. No amount of logic or reasoning can overcome strong feelings because the emotionally charged mind will always find its reasons to believe. But for people who are on the fence or who are considering but have yet to select a brand, it is absolutely necessary that the right reasons be offered in order to move them toward sales closure.

As much as it is important to interrupt patterns, build comfort, fire up one's imagination, and shift feelings, we must also satisfy the critical mind by giving people permission to act on the visceral impulses that propel us through life. What this means for marketers is at some point if you don't throw the prospective buyer logical lines or factual bones that make sense and ring true, they simply won't bite. Much as our higher-thinking neocortex jumps to conclusions, making up stories about how we are feeling, it is our critical mind that finds the justifications to support those stories, inclining us to act.

This predisposition is deeply ingrained because our minds have been trained by experience to look for reasons. It is our unconscious tendency to respond to a rationale even if it appears to be irrational, accepting factual information that doesn't always really make sense. Harvard professor Ellen Langer was one of the first social psychologists to think about the role of the unconscious processing of information. In a study Langer conducted in the late 1970s, researchers approached people in the act of using copying machines and asked if they could cut into the line and make photocopies. The experimental subjects were given different reasons for the request ranging from the sensible to the seemingly senseless, such as "because I'm in a rush" and "because I need to make copies." The researchers found out that compliance was higher when they gave a reason, even if the reason didn't really make sense. The subjects responded to the context of the request and not necessarily the specific content. Simply structuring the question with an embedded reason was sufficient to gain compliance to the request. This phenomenon was not without its limits. As Langer explained, the rationale of "because an elephant is after me" didn't cut it.[22]

When marketers structure a request for people to choose their brand, they benefit from including a reason, any reason, even if that reason is the "sheeting action" of Cascade dish detergent. It contains just enough logic consistent with a claim for virtually spotless dishes. If you don't give a reason, you are ignoring a very important component of how our emotional mind and rational mind work together, and, in turn, you are failing to address a key barrier to sealing the deal.

Once the prospect has established interest in the brand, at some phase of the purchase process you have to engage his or her frontal cortex. This is the part of the brain that plans behavior and decides whether or not to open the wallet or tighten the purse strings. You need to penetrate the critical filter that asks the questions, "Does this jibe with my past experience? Does the story hang together? Does it make sense?" If the answer is no to any of these questions, the conscious mind exercises its executive control by vetoing the suggestion and rejecting the sales pitch. The critical filter is like the gatekeeper, the bouncer at the door that decides whether or not to give permission to enter the domain of the unconscious mind.

Even though the unconscious drives behavior, it lacks the capacity for reasoning, accepting unconditionally any facts or suggestions presented to it by the conscious mind. While the unconscious mind is immensely more powerful, it is also very gullible. It responds but doesn't think. On the contrary, our conscious mind is thoughtful and skeptical but has a limited attention span. Any pitch toward the welcoming heart must be accompanied by an acknowledgment that placates the cautious cynic.

THOUGHT-STARTERS ON SATISFYING THE CRITICAL MIND

Provide facts to get excited about. We need to stop vilifying rational approaches as somehow inferior and ineffective. When advertising agencies tell marketers that rational ads don't work, they only appear self-serving and more focused on creative awards than the sales at hand. The goals are engagement and consideration in which both emotions and rationality play key roles. Rather than categorically rejecting the so-called rational, we to need find facts and figures that spark anticipatory pleasures or relevant emotions. This means looking deeper than hackneyed or bombastic claims. A detergent that is 10 percent stronger on stains probably won't cut it. Likewise, advertising a set of cutlery that cuts through solid rock without ever losing sharpness will only fall on deaf ears. Conversely, Lexus once successfully advertised gold-plated air bag connectors that in one fell swoop communicated both luxury and safety, seizing ownership of a feature not unique to the brand but equally satisfying to rational and emotional sensibilities.

Reframe support points as barriers to resistance. When designing marketing and ad strategies, don't think of the support points as a list of nice-to-know facts, think of them as consumers' barriers to action. What sticking points need to be overcome in order to give the prospect permission to buy the brand? Also make sure these points logically tie together in a single coherent narrative. For instance, if you're selling orange juice and your benefit is fresh squeezed taste, you don't want to talk about being fortified with calcium and Vitamin C because these things don't taste good.

Find your brand story. What is the narrative equivalent of your elevator pitch in your brand positioning? Not just the value proposition, but also the emotionally inspiring simple story. Once you have created your brand's narrative, break it down into a single phrase or sentence that includes both the emotional benefit and rational reason. In his documentary film *The Greatest Movie Ever Sold,* Morgan Spurlock asks marketing executives of Ban deodorant: "What are the words used to describe Ban? Ban is blank . . ." After an awkwardly uncomfortable but humorously long pause, one executive—seemingly caught off guard by the very basic query—says: "That's a great question!" Another executive finally interjects: "Superior technology." Spurlock quips: "Technology is not the way you want to describe something somebody's putting in their armpit."

The point is you should always know your brand story and be prepared to succinctly summarize it, not just the logical or technological facts but also the emotional desire that drives the brand's impetus. For example, one of the great brands I have worked on is Snapple All Natural Tea, a brand that has consistently been "made from the best stuff on earth" because it contains "healthy green tea, tasty black tea, real sugar." It's not just good; it's good for you.

Let the product do the work. When your product appears to do realistically remarkable things, showcase it. Like Dyson did in his vacuum commercials, or as Blendtec did in its viral videos of its powerfully destructive blenders. These demonstrations can help sell the product just as well as poignant tearjerkers. Apple has an effective commercial for the iPhone that turns product into pitchman. The product does the selling through a close-up demonstration of its amazing features and applications set against a simple, black background, using only an iPhone and a pair of hands.

Don't try to slip one over on them. When the conscious critical mind catches wind of attempts or perceived attempts at manipulation, marketing efforts can come back to bite you in the backside. For example, one troubling trend has been the reduction of product size without a corresponding reduction of price, or worse, with an increase. This can result in public outrage, negative online chatter, and weakened loyalty toward offending brands. Dove's famous "Real beauty" campaign came under public scrutiny and sparked controversy amid rumors that the supposedly natural, real models had been Photoshopped. Whether or not these rumors were true, it serves to underscore how a very effective campaign can be potentially undermined if there is conscious attention drawn toward potential inauthenticity, especially when extolling the benefits of "real."

Not all media attention is good attention. "Astroturfing," a term derived from the synthetic carpet designed to look like natural grass, is when a campaign planned by a corporation or other organizations is disguised as a grassroots effort. For example, in 2001 the *Los Angeles Times* accused Microsoft of astroturfing in response to the antitrust suit against the company by the US Department of Justice. Apparently hundreds of letters prepared by "Americans for Technology Leadership" were mailed to newspapers to voice disapproval of the suit. Unfortunately, some of these letters had allegedly come from incorrect addresses and dead people, putting into question the validity of the senders and the source of their claims of support for the company.[23] Another example: When Honda published photos of their new Crosstour on Facebook, negative comments about the design were countered by the positive commentary of a blogger who failed to identify his relationship with the company. He was outed by the angry crowd as the product manager at Honda.[24] And in 2012, Chick-fil-A was accused of launching a fake Facebook account to rebut criticism stemming from the announcement that The Jim Henson Company was pulling their toys from the chain because of the restaurant company president's opposition to same-sex marriage. Outspoken teen Abby Farle defended Chick-fil-A on Facebook, but when someone found her recently uploaded profile photo on a stock photography site, widespread animosity and protest toward the company ensued. Whether it was an epic corporate PR blunder or the rogue actions of someone wishing to anonymously support or further embarrass Chick-fil-A, manipulating social media is like playing with fire.[25]

Keep it simple, stupid. Among the many banal aphorisms in marketing and business, here is one worth remembering: Short and sweet is

9
STEP SIX: CHANGE THE ASSOCIATIONS

We don't see things as they are, we see them as we are.

—*Anaïs Nin*

IT WAS 1999 AND WE WERE LOST IN THE DEPTHS OF THE tropical jungle. I was being the adventurous one on this otherwise romantic trip for two, insisting that we drive the back roads from Playa del Carmen to visit the Mayan ruins of Chichen Itza. Traveling down a dusty dirt road through the dense rainforest in our four-wheel-drive rental, transported back in time to the natural terrain that once ensconced all of Mexico, we nearly forgot we were in the last year of the twentieth century, but then we were quickly snapped back into civilization. In the middle of the rainforest sat an imposing, brand new factory. Etched on its façade was the classic horse-head logo and the words Jordache Enterprises Inc. I was surprised to find that the popular jeans designer of the late 1970s and early '80s was still in business, let alone in the depths of the Yucatan Peninsula.

I rolled down the window of the truck and asked a local, "Dónde está Calle Libre?" As the young man pointed out directions, my eyes were drawn to his shirt. On it were the blue, red, and white rectangles made famous by designer Tommy Hilfiger. There was, however, one peculiar difference between his shirt and the millions of others that populated the streets of America. Instead of Hilfiger, the shirt read "Tommy Halfmaker." I soon discovered that this man was not alone. Many others were sporting the popular knock-off merchandise, from shirts to hats to backpacks, all with Hilfiger's coveted trademark albeit with a different last name. This urban style was being fabricated in the obscure seclusion of Mexico, and Halfmaker was just as popular as Hilfiger.

As we continued to drive down the busy streets of Valladolid, it struck me: Brands don't live on the racks of department stores, they live within the minds of people. The connection between a brand and its associations depends on the subjective viewpoint of the observer. To the residents of this small Mexican city, Tommy was still Tommy, but Hilfiger was now Halfmaker, and nobody cared or even noticed. Halfmaker enjoyed the same set of desirable attributes as Hilfiger did back home on the streets of Manhattan. Brand names and their associations can be both arbitrary and malleable because they live in the world of perception, not reality.

Originally known for his preppy, classic, all-American designs that appealed primarily to a niche of clean-cut, white, middle-class males, Hilfiger became wildly successful through his brash alliance with the key influencers of a diametrically opposite target segment: the inner city youth of African American hip-hop culture. Because of this partnership, Hilfiger's brand image was immensely transformed from one relegated to country clubs and yacht clubs to the influential urban streets, and later to the far-flung suburbs—and all because Tommy tapped into the growing power of the hip-hop movement.

And no one exemplified the raw and gritty talents of the city streets more than admitted ex–drug dealer turned legendary MC, the Notorious B.I.G., also known as Biggie Smalls.[1] In an open attempt to tap into the mainstreaming of the urban youth market, Hilfiger gave free wardrobes to influential rappers like Biggie and even used hip-hop bad boys Method Man of the Wu-Tang Clan and Treach of Naughty by Nature as runway models. The wardrobe gifts became de facto product placements, from which artists would give Hilfiger shout-outs at concerts and mentions in the rhymes of raps. His clothing was center stage in the prevalent rap music videos of that time, profoundly impacting popular culture and Hilfiger's sales numbers.[2] When gangsta rapper Snoop Dogg wore his red, white, and blue Hilfiger rugby shirt for an appearance on *Saturday Night Live* in 1994, sales skyrocketed overnight.

Hilfiger was intuitive enough to recognize that beneath the veneer of suburban life, those ideals of good, clean, family fun and of the American dream realized, was a desire for defiance. In the 1990s, that defiance was best translated by the street cred that hip-hop had defined. Hilfiger built his company and his designs on his brand logo knowing that it ultimately needed to stand for something bigger. As the designer explained, "It is important that my logo communicates who I am to the consumer. It has to say, 'I am about movement, energy, fun, color, quality, detail, American spirit, status, style, and value.' The brand must relate to the consumers' sensibilities. Whether they are based upon sports, music, entertainment, politics, or pop culture—it must have the cool factor."[3]

The unmistakable logo became synonymous with urban cool. And because fashion trends emanate from big cities, the brand's appeal spread from coast to coast, growing well beyond inner-city youth to varied demographics across the country and world—old and young, suburban and urban. Celebrities and public figures that included President Clinton, the Prince of Wales, Leonardo DiCaprio, and musicians and rock stars that included Michael Jackson, Bruce Springsteen, David Bowie, Elton John, and Mariah Carey wore Hilfiger designs.[4] In 1995 the Council of Fashion Designers of America named Hilfiger Menswear Designer of the Year.[5]

From 1991 to 1995 the company would net a sixfold increase in sales of $321 million with profits reaching $41 million. Hilfiger significantly outpaced industry growth in sharp contrast to the relatively poor performances by his formidable and well-established competitors of the time, like Donna Karan, Ralph Lauren, and Calvin Klein.[6] By 1999 the company was the highest-valued clothing commodity on the stock exchange, grossing more than half a billion dollars.[7] And all because Tommy Hilfiger figured out before any other designer how hip-hop could not only sell albums but an entire cultural trend.

Perhaps one of the most remarkable moments in advertising is now considered one of its most infamous. In 1924 Philip Morris introduced Marlboro to the world. At the time, it was branded as a women's cigarette, a milder, filtered version to contrast the stronger-tasting unfiltered brands that men mostly smoked. The Marlboro filter was even printed with a red band to hide lipstick stains and openly targeted feminine sensibilities with the ladylike ad slogan "Mild as May."[8]

But in 1954 all that changed. Precipitated by emerging public health concerns about the dangers of tobacco, many smokers were rethinking their allegiance to harsher unfiltered brands.[9] And Marlboro sought to leverage its distinction as a safer filtered cigarette to a wider audience beyond women. That was the year that ad executive Leo Burnett first conceived the Marlboro Man, achieving the greatest about-face in branding history. Burnett was looking for an image that would reposition and reinvent the brand for mass-market appeal. In a 1972 documentary Burnett explained how the idea for the "Marlboro Man" was first conceived in a brainstorming session when he asked his creative team, "What's the most masculine symbol you can think of?" and one of his head writers spoke up and said, "a cowboy."[10] The revered and reviled cowboy became what many industry experts consider the most brilliantly successful ad campaign of all time. Launched in 1955, the original Marlboro Man campaign featured close-up images of rugged masculine archetypes using the product. These included not only cowboys but also sailors, drill sergeants, construction workers, and other men of quintessential manly professions.[11]

The cowboy became the most popular Marlboro Man because of his ability to generate a powerfully rich set of compelling associations in the minds of many different people. Although Marlboro was originally defined as a man's cigarette by symbolizing ideal masculinity, the cowboy had wide appeal to both sexes. He embodied traits that were equally desirable to both men and women: independence, defiance, adventure, and romance. These universal, iconic, and downright sexy attributes borrowed the spirit of the Western frontier and life on the range, symbolizing the freedom and audaciousness of American culture as popularized worldwide through Western movies and television shows. Steeped with the alluring values of the American West, the ads offered intimations of strength, fearlessness, control, substance, and heroism.[12]

When the Marlboro Man was rolled out nationally in 1955, Marlboro sales jumped 3,241 percent to $5 billion, compared to its 1954 earnings when its US market share had been less than 1 percent.[13] By 1957 sales increased an additional 300 percent, going to $20 billion.[14] In 1963, when the Marlboro Country campaign began focusing solely on the symbolism of the American cowboy—using classic images of hats, boots, horses, and Western landscape—the Marlboro man became a global phenomenon and among the most widely recognized cultural symbols. By 1972 Marlboro was the leading tobacco brand in the world.[15] According to Philip Morris, it is still the number one brand of cigarette today, for both men and women, in every state of the U.S., and crossing all age groups. With a massive 42.6 percent retail market share, it has more than the combined market shares of the next 13 brands.[16]

IMPLICIT ASSOCIATIONS FOR INFERENTIAL MINDS

The evolutionary psychologist Geoffrey Miller believes that consumerism shares key parallels with narcissism, or excessive self-love. Miller observes that one's ego and self-esteem are often unconsciously linked to many of the brands we purchase. He argues that the capacity for self-absorption seems present in all ordinary humans, and often the choices we make in buying a certain brand are based primarily on its ability to help us show off to our social groups. Miller believes that two components drive the consumer mindset: status and hedonism. We show off to others in order to please ourselves, touting the indicators that advertise our biological potential as mates and friends.[17]

Humans display brands much like proud peacocks exhibit the ornamentation of their tail feathers. Peacocks spread their intricate plumage to convey to other birds their natural beauty conferred by good genes, their ability to find seeds and insects that sustain the health and integrity of their tremendous plumage, and their ability to avoid predators by negotiating and navigating the wild with such a cumbersome tail. Generally animals don't have any conscious awareness as to why they display these various indicators; the urge simply comes to them and they reap the evolutionary benefits of greater attractiveness to prospective mates.[18]

We humans also advertise our attractiveness to our fellow kind. The brands we choose to buy are the indicators of our health, wealth, and well-being and imply that we have certain traits that mark success and worth. And, like the peacock, we often have no conscious awareness of the fact that we are doing this in order to reap the evolutionary benefits of these associations in the social hierarchies in which we live. We simply have the urge to wear Prada, suggesting class, or Adidas, suggesting athleticism—and in turn promote the real benefits of our brand ornamentation: the perceptions of socioeconomic fitness and status. We show off to our tribe to make ourselves feel good by attracting attention and adulation.[19]

Great brands are like magnificent peacock tails. They communicate best through implication, because, fundamentally, our minds process information through inference. The challenge for marketers is to target and imply the traits that we unconsciously covet—the things that we so often can't or won't articulate. In the case of Hilfiger and Marlboro, it was oblique access to the concepts of rebellion and rugged independence—that elusive cool factor embodied by rappers and wranglers. These brands let people share in the intimidating badass mentality that the mainstream media made renowned and infamous. The gun-slinging outlaws and robbers and the gangstas and pimp players are all molded from the same archetype, simultaneously becoming the heroes and the villains of their respective times.

It is not just about what the brand says about the product, it is rather what it suggests about the person. The explicit message of the Marlboro Country campaign was "come to where the flavor is," but it was the flavor of the character, not the cigarette, that motivated smokers. As Mick Jagger once sang, "He can't be a man 'cause he doesn't smoke the same cigarettes as me." And women too wanted to share in the same tasty defiance that society encourages in men and condemns in women. This double standard only strengthened female resolve to claim the manly brands as their own. Likewise, it was similar insight that enabled Hilfiger to extend his brand to include a women's line, and allowed Marlboro to sell far more cigarettes to women as a men's product than it did when it spoke directly to feminine sensibilities.

THE ASSOCIATIVE MIND

When brand associations change in the minds of people, market shares shift because we learn and make decisions about brands largely driven by associative memory. Humans have the largest association cortex, which enables our species the cognitive advantage for complex mental functions beyond the mere detection of basic dimensions of sensory stimulation.[20] When marketing stimuli are processed by the mind, they don't trigger a linear sequence of conscious thoughts and ideas one after the other. In fact, a great deal of activity in the mind occurs at the same time; a single idea can simultaneously trigger many ideas, which in turn triggers many more thoughts. The tricky part for marketers is that only a few of these thoughts actually reach consciousness.[21]

The storage and retrieval of information occurs through a set of neural networks of association that become linked together in memory. This is why one thought can elicit the recall of a vast network of other interconnected thoughts, ideas, images, words, and emotions. It is not the specific word or image used in the advertising that has meaning, but rather the associations attached to it, encompassed by those thoughts in the subjectivities of people. While advertisers must remain focused on delivering a clear, consistent, coherent message, they must also recognize that this message is just the tip of the iceberg. When such a message reaches the target's mind, it must be evocative, conjuring up a rich, comprehensive set of meaningful associations below the surface.

Since brands can be reduced to memories through these associations, building these associations, both conscious and unconscious, is truly the essence of branding. It is not just about the overt art and copy of your ads, but also the subtextual meaning they generate. If you don't know the exact associations you seek to reinforce or change, you are missing one of the most important elements in branding.

When a brand consistently repeats a coherent, compelling message over a period of time, the net result is actually a physical change in the brain's circuitry at a cellular level. This rewired neural network of learned associations automatically predisposes people to think and respond in certain ways toward the brand. You want people to link your brand to a benefit without any effort. The brand's message becomes linked unconsciously. If I say, "Melts in your mouth," your mind automatically completes the thought, " . . . not in your hands." Similarly, Allstate's 48-year-old tagline, "You're in good hands with Allstate," enjoys 87 percent recognition, the most recognized ad slogan according to a 2004 survey.[22] Not only can people explicitly recall the slogan, they also are implicitly conditioned to link the brand with the feeling of being protected, the right mindset for someone thinking about buying insurance.

Freud first suggested the phenomenon of neuroplasticity, that the brain can be shaped, molded, and changed by experience. The neuropsychologist Donald Hebb theorized the basic mechanism behind it, which came to be summarized as "cells that fire together wire together." Repeatedly firing the same nerve cells rewires the brain's circuitry by increasing synaptic strength—the connections between neurons that provide a neural foundation for habits of thinking and behaving. These networks of learned associations determine the very strategies of how people approach life and choose brands.

Once these brand associations are set in the memories of people, they are not easily changed. For Tommy Hilfiger, he had the benefit of being a relative newcomer to the field of the fashion industry, and for Marlboro, before the introduction of the cowboy the brand had less than 1 percent market share.[23] As these brands spread throughout public consciousness so too did the implicit associations that would eventually become deeply rooted in the brains of individuals and subsequently within our collective cultures.

UNCONSCIOUSLY PRIMING RECEPTIVITY TO BRANDS

There is no such thing as an objective reality. When people discern product information and size up brands, they bring their own luggage and proclivities to the party. The gut reactions that help them make decisions can be reduced to their unique memories.[24] When someone says "I have a gut feeling about this," what she is really saying is, "I have seen this pattern before." Intuition is nothing more than recognition of learned events from our past that, when prompted by situational reminders, provide us with feedback on how to think, feel, or behave. The activation potential of these triggers strengthens when we experience them more often and they remain more active within our minds.

In psychology, priming refers to the ability of our minds to react to certain stimuli with increased sensitivity as a result of prior experience. For example, if you first see the word yellow, you will be slightly faster to recognize the word banana because these two words share a close relationship in memory. When one node of the associative network of memory is activated, it warms up another nearby node, making it easier and faster to retrieve that information.[25] Priming is believed to be an involuntary unconscious phenomenon because it occurs outside of conscious awareness and does not depend on the conscious retrieval of information. It relies on implicit nondeclarative memory, rather than on explicit declarative memory that we can recall consciously. Research has shown that priming can play an important role in how we make decisions.[26]

Since all of our past experiences differ, we each create our own unique set of personalized and malleable, implicitly learned associations. These learned associations often take precedence over rational evaluation. For example, Martin Lindstrom discovered that those scary warning labels about the risks of heart disease or emphysema actually stimulated the nucleus accumbens, the "craving spot" in the brains of smokers. Apparently the warning label had become associated with past pleasures of smoking rather than effectively warning people of future health risks. Similarly, Melanie Dempsey of Ryerson University and Andrew A. Mitchell of the University of Toronto conducted research that exposed participants to made-up brands paired with a set of pictures and words, some negative and some positive. After seeing hundreds of images paired with several fictitious brands, the subjects were unable to recall which brands were associated with which pictures and words, but they still expressed a preference for the positively conditioned brands. The authors of the study labeled it the "I like it, but I don't know why" effect. In a follow-up experiment the participants were presented with product information that contradicted their earlier impressions, offering them reasons to reject the products they had been conditioned to like, but they still chose the brands associated with the positive imagery. Factual information to the contrary did not undo the prior conditioning, suggesting that their product selections were driven more by unconscious conditioning rather than rational analysis.[27]

We are always reacting unconsciously to environmental signals that stimulate feelings like craving or warning, pleasure or pain. The jingle of an ice cream truck or the siren of a police car activates responses that influence our behavior toward or away from objects. Green means go. Red means stop. Jeffrey Blish, our strategy leader at Deutsch LA, will sometimes wear a necktie when he is moderating focus groups, which he uses to dictate the level of formality in the room. When he wants to relax and lower the guard of the panelists he loosens his tie. When they get a bit unruly or off topic, he slides the knot tighter and they snap back to attention. Jeffrey doesn't realize that he does this because his behavior is unconscious competence. This competence represents the highest level of learning, from which both mastery of skill and intuitive judgment arise. Brands can function much like the knot of the tie. They can be shifted back and forth to push people away from or toward the brand depending upon the associations elicited by the messages being sent out.

But just because we respond unconsciously to this stimuli doesn't mean that marketers who attempt to sneak their messages below the radar of consciousness are going to be successful in communicating their brands. While it is true that the mind learns and responds on an unconscious level to sensory associations and brand messages in the environment, it learns and responds much better when that message is clearly in the focus of our attention spotlight. In order for priming to favorably dispose your brand toward the positive, the brand concept and its storage chest of associations must first become imprinted on the minds of people. The best way to accomplish this task is through conscious attention.

Leading market researcher Ipsos ASI evaluated the impact of advertising based upon a robust sample of 97,083 respondents and an extensive array of 512 ads. In the research, subjects initially believed that they were evaluating a new television program. As part of the programming, they were also exposed to a test ad, which simulated their natural exposure to advertising. The study revealed that advertising had a significant effect on brand choice even if the message was processed at low levels of attention. But the respondents who experienced higher levels of attention to the ad—those who could spontaneously recall the test ad and accurately describe it—were over two and half times more likely to demonstrate a shift in brand choice than those who paid low attention to ads and were only able to recognize them when prompted by a description. In addition, the ads processed by the high-attention group were six times more impactful than ads processed by the ultra-low-attention group, who could neither recall nor recognize having seen the ad even though they had been exposed to it. This group of unconscious responders experienced only a 1.2 percent positive brand lift.[28]

Furthermore, when advertisers have used subliminal messages presented below the levels of consciousness, attempting to influence consumers through hidden images, words, pictures, slogans, or sounds, their efforts appear to have been a waste of resources and energy. As psychologist Timothy Wilson concludes, "Subliminal messages have little or no effect on consumer behavior or attitudes when used in ad campaigns, whereas there is considerable evidence that everyday, run-of-the-mill advertising does." Wilson adds, "Words hidden in movies do not cause people to line up at the concession stand. . . . Nor is there any evidence that implanting sexual images in cake icing increases sales, despite popular claims to the contrary. This is not to say that subliminal messages never have an effect—just that they have not been shown to do so in everyday advertising."[29]

People often confuse unconscious effect in advertising with subliminal advertising. All traditional nonsubliminal advertising has an unconscious effect, not because there are hidden messages but because we have unconscious associations to the messages communicated. Consumers are often aware of the message in the advertising—what they are unaware of is how the message influences them. Wilson points out that a prospective smoker doesn't say: "I think I'll start smoking because I want to be like the Marlboro Man I saw on a billboard. Instead adolescents learn to associate smoking with independence and rebellion with little recognition that it was advertising that helped create this association. Even when we consciously see and hear something such as an advertisement, we can be unaware of the way in which it influences us."[30]

BRANDING THE INTANGIBLE

In order to effectively brand a product you need a reference point, some sort of context out of which to identify the meaning and value of the product. Einstein's theory of relativity is a good example for understanding not only the laws of physics but also the laws of cognition and marketing. When it comes to brand perceptions, there are no absolutes. Brands are never perceived independently of other relations, as the mind is always evaluating brands relative to something else. Without this contextual comparison you simply have no sense of its worth.

Perhaps the best marketing example of the power of associative learning in marketing comes from the highly acclaimed "Intel Inside" ad campaign. Prior to this effort, Intel, the maker of premium PC chips, was confronted with a difficult challenge. To mainstream computer buyers, the brand was unknown and invisible because there simply were no points of reference in their minds on which to form judgments about the product. Even though Intel was the very engine that powered the personal computer and had become the industry standard for processors, its market position remained buried and subjugated within the brands of the products it empowered. The Intel processor was rendered not only imperceptible but also indistinguishable from the competition, which contributed to the perception of a highly commoditized market for microprocessors.

Launched in 1991, the Intel Inside® Program was a cooperative marketing program aimed to stamp the brand in the minds of end users by employing Donald Hebb's law of associative learning through repetition and persistence. By sharing advertising costs and convincing other manufacturers to place the Intel Inside trademark and logo in their marketing materials, the Intel brand experienced a remarkable leap in advertising exposure. The results of the program were immediate. In 1992, about a year after the campaign was introduced worldwide, sales rose 63 percent. From 1991 to 1995, awareness of the Intel Inside logo grew from 24 percent to an astonishing 94 percent among European PC purchasers, and by 1998 Intel controlled 90 percent of the world's market share of PC microprocessors.[31] In 2001 Intel ranked fifth on the list of the most valuable brands.[32] Intel's brand equity ballooned, going from obscurity to eventually becoming a world-class player synonymous with the computer industry. Today, the Intel Inside program is still one of the world's largest cooperative advertising campaigns, supported by thousands of PC makers licensed to use the Intel Inside logos.[33]

Not only did Intel benefit from the countless repetitions of brand exposure through PC makers' advertising, it helped them to align their products with some of the world's best and biggest computer brands, such as industry leader IBM. Today Intel remains one of the most valued and best known brands in the world, ranking in a rarefied air with Coke, Disney, and McDonald's. And in the computing industry, Intel enjoys outright ownership of its all-important associations of "quality," "technology leadership," and "reliability."[34]

COGNITIVE REFRAMES AND JUDO FLIPS

The manner in which you present brand information has primary influence on how the message is received. This framing effect creates a cognitive bias that can make the same information feel different depending on how the facts are spun. By shifting the focus of attention from the positive to the negative, marketers are able to slant the emotional coloring on top of the literal facts. This is why negative political advertisements predominate, honing in on obscure, often personal and emotionally charged transgressions of the opposing candidate, rather than talking about the bigger issues and the facts at large. And it is also why we get excited when we hear about a steak that is touted as being 90 percent fat free, and think twice about the same steak when it is claimed to contain 10 percent fat.

A great example of the tremendous power of cognitive reframing is the National Pork Board's long-standing "The other white meat" campaign. This effort debuted in 1987 with the goal of increasing consumption by dispelling pork's fatty reputation. Even though pork was perceived to have more fat than white meat chicken and turkey, pork shared an important opportunistic association with these lean protein choices. It turned white when cooked. With one simple flip of perspective, a common heuristic—that white meat is lean meat—was put to work. Pork had joined the ranks of its healthful poultry counterparts by association with a commonly shared and meaningful attribute.

Consumer research conducted prior to the launch had discovered that over 40 percent of all consumers had already subconsciously viewed pork as a white meat. Webster's dictionary even defined pork as such. After extensive pretesting of the campaign, which showed that the approach was both believable and effective, "The other white meat" campaign was born. Within seven short months an independent research company confirmed that attitudes were shifting. In the first seven months in television markets, the campaign reached 85 percent of the projected target audience with a 72 percent increase in awareness of the white-meat message. At the end of the first year of the campaign, agriculture economist Glenn Grimes of the University of Missouri said, "The apparent increase in demand for pork put $500 million in US pork producers' pockets during 1987 that wouldn't be there under normal conditions."[35] The campaign would become one of the food industry's most successful, increasing pork consumption by more than 20 percent, and last for 23 years.[36] In 2000 a study conducted by Northwestern University reported that

"The other white meat" ranked as the fifth most memorable promotional tagline in the history of contemporary advertising.[37]

The lesson for marketers is that without a meaningful associative frame of reference you simply don't have a brand. Association determines your brand's worth while context determines the meaning of those associations. It is not just what is inside the Tiffany gift box that determines the value; it is the box itself, the context in which the message is delivered, that helps to create the greatest value, making the ring and your brand shine all the brighter.

THOUGHT-STARTERS ON LEVERAGING AND CHANGING ASSOCIATIONS

Mine your brand's associative DNA. The totality of a brand is much greater than its positioning, advertisement, or package design. Recognize and tap into the entire associative architecture of the brain, the neural network of associations attached to the images, words, feelings, thoughts, and ideas that your brand evokes. In order to become fully cognizant of these associations, try breaking them out by explicit versus implicit associations. These associated qualities and features need to be discussed when you are creating the marketing approach; and the deeper dimensions can be uncovered through the use of qualitative projective techniques such as image sorts and collages to get at these hidden associations.

Another approach is to consider the neuromarketing techniques available, such as elucidating the precise points of your brand experience that trigger natural desire: the deep excitatory prompts of anticipatory pleasures. For example, NeuroFocus, a leading neuromarketing researcher, measures moment-by-moment brain wave responses to product interactions to identify what they call neurological iconic signatures (NIS), or neural high points. In one study, NeuroFocus found that when people enjoyed yogurt, the real moment of brand truth was "grasping and removing the foil covering over the top of container." The brain loved the multitude of sensations that this action produced. Once these peak moments are identified, emphasizing them, whether in advertising or through the point of sale, tends to increase ad effectiveness and sales. As NeuroFocus founder A. K. Pradeep says, "It primes [people] to desire and seek out the product between uses."[38]

Rethink forced exposures. One of the most pervasive and alarming trends in digital marketing these days is forced exposure to online advertising—those annoying pop-up windows, ads, and links that stand like roadblocks between you and your desired content. Rather than just creating awareness of the product, these intrusions train people to associate and link negative emotions like anger and frustration to the brand. After countless annoying exposures, advertisers might see an increase in brand awareness but they may also see the results of negative conditioning, i.e., the "I don't like this brand, but I don't know why" effect.

Choose the right names. Perhaps the most important thing a company can do is choose the right name for their brand. Names come with an intrinsic set of preexisting attributes, becoming the most repeated element of the brand.

Repetition is how the unconscious becomes programmed, so once you have established a mainstream brand name, it is unwise if not impossible to change the name as those hardwired associations have already set like concrete. When companies have attempted to establish more contemporary associations by changing their names, they have typically drawn only derision and confusion from customers. RadioShack failed in its attempt to shed its antiquated associations when it was rebranded as "the Shack,"[39] and similarly Pizza Hut's rebranding as "the Hut" also met with a backlash.[40] Conversely, KFC succeeded because it borrowed upon the existing nomenclature of fast-food customers, who had long been using the shortened version of Kentucky Fried Chicken in their everyday vernacular.

Dress Barn is a clothing retailer who saddled themselves with a name that implied cows and overalls more than models and runways. So they did the next best thing to changing their consumer-facing name by changing their corporate name to Ascena to reduce some of their dowdier baggage in order to better attract investors. Philip

Morris, the maker of cigarettes, also changed its corporate name to distance itself from the negative connotations of tobacco. Instead, they chose the name Altria, which sounds suspiciously like altruism, an intention the company denies.[41]

If you are in the position to choose the name of a brand or new product, make sure you explore the entire associative structure attached to the name. Choose a name that is an unblemished canvas, lacking any hidden baggage, or find one that is already linked to positive thoughts whose meaning coincides with the product you're selling.

Choose the right brand extensions. It should go without saying that it's extremely important to choose the appropriate line extensions that both reinforce the brand and help take it to new heights. Think of Nike's foray into the Air Jordan sub-brand that fit perfectly with the brand's mantra, "authentic athletic performance." At the time, no one better exemplified the highest level of athletic performance than Michael Jordan. As Magic Johnson once said, "There's Michael Jordan and then there is the rest of us."[42]

Even major marketers like Colgate can fail to understand the ramifications of their base-brand associations. The launch of Colgate Kitchen Entrees was met with obvious distaste and disappointment. From the company perspective it made sense: eat our food and then brush with our toothpaste. But people don't think that way. The thought of minty fresh toothpaste failed to whet their appetites for stir-fried chicken and vegetables.

Carefully choose endorsers. One of the easiest ways for a brand to promote its compelling attributes is through the borrowed interest of celebrity sponsorships. For example, Proactiv has become one of the leading brands of skin care treatment with a massive cultlike following thanks to a long celebrity A-list that includes Justin Bieber, Katy Perry, Britney Spears, Jessica Simpson, and P. Diddy.

But when brands align strongly with a celebrity endorsement, remember that a celebrity's swift fall from grace can have a damaging impact. Pepsi leveraged the "Choice of a new generation" through their powerful alliance with the "King of Pop," but when public attention began to focus on allegations of Michael Jackson's painkiller addiction, they severed the relationship.[43] Similarly, as Tiger Woods' public perception and golf ranks fell, so did his relationships with major advertisers. Tag Heuer, AT&T, and Gatorade all canceled their endorsement deals amid revelations of his personal life and extramarital affairs. Perhaps the most ironic twist occurred in the late '80s when the Beef Industry Council launched their "Beef . . . real food for real people" campaign featuring the likable actor James Garner, who was hired to fortify the image of beef during a time when people were becoming more health conscious. Not too long after that, Garner underwent quadruple bypass surgery.

Consider novel contexts at retail. I recently saw a picture posted on Facebook of a point-of-purchase display for condoms. Hanging on a j-hook in front of jars and jars of baby food were boxes of Trojans. Set in the context of the consequences of unprotected sex, the display worked to remind those passing down the aisle of the trials and tribulations of early parenthood. This is an intriguing example of how retailers and marketers can leverage associations. Retailers have long worked the planograms of their store shelves to match the associative context of the brain—whether it's chips alongside salsa or baby food next to condoms. In marketing your product, you must also consider what associations you want your brand to activate when the time comes for the most important moment of branding: the moment of choice.

10
STEP SEVEN: TAKE ACTION

Tell me and I'll forget; show me and I may remember; involve me and I'll understand.

—*Chinese Proverb*

ONE SNOWY MORNING THE YOUNG AND INSATIABLY CURIOUS Milton Erickson woke up early to conduct a little experiment. While walking the snow-covered pathway on his way to school, he zigzagged back and forth through the rapidly accumulating snow to create a wavy-patterned trail on the otherwise straight route. When he returned home that afternoon Milton was amused to find that others had followed his lead, tracing his absurd meanderings rather than taking the more direct route. From that early lesson, Erickson realized that people have a tendency to act without thinking, living their lives on autopilot by simply following the well-worn paths established by others. Erickson grew up to revolutionize psychotherapy, becoming the world's leading authority in medical hypnosis and one of the most effective psychotherapists ever. The unorthodox psychiatrist became legendary for his "miracle cures" that tapped into the power of his patients' unconscious minds, rapidly and often unwittingly transforming their behaviors—much like he changed the habits of his schoolmates on that snowy day.[1]

The most important step to changing our unconscious inclinations is to take action. The more frequently we walk the paths of these new behaviors, the more automatic and habitual they become, ultimately requiring little or no conscious attention or effort. The seven steps to behavior change that are described in this book are intended to be a useful model, a simplification of an extremely complex process: the manner in which our minds work to change our behavior. These seven steps are an intelligible, logical method that can help to identify and influence the dimensions that matter most to that process of change. From pattern interruption to action, this process reflects the general sequence in which behavior change occurs, both in individuals and in market environments. It aims to elucidate a rational and conscious understanding of a largely unconscious and emotional process. However, because the brain is a patchwork of distinct, conflicted, combinatorial, and often paradoxical drives, this process must always be viewed systemically as a collective whole. It is not a factory assembly line of behavioral output that can be mechanistically reduced to its sequential parts, but rather an interrelated and interactive process. The unconscious mind is always working on multiple levels, simultaneously parallel-processing information. These seven steps occur as both a linear process and an interconnected, recursive loop in which thoughts, feelings, and actions constantly and mutually influence each other.

REAL POWER

Even in the digital age, broadcast television remains the dominant media for major advertisers. The reason television commercials remain effective is that, comparatively speaking, they are still among the most neurally engaging and multisensory of media, captivating our attention on large flat-screen TVs in a typically less cluttered environment than the Internet. But, despite the industry's continued homage to the almighty 30-second commercial and the much heralded promise of the virtual and digital realm, as Marvin Gaye sang in his 1968 hit, "Ain't nothing like the real thing." One of the greatest ironies in marketing is that despite continued heavy media investments, branding does not simply occur by staring at the TV sitting in your living room, nor by surfing the Internet from your office desk. It happens in the tangible interactions of authentic human experiences.

The goal of marketing should be not only to turn thought into action via advertising, but also to turn action into thought via experience. As Timothy Wilson says, "One of the most enduring lessons of social psychology is that behavior change often precedes changes in attitudes and feelings."[2] When we leap to a new behavior, our conscious mind weaves a logically consistent narrative. We post-rationalize our actions through cognitive dissonance, seeking to reconcile the conflict and discomfort between our old ideas and our new actions so that the latter may be adjusted and conformed to our preexisting attitudes. We assign causality to our novel behaviors, often concluding that we made the conscious, considered choice to act prompted by our established attitudes and beliefs. We seek to align our personal identity to match these new behaviors.

For example, let's say the next time you visit your local coffee shop, you are offered a free cup of Tazo decaffeinated green tea instead of your usual café latte. You choose to opt for the pattern interrupt, taking the tea instead, and while enjoying the beverage, you make a mental note to consider purchasing the green tea on your next visit. You say to yourself, "I know that I have always been health conscious even though I don't always act that way." You affirm that you have indeed been thinking about cutting back on caffeine and fat. You conclude, "I guess I'm really a tea drinker after all, not the die-hard coffee fiend I used to be." You believe that it was you calling all the shots when really the response was prompted by circumstance and molded by the environment.

Does this mean marketers should put all their money into sales promotion and renounce advertising? Absolutely not. Much like Milton Erickson did for his classmates, the role of marketing is to make the path toward brand purchase the path of least resistance. Through the collective empowerment of pattern interruption, comfort, imagination, feeling, rationality, and association change, people can be given an easy pathway to take action without even having to think about it. Marketers need to leverage the full spectrum of behavioral influence so that when it comes time to take that all-important step to purchase, the audience has already established receptivity to the brand and its goals, messages, and benefits.

The essence of unconscious branding is to make the brand stand for something by laying down a patterned pathway of positively predisposed neuro-associations in the minds of people. Take Starbucks, for example. They used to effectively advertise their coffee shops, but these days they no longer need to invest heavily in brand advertising. Starbucks appears to be an anomaly in that it has spent far less on traditional advertising than other big chains but has become one of the most valued brands in the world.[3] The brand is now so strongly established that the brand name and the word "coffee" have even been removed from the logo. Leadership in premium coffee is now an unconscious connection with Starbucks, positioning them for further growth into other relevant and meaningful food and beverage areas. As marketing consultant Al Ries states, "Starbucks is following a well-worn path. Build a brand that stands for something and then try to figure out what other products you can hang the brand name on."[4]

Starbucks Coffee Company transformed the specialty coffee industry, growing from a small regional player into the undisputed leader. They did so not just by offering the best quality coffee, but also by providing an unmatched retail experience that was replicated consistently and unmistakably across the globe and all of its touch points. According to CEO Howard Schultz, the reason that Starbucks doesn't need to rely just on advertising is that it is in "over 16,000 neighborhoods around the world, in more than 50 countries, forming connections with millions of customers every day in our stores, in grocery aisles, at home, and at work."[5] The strength of their branded neural networks of associative connections is forged every day in the minds of its customers through real-world experiences in its ubiquitously consistent network of coffee shops.

What Starbucks did was piggyback on the pleasures of one of the most deep-seated and addictive cultural rituals and consumer habits: the coffee break. It was a strategy that would almost guarantee loyalty provided that the outcomes of the consumer experience remained consistently favorable. Critical to this strategy was its service orientation. Starbucks' baristas are focused on customer satisfaction and compliant to individual preferences, catering to specific whims for three shots espresso, extra hot, one pump, fat free, no whip, double cup, and more, and readily redoing customers' orders when faced with discontent. A great retail experience is the essence of their branding. For centuries, humans have relished the experience of the coffee break to relax, recharge, and socially connect. Starbucks was the first and best chain to lay claim to the actual experience, and they did so on a grand scale, providing the ideal physical environments to make these rituals not only possible but also enjoyable, offering a third locale to work and home. These authentic, in-the-flesh, physical interactions among customers, store, and baristas contributed to a strong brand valuation, which was greater than any investment in traditional media would have been.

From a neurobiological standpoint, the goal of unconscious branding is to transform neural pathways of positively predisposed brand associations into profitable behavioral pathways, bridging our thought patterns into behavioral patterns and turning thoughts about coffee into trips to Starbucks. The quicker we can animate thoughts and feelings into positive behaviors, the better. As William James once offered, "Seize the very first possible opportunity to act on every resolution you make, and on every emotional prompting you may experience in the direction of habits you aspire to gain."[6] Whether you are trying to change your life for the better or seeking to improve your marketing program, the rules of the game are identical. Brands that engage people not just in thought but in practice are best remembered, understood, and often the most successful. There is great wisdom in the Jewish principle of *na'aseh v'nishma*, which means "we will do and we will listen." According to religious belief, "practice of a commandment precedes understanding and practice is the only path to understanding."[7] The same wisdom holds true for advertisers. In order to get people to fully understand and appreciate the benefits of your brand, people must experience your product and brand firsthand. Only then will they understand its true value.

I MOVE, THEREFORE I AM

Organisms that lack movement lack brains. You will not find a brain in a tree or a flower or a cactus because those entities that have no need for movement also have no need for a brain. Take for instance the sea squirt—an aquatic animal that begins life searching for a place to live. When it discovers the right rock to permanently attach itself to, it no longer requires the services of its brain. So, waste not, want not. It makes a meal of its brain and eats it, celebrating its new-found sedentary lifestyle.[8]

It turns out Descartes did indeed have it all wrong when he said: "I think, therefore I am." If you look at the functions of the brain, it should perhaps more accurately be said that: "I move, therefore I think," according to Vittorio Gallese, Professor of Human Physiology at the University of Parma, Italy.[9] So much of our brain structures are dedicated to the systems governing movement that some even say practically all of our brain contributes in some way to our mo-tor skills. As the neuroscientist Daniel Wolpert of the University of Cambridge states: "I would argue that we have a brain for one rea-son and one reason only. And that's to produce adaptable and com-plex movement. There is no other reason to have a brain. . . . Things like sensory, memory and cognitive processes are all important, but they are only important to drive movement."[10] We are more like "hu-man doings" than we are "human beings."

Indeed, most areas of our neocortex are involved in the control of voluntary movement.[11] Our nervous system is fundamentally de-signed to perceive our environments and to take action. There are essentially three types of neurons: (1) motor neurons that carry sig-nals from the central nervous system to the outer parts of the body, controlling actions; (2) sensory neurons that take information from the outer parts of the body into the central nervous system from the senses; and (3) interneurons that connect the various neurons throughout the brain and spinal cord.[12] When we motivate people into physical action, engaging more than just their perception, cog-nition, and emotion, we involve more of their neurology, impress-ing the brand deeper into long-term memory. Not only do real-life experiences involve our vast motor systems, they vividly engage our multiple sensory systems. Through sight, sound, touch, smell, and taste, they give us more ways to firmly establish and represent the memory in the part of the brain that drives response. As doctors George I. Viamontes and Bernard D. Beitman observe in their article "Mapping the Unconscious in the Brain," "The unconscious is a vital functional core that anchors the behavioral repertoire of every organism that has a brain."[13] In other words, the path to behavior change is the path to our unconscious minds.

EXPERIENCE CHANGES EVERYTHING

The goal of marketing is to generate sales intention through positive, repetitive brand experiences, which include but also go beyond the product itself. We love Starbucks not just for its coffee, but even more so for the pleasures of the experiences it provides, an insight similar to that which inspired General Foods International Coffee television commercials many years ago when they suggested, "Celebrate the moments of our lives." All humans actually have an innate distaste for bitterness, an omnipresent characteristic of all coffees. When tasting something bitter, a common reaction for humans would be to spit it out to avoid poisoning, since bitterness signals warning of the presence of toxins.[14] This is why children don't usually like the taste of coffee and why bitter-tasting synthetic chemicals are commonly added to toxic substances, like antifreeze and denatured alcohol, to avoid accidental poisoning.[15] But thanks in part to powerful brands like Starbucks, modern humans have learned to override and transform our innate distaste for bitter flavors into a compulsory delight. We learn to associate coffee with these rituals of relaxation and socialization, as well as the pleasurable effects of caffeine. Repetitive positive experiences over time can help us to overcome our instincts, and for companies like Starbucks, it has transformed a cheap commodity into a five-dollar indulgence.

It is no surprise that some of the most successful brands in the world leverage physical experiences to their advantage. Disney gave us Disney parks. Target made discount shopping chic. Nike supported athletic aspiration, encouraging action in the sports we love. We love our cars—from our Volkswagens to our Toyotas, from our Bentleys to our Beamers—because they quite literally move us to our destinations throughout life. Apple was the first computer brand to truly comprehend that technology isn't really about technology but about what it enables individuals to do. Likewise, AT&T reached customers by poignantly suggesting they "Reach out and touch someone," even though the phone company was about helping people to communicate from afar.

But what would happen if a brand ceased talking about itself and instead chose to make action-oriented experiences the cornerstone of its marketing? And what if that brand declined its own share of voice, preferring to improve its market share by providing tangible, entertaining gatherings in lieu of amusing yet more removed advertisements? Leveraging real-life experiences can empower a brand's development and help it to achieve remarkable sales efficiency by shunning traditional marketing in favor of grassroots, experiential tactics.

Perhaps the hottest brand to fly in the face of traditional trends is Red Bull, the Austria-based company that first conceived the energy drink category. From the very beginning the brand was not without its challenges. When founder Dietrich Mateschitz was first inspired by a syrupy, medicine-like tonic that helped revitalize him after a business trip to Thailand, the concept of an energy drink was neither well known nor well received among Westerners. As Mateschitz said, "If I don't create the market, it doesn't exist."[16] When he hired a market research firm to test the product's appeal, the survey research yielded catastrophic results. Mateschitz recalls, "People didn't believe the taste, the logo, the brand name. I'd never before experienced such a disaster." He chose to ignore the research results, however, and introduced Red Bull in 1987. Once it was on the shelves, there was nothing unique or "ownable" about the product itself. Its contents were not patented. The ingredients were listed right on the can and anyone could copy or emulate it, and eventually a hundred or so imitators did, including industry giants like Coca-Cola, Pepsi, and Anheuser-Busch.[17] On top of all these pitfalls, Red Bull would retail at a huge price premium, eventually selling at around $2 for a single 8.4-ounce can, at least double what you would pay for a 12-ounce can of Coke.[18]

Despite this, Mateschitz went on to create not only a legendary brand but also a textbook case in unconscious branding. He converted market and product weaknesses into brand strengths through the empowerment of inspiring actions. Ironically, he himself hadn't been a very good student of business, taking ten years to graduate at the age of 28 from the University of Commerce in Vienna with a degree in marketing. Perhaps it was because of his fondness for the college experience, as he confessed in an interview: "Life as a student is enjoyable."[19]

Fortunately for Red Bull, sales and marketing is less about scholastic aptitude and intellectual understanding and more about emotional attunement and motivational understanding. Mateschitz's strengths were in his drive, character, and personality. He had an engaging zest for collegiate life. His friends said he liked to party, play, and pursue pretty women. Convivial, energetic, charming, and funny, he was ambitious and undaunted in both his business and life pursuits.[20] As it turned out, this rich set of traits would be instrumental to his later success as a marketing pioneer, helping him to topple traditional marketing models with an approach to branding that media alone could never capture, and forever rewriting the textbooks of marketing.

Mateschitz has what psychologist Daniel Goleman refers to as "emotional intelligence" or "the capacity for recognizing our own feelings and those of others, for motivating ourselves, and for managing emotions well in ourselves and in our relationships. It describes abilities distinct from, but complementary to, academic intelligence—the purely cognitive capacities measured by IQ."[21] In other words, Mateschitz had street smarts and not just book smarts. He had acquired emotional attunement and social savvy about the lives of college students through his own experiences as a student. Goleman believes that one's EQ, not just one's IQ, is the quality that often elevates and distinguishes great, successful leaders. Mateschitz understood that marketing is not just about understanding the numbers; it's about understanding the people. He fine-tuned this skill set through his ten years of experience at campus parties and social gatherings, more so than in the theoretical musings of classrooms and lecture halls. He went on to demonstrate an unprecedented understanding and efficiency in connecting with this cynical college demographic, a highly influential group that often resists mainstream corporate advertising but would be critical to building the Red Bull castle.

From the start, traditional marketing was summarily rejected. Initially, Red Bull avoided television, and didn't use outdoor, print, or digital ads, but chose grassroots, experiential efforts. Red Bull let people try the product free of cost through one of the most celebrated human experiences: the time-honored tradition of a good (but not necessarily old-fashioned) party. The foolproof branding plan was to give hip, young, and influential college students free cases of the energy drink and encourage them to throw their own event, a lucrative tactic that cost the marketer next to nothing. Through its alliance with the in-crowd and the alpha-partiers, Red Bull would become the dominant player in an emergent and rapidly growing category, going from obscurity to a staple at parties, bars, and clubs worldwide.

On the surface this may seem like simple sales promotion and free product sampling, but it was about neither the product nor the promotion. It was all about the social event itself. As Mateschitz explains, "We don't bring the product to the consumer, we bring the consumer to the product."[22] The goal was to create the best parties, not the best energy drink. As the brand grew so did the parties, with Red Bull becoming synonymous with high-octane fun and first-rate happenings that included huge crowds, big shots, celebrities, enormous venues, pumping music, and the ubiquitous presence of Red Bull drinks and mixers. In short, they branded the most exhilarating and social life experience of all, attracting active, on-the-go, and high-energy youth who were the primary targets.

Red Bull would later expand these tactics to bring the energetic brand to even greater experiential heights by sponsoring live events of the most intensely physical sort: extreme sports. Red Bull sponsored legions of affordable, death-defying athletes of less-than-mainstream but greatly exhilarating sports. These athletes were the up–and–coming rock stars of the newer generation, showcasing physical bravery and athletic prowess universally admired by men and desired by women. These branded iconic heroes enjoyed cultlike followings among the younger and more influential demographics. Today there are close to 500 world-class Red Bull sponsored athletes including BASE jumpers (BASE stands for buildings, antennas, spans—i.e., bridges—and earth—i.e., cliffs), cliff divers, big-wave surfers, motocross riders, snowboarders, and skateboarders, all risking life and limb in worldwide competitions and outrageous stunts.[23]

Having dispensed with the expected marketing tactics, the brand not only sponsors cutting-edge and original athletes, it has invented and hosts incredible, newfangled, and sensational competitions like "Red Bull Crashed Ice," an adrenaline-pumping combination of hockey and downhill skiing in which competitors skate, crash, tumble, and fly their way down a mountain, or the wacky "Red Bull's Flugtag" or "flying day," in which competitors seek to fly the farthest over water in their homemade flying machines.[24] Not only did these experiences grab the attention of live spectators, they also generated tons of media exposure. Ironically, by eschewing traditional up-front media spending Red Bull was able to generate much greater media impressions on the back end. As Mateschitz explained in a 2011 interview, "In literal financial terms, our sports teams are not yet profitable, but in value terms, they are. The total editorial media value plus the media assets created around the teams are superior to pure advertising expenditures."[25]

DESIGNING MEMORIES

The end goal of all marketing is the creation of empowering, inspiring memories. That's because when it comes to making purchase decisions, it is the "remembering self" that decides, not the "experiencing self." And nothing creates memories better than the simple, tried and true formula for unconscious branding employed so brilliantly by Red Bull. The three key experiential ingredients to the brand's success are novelty, physical action, and emotional stimulation. By creating novel, engaging, physically and emotionally stimulating experiences, the brand became deeply seated in the unconscious minds of its audience, the part of the mind that determines behavioral responses and brand purchases.

Marketers are not the architects of advertising. They are the architects of remembrance. Whether designing a print ad, or creating a branded experience, we are making memories, not just marketing materials. How we feel about a brand largely depends upon our memory of the experience provided by the brand, not what actually happened. Recalling the elements that made it different, that moved us either physically or emotionally, we then formulate our judgments. These are not based on the reality of these experiences but almost entirely on the peak moments and the concluding impression—whether positive or negative—the brand has produced. This tendency is what the behavioral economist Daniel Kahneman calls the "peak-end rule." In other words, marketers need to create powerful, positive, peak physical and emotional experiences that leave their audience on a high note. Mateschitz masterminded the branding of these peak experiences, delivering the highest of possible highs that are aligned not only with the sensibilities of its high-energy customers but also the characteristics and benefits of the product. He tapped into their love of wild parties and extreme sports, creating the desire for a high-energy drink that would let them play the game of life harder and better. It was this formula for fun that made Mateschitz the wealthiest man in Austria, and Red Bull the most powerful brand in the rapidly growing energy drink market that he himself had created.

According to Forbes, in 2005 Red Bull commanded a massive 80 percent market share in some countries and a 47 percent share in the US, where sales were growing at an annual rate of about 40 percent.[26] In 2010 the privately held company sold a total of 4,204 billion cans in over 161 countries, including over a billion in the US alone, earning Red Bull a total of $5.175 billion in revenue—a jump of 15.8 percent versus the previous year in a now highly competitive marketplace crowded with imitators desperate to get in on the action.[27] And the truest measure of all success is not just the numbers but the enjoyment of the journey. Mateschitz insists that he has no plans to sell or take Red Bull public because, as he puts it, "It's not a question of money. It's a question of fun."[28]

These nontraditional efforts have beat out even category-leading beverage behemoths at their own game. As Nancy F. Koehn, professor of business administration at Harvard Business School says, "In terms of attracting new customers and enhancing consumer loyalty, Red Bull has a more effective branding campaign than Coke or Pepsi. Red Bull is building a beverage brand without relying on the essential equipment of a mass-marketing campaign. Perhaps the indispensable tools of marketing aren't so indispensable after all."[29]

TAKING ACTION

Humans have the unique capacity to change consciously, physically reinventing themselves by taking action to change both mind and body. Branding is not simply about changing our opinions, attitudes, or even our behavior; it is about changing our being. Just as one must learn through experience to become a football player, a chess player, or a world-class pianist, one will only become a loyal Starbucks patron through action, by doing things again and again until it is part of who you are. We go from perceiving to feeling to thinking to doing to finally becoming. By engaging in repeated action, the body literally becomes the unconscious mind. The brand becomes ingrained in our somatic markers, and its rituals become part of our muscle memory—that is the long-term, unconscious, and procedural motor learning by which brands are insinuated into the tissues of our being.

Another universal enduring truth that drives our need for action is that humans are the only species with a conscious understanding of the bittersweet plight that is existence. As the evolutionary behavioral scientist Gad Saad maintains, "As far as we know, humans are the only species who experience existential angst due to the recognition of their mortality."[30] So much to do, so little time. Humans are uniquely blessed and cursed with this consciousness, an ability that not only confers on us the joy to fully embrace life in all its magnificent glory, but also the sobering realization that the party must some day end. As much as we may deny it, the thought looms large in the background of our behaviors, acting as a gnawing nudge that prompts us to get out and do something with our life so it doesn't idly pass us by. Great brands are the prompts that encourage our instinctive resolve to take action and live life better and more fully.

Not only do brand loyalties save us time by making purchase choices easier, they also connect us to something more fulfilling beyond the product. Brands help us seize and squeeze more out of life's moments. And lives, like brands, are not really nouns or things; they are verbs and processes, a series of actions over time. It's not about the destination. It is about the path we walk on the way to that destination. The real purpose of branding is to help us make the most of that journey by invigorating life's path with emotionally and physically gratifying moments along the way.

THIS BECOMES THAT

In 1974 psychologists Donald Dutton and Arthur Aron conducted a study in which male participants were interviewed after they walked across one of two different bridges: one, a fear-arousing suspension bridge that swayed high above a deep ravine, and the other, a safer, stable, lower bridge that failed to induce much fear in the subjects. At the end of each bridge an attractive female surveyed the male subjects and offered her phone number if they had any follow-up questions. The experimenters found that the participants who walked over the scary bridge were more likely to call the woman and ask for a date. Dutton and Aron concluded that the participants who had walked across the suspension bridge had misattributed their physiologically aroused body states as signs of attraction for the female experimenter. More so than those participants who lacked the heightened feelings of physical stimulation on the safer bridge, the suspension bridge participants mistook their sweaty palms, racing pulses, and beating hearts as signs that they liked the woman.[31]

Through my own work as a behavior change therapist, I have seen that when strong emotions and recollections are brought to the surface in clients, those same clients can redirect and attribute those feelings toward me, their bystander-therapist. These feelings can range from contentment to outrage, depending on the emotions and memories that have been stirred. This phenomenon of transference was first labeled by Freud to describe when people unconsciously transfer their attitudes and feelings from one person or situation to another. It's like when you meet someone at a party for the first time and something about him or her reminds you of one of your best friends from high school, or the friend who broke your heart in college. Without knowing anything about the person, you've already formed strong opinions that may have little basis in reality.

Because our relationships to brands are much like our relationships to people, a similar redirection of attitudes, emotions, and desires can take place with branded experiences. By these same mechanisms of misattribution and transference, a brand can become either the beneficiary or the collateral damage of someone's prior experiences. We unconsciously ascribe the feelings generated and the people encountered in those previous events to the brand itself. People prefer Red Bull over a myriad of imitators not merely because of its arousing ingredients of sugar, caffeine, amino acids, and herbal stimulants, which other products in the energy drink category commonly share, but because of the exclusive, stimulating environments of Red Bull–sponsored events. If body states, or what Damasio refers to as somatic markers, are often the keys to decision making, then by creating and activating these states, we can unconsciously convince brand buyers and encourage loyalty.

Physiological arousal has the power to transform who we are and how we make decisions. The more passionate we become, the more likely we are to give in to the desires of our deeper and sometimes uncharacteristically primal urges. For instance, behavioral economists Dan Ariely and George Lowenstein have demonstrated that levels of sexual arousal can have a profound effect on decision making. Through a study conducted at Berkeley, they found th
when male college students are in an impassioned state of heighte
sexual arousal, they indicate a much greater propensity to enga
an action they would not ordinarily consider. These young me
more than twice as likely to predict that they would engag
moral activities, and nearly twice as likely to predict that t

engage in a variety of somewhat odd sexual activities. As Ariely concludes, "Every one of us, regardless of how 'good' we are, underpredicts the effect of passion on our behavior." He adds, "Even the most brilliant and rational person, in the heat of passion, seems to be absolutely and completely divorced from the person he thought he was."[32] Likewise, when we are in highly emotional and aroused states, we are much more prone to give in to our reptilian impulses, seeking the primal excitation of wild parties and the awe-inspiring amazement of crazed extreme sports.

REAL IS MORE

As you might imagine, there is a big difference between a vicarious experience and attending the same event live. Even though the process of imagining an action involves the same neural circuitry as doing it, the intensity, richness, and vividness of that experience is never the same as when it is really happening to us. As much as we can imagine those same actions, we still know that they are not real. The discovery of mirror neurons has shed important light on this distinction. These neurons located in the frontal lobe are involved in processing empathy, imitation, and emulation. Activation of the mirror neurons is what primes the pump of desire, allowing us to vicariously envision and feel ourselves engaged in the behaviors and feelings of others. Though this is a prevailing technique employed by advertisers through the use of traditional media, these mirror neurons work best in real-life situations as compared to the shadowy substitutes delivered by broadcast, print, or digital advertising.[33] In addition, when you observe someone else doing an action, only a small subset, roughly 20 percent, of these same motor neurons will fire in your brain.[34] It is as if your brain is performing a virtual simulation of the other person's behaviors. But as when you are playing a video game, as exciting as it may be, you still know that it's not really real.

V. S. Ramachandran has expanded the theory of mirror neurons beyond motor neurons, to include sensations of touch and not just action. In other words, when you see someone being touched, neurons fire in your somatosensory cortex, located in the sensory region of your brain, which create empathy with the person being touched. Ramachandran explains that the reason you don't experience the sensation as if it were really happening to you is because of feedback signals from your sensory touch and pain receptors in your skin. These signals are sent back to your brain, vetoing the sensation by declaring, "Don't worry, you are not actually being touched." You can empathize all you want knowing that this isn't really happening, because to believe so would muddle and confuse your tactile perceptions.[35]

But Ramachandran has discovered a fascinating peculiarity that reveals profound insight into the universally social nature of our minds. If your arm is anesthetized so that you no longer can feel the sensation of touch, and you see someone being touched on their arm, you can actually feel it in your arm. Because you have no physical sensation due to the anesthesia, the feedback from your skin's sensory receptors is unable to cancel out and reject the feeling of being touched. This same effect also happens to a person with an amputated limb. When the amputee sees someone else being touched, he can actually feel it in his phantom limb because he is missing the arm containing the skin's sensory receptors, which would otherwise veto these sensory signals. Astonishingly, a person with phantom limb pain can actually experience relief of their pain symptoms by observing another person whose limbs are intact while they are being massaged. The amputee experiences the other person's massage as if it was actually happening to himself.[36]

Ramachandran calls these empathetic neurons "Gandhi neurons," arguing that all that separates ourselves from others is our skin. We really all are connected on a basic neurobiological basis, and in many ways we all share in a group consciousness of sorts. As Ramachandran puts it, "This is not in some abstract metaphorical sense. All that's separating you from him, from the other person, is your skin. Remove the skin; you experience that person's touch in your mind. You've dissolved the barrier between you and other human beings. And this, of course, is the basis of much of Eastern philosophy, and that is, there is no real independent self, aloof from other human beings, inspecting the world, inspecting other people.

You are, in fact, connected not just via Facebook and Internet; you're actually quite literally connected by your neurons. And there is a whole chain of neurons around this room, talking to each other. And there is no real distinctiveness of your consciousness from somebody else's consciousness. And this is not mumbo-jumbo philosophy. It emerges from our understanding of basic neuroscience."[37]

SOCIAL CURRENCY FOR SOCIAL ANIMALS

When we humans get together our neurons interact directly with the minds of others. Because of the nature of our shared sensory and physical experiences, which are accentuated and magnified through the power of group consciousness, the events that take place when we are among our tribal affiliates become more stimulating, more engaging, and often more memorable than when we are in isolation. This phenomenon is what likely contributes to our ability to vividly remember a live concert or sporting event, more so than if we had stayed home by ourselves, watching those same events online or on television. The power is in the sharing of the experience, which then emerges larger and more impressed in our minds.

Perhaps the greatest of humanity's truths is that we all deeply seek these connecting experiences with each other. All humans share in this innate capacity to band together with others and form groups, an instinctive desire to forge these crucial reciprocal alliances. As Gad Saad says, "Belonging to a brand community . . . only serves to accentuate that feeling of belonging, which is a central element of any social species." And after a seven-decades-long Harvard Study of Adult Development, psychiatrist George Vaillant concludes, "The only thing that really matters in life are your relationships to other people."[38]

To really understand human behavior you must take an ecological viewpoint, looking through the wider lens of the environmental context to include the social settings and not just the brain itself. Recall Herbert Simon's metaphor of the brain as a pair of scissors. As psychologist and director of the Center for Adaptive Behavior and Cognition at the Max Planck Institute for Human Development in Berlin, Gerd Gigerenzer, explains, "Just as one cannot understand how scissors cut by looking only at one blade, one will not understand human behavior by studying either cognition or the environment alone. This may seem to be common sense, yet much of psychology has gone a mentalist way, attempting to explain human behavior by attitudes, preferences, logic, or brain imaging, and ignoring the structure of the environments in which people live."[39]

There is an alarming trend in some areas of neuromarketing to encourage a reductionist view of human behavior by seeking to identify and isolate the smallest parts of the brain and searching for answers within a three-pound lump of flesh examined within the isolation of laboratory testing environments. Neuromarketing pioneer Dr. Stephen Sands once told me that one of his clients had asked him where the luxury part of the brain was. No matter how deep you peer into the most advanced brain image scans or search at the molecular level, you simply will never find it. Localization of brain function and branding on this level is as absurd as it is impossible. For marketers and laypeople, however, this question is understandable. When in doubt, we often look inward into our own minds in an attempt to find answers, but because our lives are much greater than we are, our behaviors are also rooted in something much larger than our own brains.

Whether we are connecting to our soul mate, our children, our family, our friends, our team, our co-workers, our neighbors, our countrymen, or our brand community, every one of us is, at our deepest, most unconscious level, a social animal. Identification with and acceptance of others has been critical to our survival and happiness, which makes it no surprise that brands are the physical embodiments that represent this social acceptance and this social currency. Brands become empowered through the inspiring connections of people sharing with other people, a feeling amplified manifold through the collective consciousness of brand and group affiliation. When we buy a brand that does its job, we buy into that feeling of being part of something bigger than ourselves. The objective of branding should not be to connect people to the company that sells stuff. The real role of unconscious branding is to connect people to other people. The brands that best dissolve these barriers are the ones that will not only be the most profitable but also among the most cherished.

THOUGHT-STARTERS ON LEVERAGING ACTION

Transform business operations into branding tools. The era of simply buying brand recognition, familiarity, and market share dominance through big, branded advertising and huge media budgets is long gone. That doesn't mean brand advertising can no longer play a critical role, but it does mean that you need to rethink what your "brand advertising" entails. If your brand is being defined by your actions as a company, what are you doing to make those actions not just exercises in business operations but also tools in marketing? How does your brand experience match up and fit in with your marketing communications? Think of all those customer experiences not only as business opportunities but also as additional forms of messaging and media. What you do speaks volumes because it ultimately determines the experiences and impressions that your brand leaves with your prospects.

Get physical. Consider shifting some of your media budget to experiential marketing. Such branded events are often considered second-rate tactics and afterthoughts in the planning process, but they are fundamental to branding. Marketers need to do more than simply sponsor existing events. They need to create new ones that both demonstrate the brand's strategy in action and provide real, tangible benefits to customers by representing the dimensions that differentiate the product. Start with your product and brand benefits and build an experience that matches hand-in-glove, much like Red Bull created high-energy experiences to match their high-energy drinks.

Design memories. When you are designing brand experiences, such as the purchase process, the online user experience, or customer service interactions, use the "peak-end rule" suggested by Kahneman.[40] When identifying ways to improve these processes, clearly define the peak experience you wish to create, and how you can conclude the total experience on the best possible note. What can you do to surprise and delight your customers? How can you leave them satisfied and wanting more? Both criteria will weigh disproportionately high in their overall brand impression, and poor delivery along either dimension can negate or compromise the brand experience. For instance, a flawless, first-rate stay at a resort hotel punctuated with the unexpected delivery of flowers and a free bottle of champagne will all be quickly forgotten if you screw up the in-room breakfast dining order on the day of departure.

Be consistent in product delivery. Because the unconscious mind becomes programmed by repetition of the exact same action over and over again, make sure your brand interactions are identical across touch points. This is not just the look and feel of your communications, but the manner in which the customer physically interacts with your product or service. For example, Starbucks customers know the drill no matter what city or town they are in. Model every retail, brand, and purchase experience after a single ideal experience and replicate it identically throughout the network.

Leverage social brands. Social media is all the rage in marketing these days—both the medium and the message are about our nature as social animals. Before we think about using social or even traditional media, we first must remember that it is the brand that is communal in nature. We need to put the human before the app or ad, and the cart before the horse. Before developing creative and media plans, particularly of the social variety, you need to identify the social DNA of your brand. What are the traits that are being displayed by category users? And what motivating and differentiating traits would you like your customers to display as outcomes of purchasing your brand? What common collective experiences does your brand empower? In the end, you need to inspire deep meaningful connections between your customers and other people, improving their life success on the way to improving your business success.

Leverage these seven steps. This process is intended not only to inspire marketing communications but also to precede and inform strategy development. Before you develop your brand strategy, write these seven steps on a single sheet of paper and fill in briefly what has to happen to accomplish each. What is the convention or pattern your brand needs to interrupt to get noticed? What needs to be done to make people comfortable to consider buying it? What do you want them to imagine as the benefits and outcomes of buying and using your brand? What are the key emotions and feelings you need to shift to gain interest? What logical support points help them overcome their resistance to buying the brand? What brand associations do you need to change or reinforce? And how can you physically engage your audience beyond just communications to experience your brand so that they may understand how it can make their lives better? With this as a backdrop, your strategy development process will become much more focused, empowered, inspired, and actionable.

Recognize these seven steps. Every day we wake up wearing two hats: marketer and customer. We sell our wares in the market, we sell ourselves in our social groups, and we participate as so-called consumers. Now that you are aware of the influence of these seven steps—interrupt the pattern; create comfort; lead the imagination; shift the feeling; satisfy the critical mind; change the associations; take action—you will find real world evidence of them everywhere. Buyer and seller beware.

The goal of this book is to uncover these patterns in our nature and our cultures so that we all can leverage them, and are not leveraged by them. Only through conscious knowledge of this process can we begin to make better brands and make better-informed purchase decisions. The brands that prevail amidst this leveled playing field of equally enlightened marketers and customers will be those that create real value. When we all are aware of the real causes of our deeds, we can inspire real progress on both sides of the free market fence.

AFTERWORD

I BEGAN THIS JOURNEY BECAUSE OF A DEEP CURIOSITY ABOUT the vast powers of the unconscious. Ironically, I discovered that the real power actually lies in consciousness. There is so much more to the phrase "change your mind." Science now tells us that we have the ability to not only change our thoughts but also our brains. Through plasticity, a biological phenomenon that allows us to reinvent ourselves through conscious effort, learning, and new experiences, we can quite literally create new realities. Likewise, the process of writing this book has changed who I am. It developed in me the sensitivity to see things that always existed but that I never noticed, and it created for me new experiences that I'd never before imagined.

The challenge comes in that it is so much easier and more natural to fall back on the automatic patterns of the familiar, the routine, and the unconscious; to keep doing the same things over and over again while really going nowhere. Nature has stacked the deck in favor of the status quo, but she also has given us a unique gift by providing us with access to a sliver of thoughts that we can mold. The focus of our attention really does change everything. Through constant, relentless effort and attention, and by switching our thoughts from the anxious, primitive centers to the resourceful, enlightened circuits of contemplative awareness, we can learn to subordinate biological interests that no longer serve us very well and, instead, to shape our own destiny.

It's been said that there are two ways to win: beat the competition or achieve your own goal. If you are driven by a desire for the former, you will be hijacked by your genes' basic programs, wired to succeed in environments that have little relevance in today's world. And you will not be alone. Much of the business world continues to operate in the mind that reinforces fear and aggression: the physical, reptilian, unthinking brain that seeks domination over others. What we don't realize is that by relying on these self-serving, primitive instincts we are quite literally shutting down our capacity to see and generate novel solutions.

The future of marketing and branding depends on our capability to shift from this competitive mindset to a creative mindset. We need to live in the conscious presence of the frontal lobe, the part of the mind that doesn't fear that the other guy will steal our slice of the market share pie, but envisions ways to bake a bigger pie. By quieting the selfish impulses of the body you'll begin to evolve and engage the mind that is "no body" and "beyond self" and you will create bigger and better outcomes for everyone.

It is the competitive mindset that keeps us marketers awake at night worrying over the bewildering pace of digital change in the media landscape and what it means for our survival. We need to stop paying attention to the environment alone—to the bleeding-edge apps and technologies that abound—and realize that our minds and our immaterial thoughts actually have a strong hand in constructing our physical environment. We should not be distracted by today's cultural expressions, but should focus on the innovative answers that have yet to be conceived. And in order to do so, we should pay more attention to new understandings of human behavior. When you truly understand people at the depths of these new levels, everything else becomes so much easier and much more rewarding.

And this is not woo-woo new-age spirituality or philosophical psychobabble. This new view of humanity emerges from a hard scientific understanding of the neurosciences. Instead of looking in fear at the problems of today's circumstances, have the courage and creativity to look beyond them.

ACKNOWLEDGMENTS

EMBRACING THE ELUSIVE INTANGIBLE MYSTERIES OF THE UN-conscious in an industry that's focused on hard facts and numbers has drawn its fair share of criticism along the way. I was inspired by the German philosopher Arthur Schopenhauer who once said, "All truth passes through three stages: First, it is ridiculed. Second, it is violently opposed. Third, it is accepted as being self-evident."

One time, I was asked to review advertising in development and provide feedback on the relative strengths and weaknesses of campaign options through the lens of my seven steps. When I sent my thoughts out in an email, a clever, good-natured digital creative director converted the text of my observations into speech, sharing the audio file with the group replete with a stilted robotic voice that made me laugh out loud. But when the snickering and wisecracks about my neuroanatomical references and hypnosis demonstrations turned into outrage and table pounds, that's when I knew I was getting somewhere. We all at times are quick to judge new ideas that threaten old comfortable ways of thinking. But we are sometimes equally compliant to jump on the bandwagon of popular belief when the tide shifts. I acknowledge not only those who supported this endeavor but also those who challenged it, since they helped strengthen my resolve and deepen my inquiry.

I am most grateful that Jim Levine supported this project when it was just a working title and a rough proposal. Thanks to Kerry Sparks and Elizabeth Fisher at the Levine Greenberg Literary Agency for being so helpful and responsive throughout this process. My editor

Laurie Harting was among the first to find originality in my ideas and best qualified to help bring them to my audience. Thanks also to the many other smart and dedicated people at Palgrave Macmillan including: Alan Bradshaw, Lauren Dwyer, Andrew Varhol, and Roberta Melville. I am fortunate that Dan Smetanka taught me about the publishing business and introduced me to Kristen McGuiness who helped me at every step from proposal to endless endnote, adding structure, fluency and thoughtful input from Intro to Afterword. Jon Ritt not only brilliantly designed the cover of this book, but he also demonstrated the power of the branding principles contained within it. I am truly grateful for Anna Villano, my parents, Marie-Louise and Robert, and my siblings, Viviane, Connie, and Robert.

I must acknowledge the authorities in the cognitive and behavioral sciences, the amazing doctors, scientists, and professors who are far more qualified than myself to make these arguments and without whom this book could not have been written. Some of them I have had the pleasure of meeting; all of which I have had the benefit of learning from their work. I respectfully recognize: Antonio Damasio, Joseph LeDoux, V.S. Ramachandran, Richard Dawkins, Steven Pinker, Leda Cosmides, John Tooby, Daniel Kahneman, Dan Ariely, Timothy Wilson, Geoffrey Miller, Read Montague, Chris Frith, Matt Ridley, David Eagleman, Paul Zak, Rob Kurzban, Paul Ekman, Edward O. Wilson, Giacomo Rizzolatti, Eric Kandel, Robert Trivers, John-Dylan Haynes, George Loewenstein, Baba Shiv, Douglas Hofstadter, Michael Gazzaniga, Gerd Gigerenzer, Gad Saad, Daniel Goleman, Robert Cialdini, Mark Turner, Louann Brizendine, Naomi Eisenberger, David Buss, Mihaly Csikszentmihalyi, Robin Dunbar, Paul Bloom, Andrew Newberg, Bianca Wittman, Emrah Düzel, Nico Bunzeck, John Medina, Allen MacNeill, Thomas Crook, Beatrice de Gelder, Wolfram Schultz, Greg Stephens, Joshua Brown, Barry Schwartz, Ellen Langer, Jeff Brown, Mark Fenske, George Viamontes, Bernard Beitman, Robert Provine, Vittorio Gallese, Daniel Wolpert, Christopher Chabris, Daniel Simons, Dylan Evans, John Sarno, and more . . .

Thanks to George Kappas and his staff at HMI College of Hypnotherapy for teaching me about the unconscious mind and helping people lead better more fulfilling lives. I would also like to acknowledge the pioneering work of his father, the late Dr. John Kappas, a founder of the profession of hypnotherapy who intuited the inner workings of the mind about half a century ago. The revolutionary work of the late Dr. Milton Erickson was also highly influential to this book, and I respect his contributions to the hypnosis, medical, and psychiatric communities in offering people better, quicker paths toward mental and emotional wellbeing.

Behind every great ad or marketing effort there is always a great client so I would like to thank my many great clients past and present, especially the people at Volkswagen with whom I have spent much of my time in recent years, including: Jonathan Browning, Tim Mahoney, Kevin Mayer, Justin Osborne, Brian Thomas, Jeff Sayen, Steve Neder, and Tim Ellis.

And last but never least, many thanks go to my many good friends and colleagues at Deutsch LA. I have worked at a few good ad agencies but none as original, intelligent, and capable as Deutsch. Our philosophy for hiring people with "big brains, big hearts, thick skin, who are two degrees off-center" has assembled one of the most creative and innovative teams in the business. Special thanks to Mike Sheldon, Eric Hirshberg, Jeffrey Blish, Mark Hunter, Kim Getty, Kyle Acquistapace, Winston Binch, Vic Palumbo, Chad Saul, Jeff Sweat, Tom Else, Michael Kadin, Matt Ian, Eric Springer, Monica Jungbeck, Chris Carter, Nargis Pirani, Bryan Clurman, Stuart Foster, Bud Caddell, David Povill, Ryan McLaughlin, Craig Melchiano, and all the other great Deutschers that make our agency what it is today.

AUTHORS NOTE:

For More information about Unconscious Branding go to:

http://www.unconsciousbranding.com

NOTES

INTRODUCTION

1. Martin Lindstrom, *Buyology* (New York: Broadway Books, 2008), p. 20.
2. ESOMAR, *Global Market Research 2011, An ESOMAR Industry Report in cooperation with KPMG Advisory* (Amsterdam: ESOMAR, 2011).
3. Mark Dziersk, "Six Ways to Avoid Landing in the Product Failure Bin," fastcompany
   .com, May 29, 2009, accessed May 23, 2012, http://www.fastcompany.com/blog
   /mark-dziersk/design-finds-you/6-ways-avoid-landing-product-failure-bin.
4. Ginger Campbell, MD, "Interview with Neuropsychologist Dr. Chris Frith, Author
   of Making Up the Mind: How the Brain Creates Our Mental World," Brain Science Podcast, May 8, 2009, accessed May 23, 2012, http://www.brainsciencepodcast
   .com/storage/transcripts/bsp-year-3/57-brainscience-Frith.pdf.
5. Gerald Zaltman, *How Customers Think* (Boston: Harvard Business School Press, 2003), p. xiii.

CHAPTER 1

1. William M. O'Barr, "'Subliminal' Advertising," *Advertising & Society Review* 6, no. 4 (2005), accessed May 24, 2012, http://muse.jhu.edu/journals/asr/v006/6.4unit03
   .html.
2. Ibid.
3. Ibid.
4. Richard Gafford, "The Operational Potential of Subliminal Perception," cia.gov, September 18, 1995, accessed May 24, 2012, https://www.cia.gov/library/center-for
   -the-study-of-intelligence/kent-csi/vol2no2/html/v02i2a07p_0001.htm.
5. Fred Danzig, "Subliminal Advertising—Today It's Just Historic Flashback for Researcher Vicary," *Advertising Age*, September 17, 1962, pp. 72-73.
6. O'Barr, "'Subliminal' Advertising."
7. Brandon Keim, "Brain Scanners Can See Your Decisions Before You Make Them," Wired.com, April 13, 2008, accessed May 24, 2012, http://www.wired.com/science
   /discoveries/news/2008/04/mind_decision.
8. John A. Byrne, "The 12 greatest entrepreneurs of our time," money.cnn.com, accessed June 2, 2012, http://money.cnn.com/galleries/2012/news/companies/1203
   /gallery.greatest-entrepreneurs.fortune/2.html. On iPad's success, Walter Isaacson, *Steve Jobs* (New York: Simon and Schuster, 2011), p. 478.
9. Posit Science, "Types of Memory," positscience.com, accessed May 22, 2012, http://
   www.positscience.com/about-the-brain/brain-facts/types-of-memory.
10. Coca-Cola Company, "Teaching the World to Sing," cocacolacompany.com, accessed May 22, 2012, http://www.thecoca-colacompany.com/heritage/ourheritage
    .html.

11. Kim Bhasin, "15 Facts about Coca-Cola That Will Blow Your Mind," business insider.com, June 9, 2011, accessed May 24, 2012, http://www.businessinsider.com/facts-about-coca-cola-2011-6?op=1#ixzz1qLF60Zqf.

12. Figures according to Steve Neder, Volkswagen, "Agency Sales and Business Review 2011 Presentation," Jan 23, 2012, Herndon, Virginia.

13. David Brooks, "The Social Animal," ted.com, March 14, 2011, accessed May 24, 2012, http://blog.ted.com/2011/03/14/the-social-animal-david-brooks-on-ted-com/.

14. Steven Pinker, *The Blank Slate: The Modern Denial of Human Nature* (New York: Viking, 2002).

15. Ruben Gur, Harold Sackeim, and Joanna Starek, "Lying to Ourselves," radiolab.org, accessed May 24, 2012, http://www.radiolab.org/2008/mar/10/lying-to-ourselves/.

16. David Eagleman, *Incognito* (New York: Pantheon, 2011), p. 8.

17. A. K. Pradeep, *The Buying Brain* (New Jersey: Wiley & Sons, 2010), p. 4.

18. Marc Gravelle, lecture entitled "Hypno Diagnostics," September 14, 2006, Hypnosis Motivation Institute, Tarzana, CA.

19. John Medina, *Brain Rules: 12 Principles for Surviving and Thriving at Work, Home, and School* (Seattle: Pear Press, 2008).

20. Jane Bloomfield & Greg Nyalisy, Hall & Partners, "The Future of Research for Advertising," *Admap,* October 2008, p. 24.

21. Dan Ariely, *Predictably Irrational* (New York: Harper Collins, 2010), p. 167.

22. Ross Tomlin, "Neuroscience breaks down soft drink 'battle' inside brain," bioed online.com, November 2004, accessed May 24, 2012, http://www.bioedonline.org/from-the-labs/article.cfm?art=283.

23. Ibid.

24. Jonah Lehrer, *How We Decide* (New York: Houghton Mifflin, 2009), p. 41.

25. Russell Poldrack, "Multitasking: The Brain Seeks Novelty," huffingtonpost.com, October 28, 2009, accessed May 24, 2012, http://www.huffingtonpost.com/russell-poldrack/multitasking-the-brain-se_b_334674.html.

26. Ariely, *Predictably Irrational,* p. 167.

27. Ross Tomlin, "Neuroscience breaks down soft drink 'battle' inside brain," bioed online.com, November 2004, accessed May 24, 2012, http://www.bioedonline.org/from-the-labs/article.cfm?art=283.

28. Food Safety News Desk, "FDA Urged to Ban Cola Caramel Coloring," foodsafety news.com, February 17, 2011, accessed May 24, 2012, http://www.foodsafetynews.com/2011/02/cspi-urges-fda-to-ban-popular-ingredient-caramel-coloring/.

29. John Medina, *Brain Rules: 12 Principles for Surviving and Thriving at Work, Home, and School* (Seattle: Pear Press, 2008), p. 210.

30. "Stone Age Minds: A conversation with evolutionary psychologists Leda Cosmides and John Tooby with Paul Feine," Aug. 5, 2010, accessed August 18, 2012, http://reason.com/reasontv/2010/08/05/leda-and-john-short.

31. David Eagleman, *Incognito* (New York: Pantheon, 2011), p. 6.

32. G. A. Miller, "The magical number seven, plus or minus two: Some limits on our capacity for processing information," *Psychological Review* 63, 81–97, 1956.

33. "Reading Your Mind," *60 Minutes,* CBS News, January 4, 2009.

34. Laura Burkitt, "Neuromarketing: Companies Use Neuroscience for Consumer Insights," forbes.com, October 29, 2009, accessed May 24, 2012, http://www.forbes.com/forbes/2009/1116/marketing-hyundai-neurofocus-brain-waves-battle-for-the-brain.html. Haley, Russell I. and Baldinger, Allan L., "ARF Copy Validity Project," Journal of Advertising Research, November 2006, pp. 114-135.

35. Wikipedia, "Pets.com," wikipedia.com, accessed May 22, 2012, http://en.wikipedia.org/wiki/Pets.com.

36. Chuck Stogel, "It's Insane! Crazy Eddie Returns," adweek.com, April 14, 2009, accessed May 24, 2012, http://www.adweek.com/news/advertising-branding/its-insane-crazy-eddie-returns-105601.

37. Jonah Lehrer, *How We Decide* (New York: Houghton Mifflin, 2009).

38. Bas van Rijn, "Lust for sex depends on size of brain," stunning-stuff.com, February 13, 2004, accessed May 24, 2012, http://www.stunning-stuff.com/read-weird-news -stories/28.html?ci=5.

39. A. K. Pradeep, *The Buying Brain* (New Jersey: Wiley & Sons, 2010).

40. Gad Saad, *The Consuming Instinct* (New York: Prometheus Books, 2011), p. 26.

41. The Quotations Page, accessed August 18, 2012. http://www.quotationspage.com /quote/5154.html

42. Good Reads, "C.G. Jung," goodreads.com, accessed May 25, 2012, http://www.good reads.com/quotes/show/44379.

CHAPTER 2

1. A. Edward O. Wilson, *On Human Nature* (Cambridge, MA: Harvard University Press, 1978), p.167.

2. A. Hill, S. Ward, A. Deino, G. Curtis, R. Drake, "Earliest Homo," *Nature* 1992, 355 (6362): 719-722. Leda Cosmides and John Tooby, *Evolutionary Psychology: A Primer* (Santa Barbara: Univ. of California, Santa Barbara, 1997), p 12.

3. John Stevenson, "The Evolution of the Human," onelife.com, accessed May 22, 2012, http://www.onelife.com/evolve/manev.html.

4. Leda Cosmides and John Tooby, *Evolutionary Psychology: A Primer* (Santa Barbara: Univ. of California, Santa Barbara, 1997), p. 12.

5. Ibid., p. 12.

6. Ibid., p. 12.

7. Avi Dan, "VW's CMO Mahoney on Becoming America's Fastest Growing Car Company," forbes.com, April 4, 2012, accessed May 24, 2012, http://www.forbes.com /sites/avidan/2012/04/04/vw-cmo-tim-mahoney-on-how-it-became-americas-fastest -growing-car-company/.

8. Allan MacNeill, *The Modern Scholar: Evolutionary Psychology: The Science of Human Nature* (Maryland: Recorded Books, 2010).

9. Steven Pinker, *The Blank Slate* (New York: Penguin Books, 2002), pp. 40-41.

10. AOL Autos Staff, "The Best Selling Cars in America: November 2010," autos .aol.com, December 2, 2010, accessed May 24, 2012, http://autos.aol.com/gallery /best-selling-cars/.

11. U.S. Food and Drug Administration, "Facts about Generic Drugs," fda.gov, May 14, 2012, accessed May 24, 2012, http://www.fda.gov/Drugs/ResourcesForYou/Consum ers/BuyingUsingMedicineSafely/UnderstandingGenericDrugs/ucm167991.htm.

12. InBev Annual Report 2006, "Stella Artois," ab-inbev.com, accessed May 22, 2012, accessed May 24, 2012, http://www.ab-inbev.com/annualreport2006/stella_artois .cfm.

13. Robert Cialdini, *Influence* (New York: HarperBusiness, 2006), p. 20.

14. Holy Bible, Matthew 7:12.

15. Helen Briggs, "Altruism 'in-built' in humans," bbc.com, March 3, 2006, accessed May 24, 2012, http://news.bbc.co.uk/2/hi/science/nature/4766490.stm.

16. Kapil Bawa and Robert Shoemaker, "The Effects of Free Sample Promotions on Incremental Brand Sales," *Marketing Science,* Summer 2004, pp. 345-363.

17. http://epublications.marquette.edu/cgi/viewcontent.cgi?article=1202&context=mulr.

18. Robert L. Trivers, "The Evolution of Reciprocal Altruism," *The Quarterly Review of Biology* 46, no. 1, March 1971, pp. 35-57.

19. Robert Cialdini, *Influence,* p. 20.

20. James G. Enloe, "Hunter-Gather Food Sharing," uiowa.edu, 2003, accessed May 24, 2012, http://www.uiowa.edu/~zooarch/enloehuntergath.pdf.

21. John Cloud, "Competitive Altruism," time.com, June 3, 2009, accessed May 24, 2012, http://www.time.com/time/health/article/0,8599,1902361,00.html.

22. Tim Nudd, "Apple's 'Get a Mac,' the Complete Campaign," adweek.com, April 13, 2011, accessed May 27, 2012, http://www.adweek.com/adfreak/apples-get-mac -complete-campaign-130552.

23. Mac News, "Apple is 'World's Most Valuable Brand,'" macnews.com, accessed May 22, 2012, http://www.macnews.com/2012/03/19/apple-worlds-most-valuable-brand.

24. Leda Cosmides and John Tooby, "Center for Evolutionary Psychology," psych.ucsb .edu, accessed May 22, 2012, http://www.psych.ucsb.edu/research/cep/cep.html.

25. Douglas Van Praet interview with Robert Kurzban, Associate Professor of Psychology at University of Pennsylvania, January 19, 2011, at Chapman University, Orange California.

26. "Last Human Standing," PBS, aired August 31, 2011.

27. Steven Pinker, *The Blank Slate: The Modern Denial of Human Nature* (New York: Viking, 2002).

28. QSR Magazine, "Biggest Fast Food Companies in Industry by Rank," qsrmagazine .com, August 2011, accessed May 24, 2012, http://www.qsrmagazine.com/reports /top-50-sorted-rank.

29. David M. Buss, *The Evolution Of Desire: Strategies Of Human Mating* (New York: Basic Books, 1994), p. 14.

30. David J. Linden, *The Accidental Mind* (Cambridge: Harvard University Press, 2007), p. 7.

31. Allan MacNeill, The Modern Scholar: Evolutionary Psychology: The Science of Human Nature, (Maryland: Recorded Books, 2010).

32. John Medina, *Brain Rules* (Seattle: Pear Press, 2008), p. 7.

33. Edward Geehr, "Do Calorie Counts on Restaurant Menus Work?" healthbistro .com, February 2, 2011, accessed May 24, 2012, http://healthbistro.lifescript.com /2011/02/02/do-calorie-counts-on-restaurant-menus-work/.

34. Louann Brizendine, *The Male Brain* (New York: Broadway Books, 2010), p. 34

35. Robert Wright, *The Moral Animal* (New York: Vintage Books, 2005), p. 58.

36. UPI, "Study shows chimps exchange meat for sex," upi.com, April 8, 2009, accessed May 27, 2012, http://www.upi.com/Science_News/2009/04/08/Study-shows -chimps-exchange-meat-for-sex/UPI-44101239238066/#ixzz1K7n9MNYF.

37. Adam Waytz, "The Psychology of Social Status," scientificamerican.com, December 8, 2009, accessed May 24, 2012, http://www.scientificamerican.com/article .cfm?id=the-psychology-of-social.

38. Robert O. Deaner, Amit V. Khera and Michael L. Platt, "Monkeys Pay Per View: Adaptive Valuation of Social Images by Rhesus Macaques," Current Biology, Volume 15, Issue 6, March 29, 2005, pp. 543-548.

39. Stuart Wolpert, "Researchers find genetic link between physical pain and social rejection," UCLA Newsroom, August 17, 2009, accessed May 24, 2012, http://news room.ucla.edu/portal/ucla/a-genetic-link-between-pain-and-98593.aspx.

40. Ibid.

41. Naomi Eisenberger, Jaana Juvonen and Thomas Bradbury, "The Science of Relationships: From Romance to Rejection," virtualprofessors.com, July 5, 2010, accessed May 24, 2012, http://www.virtualprofessors.com/the-science-of-relationships -from-romance-to-rejection.

42. Daniel Lametti, "Mirroring Behavior," scientificamerican.com, June 9, 2009, accessed May 24, 2012, http://www.scientificamerican.com/article.cfm?id=mirroring -behavior.

43. Ibid.

44. Lindstrom, *Buyology* (New York: Crown Business, 2008).

45. Leah Eisenstadt, "Empathy on the Brain," bu.edu, accessed May 22, 2012, http:// www.bu.edu/sjmag/scimag2005/features/mirrorneurons.htm.

46. The One Club, "Best of Digital Decade," oneclub.org, accessed May 22, 2012, http://www.oneclub.org/DigitalDecade/.

47. Forbes, "Best-Ever Social Media Campaigns," forbes.com, August 17, 2010, accessed May 24, 2012, http://www.forbes.com/2010/08/17/facebook-old-spice-farm ville-pepsi-forbes-viral-marketing-cmo-network-social-media_slide.html.

48. The Associated Press, "'Paranormal Activity' an Abnormal Success," cbsnews .com, October 14, 2009, accessed May 24, 2012, http://www.cbsnews.com/stories /2009/10/14/entertainment/main5383879.shtml.

49. "PunchDub Quantitative Study Results," Nelson Tao, Deutsch Data Strategy, Reported May 20, 2010, Surveys conducted 5/17-5/20, 2010.

50. Sands Research, "Sands Research Announces Results of Neuromarketing Study Ranking Effectiveness Of 2010 Super Bowl Commercials," sandsresearch.com, February 24, 2010, accessed May 24, 2012, http://www.sandsresearch.com/PressRelease _SB2010.aspx[0].

51. Geoffrey Miller, *Spent* (New York: Viking Press, 2009).

52. The Associated Press, "Number of active users at Facebook over the years," cbsmews.com, May 17, 2012, accessed May 24, 2012, http://www.cbsnews .com/8301-505250_162-57436609/number-of-active-users-at-facebook-over-the -years/.

53. CBS News, *60 Minutes,* "Mark Zuckerberg and Facebook, Part I," December 5, 2010.

54. The One Club, "Best of Digital Decade," oneclub.org, accessed May 22, 2012, http://www.oneclub.org/DigitalDecade/.

CHAPTER 3

1. Keith Oatley, *Emotions: A Brief History* (New Jersey: Wiley-Blackwell, 2004), p. 53.

2. Crystalinks, "Reptilian Brain," crystalinks.com, accessed May 22, 2012, http:// www.crystalinks.com/reptilianbrain.html.

3. Cralle Physical Therapy, "Excerpt from Smart Moves," raycralle.com, January 14, 2012, accessed May 24, 2012, http://www.raycralle.com/index.php?option=com _content&view=article&id=201:excerpt-from-smart-moves&catid=88:articles& Itemid=27.

4. David J. Linden, *The Accidental Mind* (Cambridge: Harvard University Press, 2007), p. 9.

5. Antonio Damasio, *Self Comes to Mind* (New York: Pantheon, 2010), p. 74.

6. Paul D. Maclean, *The Triune Brain in Evolution* (New York: Springer Publishing, 1990).

7. Jonah Lehrer, *How We Decide* (New York: Houghton Mifflin, 2009), p. 18.

8. Joe Dispenza, *Evolve Your Brain* (Florida: HCI Books, 2007), p. 136-137.

9. Daniel Goleman, *Emotional Intelligence* (New York: Bantam Books, 2006), p. 20.

10. Austin Allen, "Big Think Interview with Joseph LeDoux," bigthink.com, June 24, 2010, accessed May 24, 2012, http://bigthink.com/ideas/20451.

11. Julia Layton, "How Fear Works," howstuffworks.com, accessed May 22, 2012, http://health.howstuffworks.com/mental-health/human-nature/other-emotions /fear1.htm.

12. Hamish Pringle and Peter Field, *Brand Immortality* (Philadelphia: Kogan Page, 2009).

13. Paul D. Maclean, *The Triune Brain in Evolution* (New York: Springer Publishing, 1990).

14. Richard Cytowic. *The Neurological Side of Neuropsychology* (Boston: Massachusetts Institute of Technology, 1996), p.107.

15. Brain Explorer, "Prefrontal Cortex," brainexplorer.com, accessed May 22, 2012, http://www.brainexplorer.org/glossary/prefrontal_cortex.shtml.

16. Renate Nummela and Geoffrey Caine, *Making Connections: Teaching and the Human Brain* (Nashville, TN: Incentive Publications, 1990).

17. Paul D. Maclean, *The Triune Brain in Evolution* (New York: Springer Publishing, 1990).

18. Steven Pinker, *How the Mind Works* (New York: W.W. Norton & Company, 1999).

19. David J. Linden, *The Accidental Mind* (Cambridge: Harvard University Press, 2007).

20. Richard Dawkins, *The Selfish Gene* (New York: Oxford University Press, USA, 1989), p. 192.

21. Ibid., p. 258.

22. Kate Murphy, "First Camera, Then Fork," nytimes.com, April 6, 2010, accessed May 24, 2012, http://www.nytimes.com/2010/04/07/dining/07camera.html.

23. Megan O'Neill, "The 7 Most Viral YouTube Video Topics of All Time," socialtimes .com, April 12, 2010, accessed May 24, 2012, http://www.socialtimes.com/2010/04 /youtube-video-topics/.

24. *Forbes,* "Best-Ever Social Media Campaigns," forbes.com, August 17, 2010, accessed May 24, 2012, http://www.forbes.com/2010/08/17/facebook-old-spice-farm ville-pepsi-forbes-viral-marketing-cmo-network-social-media_slide_8.html.

25. Antonio Damasio, "This Time with Feeling," The Aspen Institute, July 4, 2009, accessed May 24, 2012, http://fora.tv/2009/07/04/Antonio_Damasio_This_Time_With _Feeling.

26. Richard Stalker, "Kate Upton Ad Creates Big Returns for Carl's Jr.," webpronews .com, April 2, 2012, accessed May 24, 2012, http://www.webpronews.com /kate-upton-ad-creates-big-returns-for-carls-jr-2012-04.

27. Michael Dawson, "The Marketing Front: The Real Essence of Advertising," spin-watch.org.uk, December 13, 2005, accessed May 24, 2012, http://www.spinwatch .org.uk/-articles-by-category-mainmenu-8/42-media-spin/202-the-marketing-front -the-real-essence-of-advertising.

28. Martha Lagace, "Connecting with Consumers Using Deep Metaphors," hbswk.edu, May 5, 2008, accessed May 24, 2012, http://hbswk.hbs.edu/item/5871.html.

29. *Hollywood Reporter,* "TiVo: Jackson Stunt Most Replayed Moment Ever," cnn .com, February 3, 2004, accessed May 24, 2012, http://www.cnn.com/2004/TECH /ptech/02/03/television.tivo.reut/index.html.

30. Barry Miles, *Paul McCartney: Many Years From Now* (New York: Henry Holt & Company, 1997), p. 499.

31. Alison Jones, "James Cameron and the Lace G-Strings," sundaymercury.net, December 20, 2009, accessed May 24, 2012, http://blogs.sundaymercury.net/anorak -city/2009/12/james-cameron-and-the-lace-g-s.html.

32. Oliver Chiang, "Call of Duty: Black Ops Claims 'Biggest Entertainment Launch in History,'" forbes.com, November 11, 2010, accessed July 8, 2012, http://www .forbes.com/sites/oliverchiang/2010/11/11/call-of-duty-black-ops-claims-biggest -entertainment-launch-in-history/. Keith Stuart, "Modern Warfare 3 smashes enter-tainment launch records," guardiannews.com, November 11, 2011, accessed July 7, 2012, http://www.guardian.co.uk/technology/gamesblog/2011/nov/11/

33. Interview with Eric Hirshberg, CEO of Activision, NBC, "Late Night with Jimmy Fallon," June 13, 2011.

34. *Forbes,* "Best-Ever Social Media Campaigns," forbes.com, August 17, 2010, accessed May 24, 2012, http://www.forbes.com/2010/08/17/facebook-old-spice-farm ville-pepsi-forbes-viral-marketing-cmo-network-social-media_slide_2.html.

35. Steven Pinker, "The History of Violence," *The New Republic,* March 19, 2007.

36. Ethan Gilsdorf, "Geek Pride," psychologytoday.com, November 17, 2010, accessed July 7, 2012, http://www.psychologytoday.com/blog/geek-pride/201011/violent -video-games-are-good-you.

37. Ian Sample, "Blind Man Amazes Scientists with His Ability to Detect Objects He Cannot See," guardian.co.uk, December 23, 2008, accessed May 24, 2012, http:// www.guardian.co.uk/science/2008/dec/23/neuroscience.

38. Kate Devin, "Blind Man Navigates Obstacle Course Using 'Blindsight,'" telegraph .co.uk, December 22, 2008, May 24, 2012, http://www.telegraph.co.uk/news/news topics/howaboutthat/3902864/Blind-man-navigates-obstacle-course-using-blind sight.html.

39. Sample, "Blind Man Amazes Scientists With His Ability To Detect Objects He Cannot See."

40. V. S. Ramachandran, "Ramachandran On How 'Blind-Sight' Gives Us Clues About The Nature Of Consciousness," youtube.com, December 23, 2008, accessed May 24, 2012, http://www.youtube.com/watch?v=RuNDkcbq8PY.[0]

41. Ibid.

42. Ibid.

43. William James, *The Principles of Psychology, Vol. 2* (New York: Henry Holt (Reprinted Bristol: Thoemmes Press, 1999), pp. 449-450.

44. Jonah Lehrer, *How We Decide* (New York: Houghton Mifflin, 2009), p. 23.
45. John Brockman, "Parallel Memories: Putting Emotions Back Into the Brain. A Talk with Joseph LeDoux," edge.org, February 17, 1997, accessed May 24, 2012, http://www.edge.org/3rd_culture/ledoux/ledoux_p4.html.
46. Joseph LeDoux, "Joseph LeDoux and The Amygdaloids at 92nd Street Y," youtube.com, May 2, 2008, accessed May 24, 2012, http://www.youtube.com/watch?v=zmrm4-hYiNw.
47. Austin Allen, "Big Think Interview with Joseph LeDoux," bigthink.com, June 24, 2010, accessed May 24, 2012, http://bigthink.com/ideas/20451.
48. Martin Lindstrom, *Brandwashed* (New York: Crown Business, 2011), p. 66.
49. Max Miller, "More Ideas from LeDoux," bigthink.com, September 16, 2010, accessed May 24, 2012, http://bigthink.com/ideas/24131.
50. Jad Abumrad & Robert Krulwich, "Seeing Imposters: When Loved Ones Suddenly Aren't," npr.org, March 30, 2010, accessed May 24, 2012, http://www.npr.org/templates/story/story.php?storyId=124745692.
51. Lehrer, *How We Decide*, pp. 14-15.
52. Ibid.
53. Antonio Damasio, "When Emotions Make Better Decisions," The Aspen Institute, July 4, 2009, accessed May 24, 2012, http://www.youtube.com/watch?v=1wup_K2WN0I&feature=relatedDamasio.
54. Martin Lindstrom, "Your Love Your iPhone. Literally," nytimes.com, September 30, 2011, accessed May 24, 2012, http://www.nytimes.com/2011/10/01/opinion/you-love-your-iphone-literally.html.
55. Charles T. Blair-Broeker, Randal M. Ernst, and David G. Myers, *Thinking About Psychology: The Science of Mind and Behavior* (New York: Worth Publishers, 2003), p. 118.
56. Antonio Damasio, "What role do emotions play in consciousness?" youtube.com, November 10, 2010, accessed May 24, 2012, http://www.youtube.com/watch?v=Aw2yaozi0Gg.
57. Antonio Damasio, *Descartes' Error* (New York: Harper Perennial, 1995).

CHAPTER 4

1. David Baude, "Super Bowl 2011 Is Most Watched Program EVER," huffingtonpost.com, February 7, 2011, accessed May 24, 2012, http://www.huffingtonpost.com/2011/02/07/super-bowl-2011-ratings-s_n_819559.html.
2. Tim Nudd, "The 10 Best Commercials of 2011," adweek.com, November 28, 2011, accessed May 24, 2012, http://www.adweek.com/news/advertising-branding/10-best-commercials-2011-136663?page=10.
3. Sands Research, "VW Darth Vader Achieves Highest Score To Date On Sands Research Annual Super Bowl Ad Neuro Ranking," sandsresearch.com, February 16, 2011, accessed May 24, 2012, http://sandsresearch.com/PressRelease_SRI_SB2011.aspx.
4. Ibid.
5. Webinar hosted by Sean Scott (Ameritest) and Dr. Steven Sands (Sands Research), "Finding the Sweet Spot Between Neuroscience and Quantitative Research," attended on June 23, 2011.
6. Bob Garfield, "Ad Age Advertising Century: The Top 100 Campaigns," adage.com, March 29, 1999, accessed May 24, 2012, http://adage.com/century/campaigns.html.
7. Thomas Politzer, "Vision Is Our Dominant Sense," brainline.org, November 2008, accessed May 24, 2012, http://www.brainline.org/content/2008/11/vision-our-dominant-sense.html.
8. Nufflied Department of Clinical Neurosciences, "Vision Group Research," accessed May 23, 2012, http://www.fmrib.ox.ac.uk/vision/vision-group-research-2.
9. Jonah Lehrer, "How We Decide," scienceblogs.com, January 22, 2009, accessed May 27, 2012, http://scienceblogs.com/cortex/2009/01/22/how-we-decide/.
10. David Eagleman, *Incognito* (New York: Pantheon, 2011), p. 44.

11. Ibid., p. 48.

12. Ibid., p. 47.

13. John Medina, *Brain Rules: 12 Principles for Surviving and Thriving at Work, Home, and School* (Seattle: Pear Press, 2008).

14. Bernard J. Baars and Nicole M. Gage, *Cognition, Brain, and Consciousness: Introduction to Cognitive Neuroscience* (Waltham, MA: Academic Press, 2007), p. 173.

15. David J. Linden, *The Accidental Mind* (Cambridge: Harvard University Press, 2007), pp. 94-97.

16. Jonah Lehrer, *How We Decide* (New York: Houghton Mifflin, 2009).

17. *Advertising Age,* "Ad Age Advertising Century: Top 10 Icons," adage.com, March 29, 1999, accessed May 24, 2012, http://adage.com/century/ad_icons.html.

18. Russell Poldrack, "Multitasking: The Brain Seeks Novelty," huffingtonpost.com, October 28, 2009, accessed May 24, 2012, http://www.huffingtonpost.com/russell-poldrack/multitasking-the-brain-se_b_334674.html.

19. Wellcome Trust, "Neuroscientists Discover A Sense Of Adventure," sciencedaily.com, June 25, 2008, accessed May 24, 2012, http://www.sciencedaily.com/releases/2008/06/080625122945.htm.

20. University College London, "Novelty Aids Learning," sciencedaily.com, August 4, 2006, accessed May 24, 2012, http://www.sciencedaily.com/releases/2006/08/060804084518.htm.

21. Ibid.

22. Ibid.

23. Lehrer, *How We Decide,* p. 35.

24. Simon Small, "Who Is In Control of Your Brand?" simonsmall.com, August 12, 2010, accessed May 24, 2012, http://from.simontsmall.com/index.php/2010/08/12/old-spice-campaign-case-study/.

25. Jose Vega, M.D., Ph.D., "Thalamus," about.com, November 7, 2008, accessed May 24, 2012, http://stroke.about.com/od/glossary/g/Thalamus.htm.

26. Email from Brian Thomas, General Manager, Volkswagen, May 24, 2012, Herndon, Virginia.

27. Lehrer, *How We Decide,* pp. 36-39 and 54.

28. Volkswagen, "The Fun Theory Case Study," youtube.com, April 7, 2011, accessed May 24, 2012, http://www.youtube.com/watch?v=Ihai50diA7o.

29. Editor, "Have You Lost Your Mind? If Not, Would You Like To?," westranchbeacon.com, April 11, 2012, accessed May 24, 2012, http://westranchbeacon.com/2012/04/the-john-boston-report-have-you-lost-your-mind-if-not-would-you-like-to/.

30. Caryn Ganz, " Meet the Mystery Meat Dress: Lady Gaga Explains Rare VMAs Outfit," yahoo.com, September 12, 2010, accessed May 25, 2012, http://new.music.yahoo.com/blogs/stopthepresses/279379/meet-the-mystery-meat-dress-lady-gaga-explains-rare-vmas-outfit/.

31. Dorothy Pomerantz, "Lady Gaga Tops Celebrity 100 List," forbes.com, May 18, 2011, accessed May 25, 2012, http://www.forbes.com/2011/05/16/lady-gaga-tops-celebrity-100-11.html.

32. Daniel Pink, *Drive* (New York: Penguin, 2011), p. 106.

33. Terry O'Reilly, "The Age of Persuasion," cbc.ca, June 11, 2011, accessed May 25, 2012, http://www.cbc.ca/ageofpersuasion/episode/season-5/2011/06/11/season-five-terrys-book-club-1/.

34. Cici's Pizza, "Our Story," cicispizza.com, January 8, 2012, accessed May 25, 2012, http://www.cicispizza.com/about-us/our-story.

35. Webinar, Scott and Sands, "Finding the Sweet Spot Between Neuroscience and Quantitative Research."

CHAPTER 5

1. CNN Money, "Global 500 2008," cnn.com, accessed May 23, 2012, http://money.cnn.com/magazines/fortune/global500/2008/index.html.

2. Tom Murse, "When Did the Great Recession End?" about.com, October 24, 2010, accessed May 25, 2012, http://usgovinfo.about.com/od/moneymatters/a/When-Did-The-Great-Recession-End.htm.

3. Brian Ross and Joseph Rhee, "Big Three CEOs Flew Private Jets to Plead for Public Funds," abcnews.com, November 19, 2008, accessed May 25, 2012, http://abcnews.go.com/Blotter/WallStreet/story?id=6285739&page=1.

4. Jonathan Stein, "Throw the Bums Out (of Detroit)," motherjones.com, November 19, 2008, accessed May 25, 2012, http://motherjones.com/mojo/2008/11/throw-bums-out-detroit.

5. Brian Ross and Joseph Rhee, "Big Three CEOs Flew Private Jets to Plead for Public Funds," abcnews.com, November 19, 2008, accessed May 25, 2012, http://abcnews.go.com/Blotter/WallStreet/story?id=6285739&page=1.

6. Ali Frick, "Rep. Ackerman: Auto Execs' Private Jet Travel Like Guy At 'The Soup Kitchen In High Hat And Tuxedo,'" thinkprogress.com, November 19, 2008, accessed May 25, 2012, http://thinkprogress.org/politics/2008/11/19/32576/big3-private-jets/.

7. Brian Ross and Joseph Rhee, "Big Three CEOs Flew Private Jets to Plead for Public Funds," abcnews.com, November 19, 2008, accessed May 25, 2012, http://abcnews.go.com/Blotter/WallStreet/story?id=6285739&page=1.

8. Frick, "Rep. Ackerman: Auto Execs' Private Jet Travel Like Guy At 'The Soup Kitchen In High Hat And Tuxedo.'"

9. Mark D. White, "Jerry Evensky on Adam Smith, trust, and the Great Recession," economicsandethics.org, June 1, 2011, accessed May 25, 2012, http://www.economicsandethics.org/2011/06/jerry-evensky-on-adam-smith-trust-and-the-great-recession.html.

10. Stephen Covey, *The 7 Habits of Highly Effective People* (New York: Free Press, 1990), p. 273.

11. Seth Feigerman, "Why You Shouldn't Shop While Relaxed," mainstreet.com, August 26, 2011, accessed May 25, 2012, http://www.mainstreet.com/article/smart-spending/why-you-shouldn-t-shop-while-relaxed.

12. Roger Dolley, "The Relaxation Effect," neurosciencemarketing.com, August 8, 2011, http://www.neurosciencemarketing.com/blog/articles/whats-better-than-an-excited-customer.htm.

13. Advertising Research Foundation, "Reinvention: Chapter 1," amazonaws.com, accessed May 25, 2012, http://thearf-org-aux-assets.s3.amazonaws.com/ogilvy/cs2010/General%20Motors_CaseStudy.pdf.

14. Richard Dawkins, "Why the Universe Seems So Strange," TEDGlobal 2005, June 2005, accessed May 25, 2012, http://www.ted.com/talks/lang/eng/richard_dawkins_on_our_queer_universe.html.

15. Robert Wright, *The Moral Animal* (New York: Vintage Books, 1995), p. 278.

16. Ibid., p. 208.

17. Rob Fuggetta, "Customer Trust in the Social Media Age," TedxConstitutionDrive, Menlo Park, CA, December 22, 2010_, May 25, 2012, http://www.youtube.com/watch?v=5VuwMRMv-uc.

18. Ibid.

19. Tori DeAngelis, "The Two Faces of Oxytocin," apa.com, February 2008, accessed May 25, 2012, http://www.apa.org/monitor/feb08/oxytocin.aspx.

20. Reuters, "Breast-feeding triggers pulses of feel-good hormone," reuters.com, July 17, 2008, accessed May 25, 2012, http://www.reuters.com/article/idUSN1746293720080718.

21. Adam Penenberg, "Social Networking Affects Brains Like Falling in Love," fastcompany.com, July 1, 2010, accessed May 25, 2012, http://www.fastcompany.com/magazine/147/doctor-love.html.

22. Leda Cosmides and John Tooby, "Stone Age Minds," youtube.com, August 5, 2010, accessed May 25, 2012, http://www.youtube.com/watch?v=nNW_B8EwgH4.

23. Ibid.

24. Penenberg, "Social Networking Affects Brains Like Falling in Love."

25. Associated Press, "Scientists study 'Trust in a Bottle,'" msnbc.com, June 1, 2005, accessed May 25, 2012, http://www.msnbc.msn.com/id/8059069/ns/health-mental _health.

26. Louann Brizendine, *Female Brain* (New York: Three Rivers Press, 2007), p. 94.

27. Joanne Oatts, "Hormone Increases Advertising Influence," marketingweek.com, November 15, 2010, accessed May 25, 2012, http://www.marketingweek.co.uk /disciplines/advertising/hormone-increases-advertising-influence/3020523.article.

28. Leah Zerbe, "Boost Your Love Hormone Levels . . . Naturally," rodale.com, accessed May 23, 2012, accessed May 25, 2012, http://www.rodale.com/oxytocin.

29. Paul Zak, "Trust, Morality—and Oxytocin," filmed July 2011, TEDGlobal 2011, Edinburgh, Scotland.

30. David Macaray, "The Secret of Southwest Airlines," counterpunch.com, April 1, 2010, accessed May 25, 2012, http://www.counterpunch.org/2010/04/01/the -secret-of-southwest-airlines/.

31. *The Economist,* "Smiles and free peanuts," economist.com, June 2, 2011, accessed May 25, 2012, http://www.economist.com/node/18774997.

32. Macaray, "The Secret of Southwest Airlines."

33. Gary Kelly, "Let the Summer Travel Season Begin," southwest.com, May 2012, accessed May 25, 2012, http://www.southwest.com/assets/pdfs/about-southwest/garys -greeting.pdf.

34. Focus Editors, "Top 10 Big Brother Companies: Ranking the Worst Consumer Privacy Infringers," accessed May 23, 2012, http://www.focus.com/fyi/top-10-big -brother-companies-privacy-infringement/.

35. Dave Rosenberg, "Study: Amazon.com is Most Trusted Brand in U.S.," cnet.com, February 22, 2010, accessed May 23, 2012, http://news.cnet.com/8301-13846_3 -10457727-62.html.

36. Andrea James, "Amazon's Jeff Bezos on Kindle, Advertising, and Being Green," seattlepi.com, May 28, 2009, accessed May 23, 2012, http://blog.seattlepi.com /amazon/2009/05/28/amazons-jeff-bezos-on-kindle-advertising-and-being-green/.

37. Chris Anderson, "The Zen of Jeff Bezos," wired.com, January 2005, accessed May 23, 2012, http://www.wired.com/wired/archive/13.01/bezos.html.

38. John G. Kappas, Ph.D., Founder, Hypnosis Motivation Institute, a non-profit nationally accredited college and clinic of hypnotherapy, Tarzana, California.

39. Margalit Fox, "Robert Zajonc, Who Looked at Mind's Ties to Actions, Is Dead at 85," December 6, 2008, accessed May 25, 2012, http://www.nytimes.com/2008/12/07 /education/07zajonc.html?_r=1&pagewanted=print.

40. Shankar Vendantam, *Hidden Brain* (New York: Spiegel & Grau, 2010), p. 28.

41. Noah J. Goldstein, Steve J. Martin and Robert B. Cialdini, *Yes!* (New York: Free Press, 2008), pp. 114-115.

42. Miguel Brendl, "Name-letter Branding," Kellogg.northwestern.edu, November 2009, http://insight.kellogg.northwestern.edu/index.php/Kellogg/article/name-letter _branding.

43. David Brooks, *The Social Animal* (New York: Random House, 2011), p. 208.

44. Goleman, *Social Intelligence,* pp. 70-71.

45. Brooks, *The Social Animal,* p. xv.

46. Ken Schuman, "Michaelangelo's Hidden Message," michaelangelomethos.com, accessed May 23, 2012, http://michelangelomethod.com/articles/michelangelo_hidden _message.html.

47. Ibid.

48. Oliver Chiang, "Call of Duty: Black Ops Claims 'Biggest Entertainment Launch in History,'" forbes.com, November 11, 2010, accessed July 8, 2012, http:// www.forbes.com/sites/oliverchiang/2010/11/11/call-of-duty-black-ops-claims -biggest-entertainment-launch-in-history/

49. Best Media Info Bureau–Delhi, "Nike launches 'Find your greatness' campaign," bestmediainfo.com, July 30, 2012, accessed August 1, 2012, http://www.best mediainfo.com/2012/07/nike-launches-find-your-greatness-campaign/. Mallory Russell, "Nike Ambushes Adidas on World Stage . . . Again," AdAgeDIGITAL, July

31, 2012, accessed August 18, 2012, http://adage.com/article/the-viral-video-chart
/nike-ambushes-adidas-world-stage/236400/.

50. Goleman, *Social Intelligence,* pp. 357-358.

51. Marketing Vox, "Grand EFFIE Goes to Dove's 'Real Beauty,'" marketingvox
.com, June 8, 2006, accessed May 25, 2012, http://www.marketingvox.com/grand
_effie_goes_to_doves_real_beauty-021934/.

52. Tom Layfield, "The Top 10 Best Social Media Marketing Campaigns of All Time,"
acquisitionengine.com, accessed May 23, 2012, http://www.acquisitionengine.com
/top-10-best-social-media-marketing-campaigns-all-time/.

53. Adam Bryan, "The Media Business: Advertising—Addenda; Awards Presented At 2
Ceremonies," nytimes.com, March 17, 1993, accessed May 25, 2012, http://www
.nytimes.com/1993/03/17/business/the-media-business-advertising-addenda-awards
-presented-at-2-ceremonies.html.

54. Dan Vergano, "Mind Meld: Brain cells synchronize during good conversations,"
usatoday.com, July 27, 2010, accessed May 25, 2012, http://content.usatoday
.com/communities/sciencefair/post/2010/07/mind-meld-neurons-conversation
-brain/1.

55. John Whitfield, "Copycat Waitresses Get Bigger Tips," bioedonline.org, July 4,
2003, accessed May 25, 2012, www.bioedonline.org/news/news.cfm?art=401.

56. Rick B. van Baaren, "The Parrot Effect," Cornell Hospitality Quarterly, February
2005, accessed May 25, 2012, http://cqx.sagepub.com/content/46/1/79.abstract.

57. Jesse Stanchak, "What Does the Decline of Peer Trust Mean for Social Marketing?" smartblogs.com, February 8, 2010, accessed May 25, 2012, http://smart
blogs.com/socialmedia/2010/02/08/what-does-the-decline-of-peer-trust-mean-for
-social-marketing/.

58. Michael Bush, "In Age of Friending, Consumers Trust Their Friends Less," adage.
com, February 8, 2010, accessed May 25, 2012, http://adage.com/article/news/
social-media-consumers-trust-friends/141972/.

59. Greg Ferenstein, "The Science of Building Trust with Social Media," mashable
.com, February 24, 2010, accessed May 25, 2012, http://mashable.com/2010/02/24
/social-media-trust/.

60. Pete Cashmore, "Southwest Tweets, Blogs Apology to Kevin Smith," mashable
.com, February 14, 2010, accessed May 25, 2012, http://mashable.com/2010/02/14
/southwest-kevin-smith/.

61. Ferenstein, "The Science of Building Trust with Social Media."

62. Hara Estroff Marano, "The Benefits of Laughter," psychologytoday.com, April 29,
2003, accessed May 25, 2012, http://www.psychologytoday.com/articles/200304
/the-benefits-laughter.

63. James Gorman, "Scientists Hint at Why Laughter Feels So Good," nytimes.com,
September 13, 2011, accessed May 25, 2012, http://www.nytimes.com/2011/09/14
/science/14laughter.html.

64. Cindy Solliday-McRoy, "Laughter Is the Best Emotional Medicine," livestrong.
com, April 26, 2011, accessed May 25, 2012, http://www.livestrong.com/article
/12141-laughter-best-emotional-medicine/.

65. Molly Edmonds, "Is Laughter Contagious?" tlc.com, accessed May 23, 2012,
http://health.howstuffworks.com/mental-health/human-nature/happiness/laughter
-contagious.htm.

66. Mike Sacks, "Canned Laughter: Ben Glenn II, Television Historian," theparis
review.org, July 20, 2010, accessed May 25, 2012, http://www.theparisreview.org
/blog/2010/07/20/canned-laughter-ben-glenn-ii-television-historian/.

67. Russell I. Haley and Allan L. Baldinger, "ARF Copy Validity Project," *Journal of
Advertising Research,* November 2006, accessed May 25, 2012, pp. 114-135, http://
www.aeforum.org/aeforum.nsf/b6f532dc08e2a32e80256c5100355eab/39d4869ae
7d09e92802567f600405431/$FILE/acut0066.pdf.

68. Alexander Gelfand, "Long-Promised, Voice Commands Are Finally Going Mainstream," wired.com, June 4, 2008, accessed May 25, 2012, http://www.wired.com
/software/coolapps/news/2008/06/speech_tech.

69. Anne Aula, Rehan Khan, and Zhiwei Guan, "Frowns, Sighs, and Advanced Queries—How Does Search Behavior Change as Search Becomes More Difficult," google research.com, September 17, 2010, accessed May 25, 2012, googleresearch.blog spot.com/2010/09/frowns-sighs-and-advanced-queries-how.html.

70. Alix Spigel, "When the 'trust hormone' is out of balance," npr.org, July 17, 2010, accessed May 25, 2012, http://www.npr.org/templates/story/story.php?storyId=1261 41922.

71. Roger Dolley, "The Relaxation Effect," neurosciencemarketing.com, August 8, 2011, accessed May 25, 2012, http://www.neurosciencemarketing.com/blog/articles /whats-better-than-an-excited-customer.htm.

72. Editor, "Increase Sales with Color, Sound, Taste, Smell and Touch," marketingprofs .com, March 8, 2001, accessed May 25, 2012, http://www.marketingprofs.com/web news/2/news3-8-01.asp.

73. Ibid.

74. Hugh Mackay, "Life's an adventure, or is it?," theage.com.au, December 4, 2004, accessed May 25, 2012, http://www.theage.com.au/news/Hugh-Mackay/Lifes-an -adventure-or-is-it/2004/12/03/1101923331151.html.

CHAPTER 6

1. Tessa Fisher, "Shirley Polykoff," Jewish Women's Archive, accessed May 23, 2012, http://jwa.org/encyclopedia/article/polykoff-shirley.

2. Robert McG. Thomas, Jr., "Ad Writer Whose Query Colored a Nation," nytimes .com, June 08, 1998, accessed May 23, 2012, http://www.nytimes.com/1998/06/08 /nyregion/shirley-polykoff-90-ad-writer-whose-query-colored-a-nation.html.

3. Center for Applied Research, "Mini-case study. Nike's 'Just Do It' Advertising Campaign," cfar.com, accessed May 23, 2012, http://www.cfar.com/Documents/nike cmp.pdf.

4. Brent Hunsberger, "Nike's 'Just Do It' Slogan Celebrates 20 Years: The Iconic Saying, Now 20, Is Featured in the Company's Olympics Campaign," oregonlive.com, July 18, 2008, accessed May 25, 2012, http://www.oregonlive.com/business/oregonian /index.ssf?/base/business/1216353305226620.xml&coll=7.

5. Eleftheria Parpis, "On the Spot: Dan Wieden," adweek.com, May 22, 2009, accessed May 25, 2012, http://www.adweek.com/news/advertising-branding/spot-dan -wieden-101196.

6. Brent Hunsberger, "Nike Celebrates 'Just Do It' 20th Anniversary with New Ads," oregonlive.com, July 17, 2008, accessed May 25, 2012, http://blog.oregonlive.com /playbooksandprofits/2008/07/nike_celebrates_just_do_it_20t.html.

7. Ibid.

8. Quotation Vault, "Sigmund Freud," quotationvault.com, accessed May 23, 2012, http://www.quotationvault.com/author/Sigmund_Freud.

9. Douglas Van Praet interview with Paul Zak, Professor of Economics and Department Chair at Claremont Graduate University, January 4, 2011, Claremont, California.

10. Jim Afremow, PhD., LPC, "Trust the Talent," psychologytoday.com, September 3, 2011, accessed May 25, 2012, http://www.psychologytoday.com/blog/trust -the-talent/201109/visualize-actualize.

11. F. Lebon, C. Collet, and A. Guillot, "Benefits of Motor Imagery Training on Muscle Strength," *Journal of Strength and Conditioning Research*, June 2010, pp. 1680-87.

12. Marketing Campaign Case Studies, "Silhouette Campaign," marketing-case-studies .blogspot.com, February 28, 2008, accessed May 25, 2012, http://marketing-case -studies.blogspot.com/2008/02/silhouette-campaign.html.

13. Deutsch Inc., "Beliefs," deutschinc.com, accessed May 23, 2012, accessed May 25, 2012, http://www.deutschinc.com/#!/about/beliefs.

14. Noah Joseph. "Toronto Porsche Dealer Redefines Direct Marketing," Carbuzz.com, July 31, 2012, accessed August 1, 2012, http://www.carbuzz.com/news/2012/7/31 /Toronto-Porsche-Dealer-Redefines-Direct-Marketing-7710046/.

15. Mark Turner, "The Way We Imagine," *In Imaginative Minds,* edited by Ilona Roth (London: Oxford University Press & The British Academy, 2007), pp. 213–236.

16. Mark Turner, "Blending & Conceptual Integration," markturner.com, accessed May 23, 2012, http://markturner.org/blending.html.

17. Steven Pressfield, *The War of Art* (New York: Rugged Land, 2002).

18. Jonah Lehrer, "Harold and the Purple Crayon," The Frontal Cortex, August 17, 2009, accessed May 25, 2012, http://scienceblogs.com/cortex/2009/08/17/childhood-rituals/.

19. David Brooks, *The Social Animal* (New York: Random House, 2011), p. 350.

20. David Jary and Julia Jary, *Collins Dictionary of Sociology* (New York: Harper-Collins, 1995), p. 93.

21. Wikipedia, "The Sims," wikipedia.com, accessed May 23, 2012, http://en.wikipedia.org/wiki/The_Sims.

22. James Brightman, "The Sims 3 Is Best-Selling PC Game Worldwide in 2009," industry gamers.com, January 22, 2010, accessed May 25, 2012, http://www.industrygamers.com/news/the-sims-3-is-best-selling-pc-game-worldwide-in-2009/.

23. Charles Howe, "Fantasy Football: Is It Ruining the NFL?" bleacherreport.com, August 30, 2010, accessed May 25, 2012, http://bleacherreport.com/articles/446740-fantasy-football-is-it-ruining-the-nfl.

24. Daniel H. Pink, *A Whole New Mind* (New York: Riverhead Books, 2005), p. 101.

25. Scott West and Mitch Anthony, *Storyselling for Financial Advisors* (Chicago: Dearborn Financial Publishing, Inc., 2000), p. 181.

26. Figures according to Steve Neder, Volkswagen, "Agency Sales and Business Review 2011 Presentation," Jan 23, 2012 Herndon, Virginia.

27. Volkswagen, "Volkswagen Selected as Clio Awards 2012 Global Advertiser of the Year," May 4, 2012, accessed May 25, 2012, http://media.vw.com/press release/1053/1/volkswagen-selected-clio-awards-2012-global-advertiser-year.

28. Carl Jung, *Man and his Symbols* (New York: Dell, 1968), p. 41.

29. Human Origins Initiative of the Smithsonian Institution's National Museum of Natural History, "Language and Symbols," humanorigins.si.edu, accessed May 23, 2012, http://humanorigins.si.edu/human-characteristics/language.

30. Alex Riley and Adam Boome, "Superbrands' Success Fuelled By Sex, Religion And Gossip," bbc.co.uk, May 16, 2011, accessed May 25, 2012, http://www.bbc.co.uk/news/business-13416598.

31. Martin Lindstorm, *Buyology* (New York: Crown Business, 2008), p. 124.

32. Lauriane Zonco, "On the Cutting Edge," swissstyle.com, accessed May 23, 2012, http://www.swissstyle.com/victorinox-cutting-edge.

33. Alexandra Kalinina, Anne Schär, Dijana Ukic, Victorinox Intercultural Stakeholder Management Groupwork, imu.unibe.ch, accessed May 23, 2012, http://www.marketing.imu.unibe.ch/download/lehre/intstake/10_Victorinox.pdf.

34. V. S. Ramachandran, "V. S. Ramachandran On Your Mind," TED Talks 2007, March 2007, accessed May 27, 2012, http://www.ted.com/talks/vilayanur_ramach andran_on_your_mind.html.

CHAPTER 7

1. Donald T. Phillips, *Run to Win* (New York: St. Martin's Griffin, 2002).

2. Family of Vince Lombardi, "Famous Quotes by Vince Lombardi," vincelombardi.com, accessed May 23, 2012, http://www.vincelombardi.com/about.html.

3. Nadia Gilani, "Christianity Is Still the Largest Religion in the World but Followers Have Moved Away from Europe," dailymail.co.uk, December 22, 2011, accessed May 25, 2012, http://www.dailymail.co.uk/news/article-2077272/Christianity-largest-religion-world-despite-shift-away-Europe.html.

4. George Weigel, "World Religions by the Numbers," catholiceducation.org, accessed May 23, 2012, http://www.catholiceducation.org/articles/facts/fm0010.html.

5. Ralph Waldo, "Is the Catholic Church the Richest Organization in the World?" dailypaul.com, September 16, 2009, accessed May 25, 2012, http://www.dailypaul.com/107294/is-the-catholic-church-the-richest-organization-in-the-world.

6. Steven Pinker, "The Evolutionary Psychology of Religion," harvard.edu, October 29, 2004, accessed May 25, 2012, http://pinker.wjh.harvard.edu/articles/media/2004_10_29_religion.htm.

7. Fiona Macrae, "Brains 'Are Hardwired to Believe in God and Imaginary Friends,'" dailymail.com, February 5, 2009, accessed May 25, 2012, http://www.dailymail.co.uk/sciencetech/article-1136482/Brains-hardwired-believe-God-imaginary-friends.html.

8. A. Chris Gajilan, "Are Humans Hard-Wired for Faith?" cnn.com, April 4, 2007, accessed May 25, 2012, http://articles.cnn.com/2007-04-04/health/neurotheology_1_scans-frontal-lobe-sensory-information?_s=PM:HEALTH.

9. Sharon Begley, "(Un)wired for God," newsweek.com, August 12, 2009, accessed May 25, 2012, http://www.thedailybeast.com/newsweek/2009/08/12/un-wired-for-god.html.

10. Macrae, "Brains 'Are Hardwired To Believe in God and Imaginary Friends.'"

11. National Conference of Catholic Bishops, "Canon 284—Clerical Dress," usccb.com, accessed May 23, 2012, http://www.usccb.org/beliefs-and-teachings/what-we-believe/canon-law/complementary-norms/canon-284-clerical-dress.cfm.

12. Derrick Daye, "Great Moments in Branding: Roy Disney's Speech," brandingstrategyinsider.com, January 30, 2008, accessed May 25, 2012, http://www.brandingstrategyinsider.com/2008/01/great-moments-3.html.

13. "Costco's Secrets Revealed," ABC News, March 29, 2010, accessed May 25, 2012, http://abcnews.go.com/GMA/YourMoney/video/costcos-success-secrets-revealed-10228994.

14. Antonio Damasio, "How Our Brains Feel Emotion," bigthink.com, October 19, 2010, accessed May 25, 2012, http://bigthink.com/ideas/23022.

15. Ron Shachar, Tulin Erdem, Keisha M. Cutright, Gavan J. Fitzsimons, "Brands: The Opiate of the Nonreligious Masses?," *Marketing Science,* September 24, 2010, pp. 1–19.

16. Damasio, "How Our Brains Feel Emotion."

17. Lauriane Zonco, "On the Cutting Edge," swissstyle.com, accessed May 23, 2012, http://www.swissstyle.com/victorinox-cutting-edge.

18. Roger Dooley, "Connect Emotionally to Boost Sales," neurosciencemarketing.com, September 1, 2011, May 25, 2012, http://www.neurosciencemarketing.com/blog/articles/connect-emotionally.htm.

19. Terry Galanoy, "Don't Inhale that New Car Smell," cnn.com, July 31, 2008, accessed May 25, 2012, http://edition.cnn.com/2008/LIVING/wayoflife/07/31/aa.new.car.smell/.

20. George Carlin, "You Are All Diseased," HBO, New York, February 6, 1999.

21. Peter De Vries, *The Mackerel Plaza* (New York: Oxford University Press, 1958).

22. Macrae, "Brains 'Are Hardwired To Believe In God And Imaginary Friends.'"

23. Douglas Van Praet interview with Robert Kurzban, Associate Professor of Psychology at University of Pennsylvania, January 19, 2011, at Chapman University, Orange California.

24. "Scientists Prove Einstein's Theory of Relativity Wrong?," *IBN Live,* November 20, 2011, http://ibnlive.in.com/videos/204110/scientists-prove-einsteins-theory-of-relativity-wrong.html.

25. Walter Isaacson, *Steve Jobs* (New York: Simon & Schuster, 2011), pp. 117-119[0].

26. Daniel Pink, *Drive,* p. 137.

27. Robert Dilts, "Neurological Levels," integratedsociopsychology.net, accessed May 23, 2012, http://www.integratedsociopsychology.net/neurological_levels.html.

28. Irfan Iftekhar, "Best Advertising Slogans," newzglobe.com, October 20, 2011, accessed May 25, 2012, http://www.newzglobe.com/article/20111020/best-advertising-slogans.

29. Ibid.

30. Think Exist, "Albert Einstein," thinkexist.com, accessed May 25, 2012, http://thinkexist.com/quotation/no_problem_can_be_solved_from_the_same_level_of/222376.html.

31. Dilts, "Neurological Levels."
32. Figures according to Steve Neder, Volkswagen, "Agency Sales and Business Review 2011 Presentation," Jan 23, 2012, Herndon, Virginia.
33. Avi Dan, "VW's CMO Mahoney on Becoming America's Fastest Growing Car Company," forbes.com, April 4, 2012, accessed May 25, 2012, http://www.forbes.com/sites/avidan/2012/04/04/vw-cmo-tim-mahoney-on-how-it-became-americas-fastest-growing-car-company/.
34. Steve Jobs, Commencement address at Stanford University, June 12, 2005.
35. Jeff Brown and Mark Fenske, *The Winner's Brain* (Cambridge: De Capo Press, 2010).
36. Roger Dooley, "Smiles Really DO Boost Sales," neurosciencemarketing.com, October 26, 2007, accessed May 25, 2012, http://www.neurosciencemarketing.com/blog/articles/smiles-boost-sales.htm.

CHAPTER 8

1. Antonio Damasio, *The Feeling of What Happens* (New York: Mariner Books, 2000), p. 40.
2. Jonah Lehrer, "The New State of Mind," *Seed Magazine,* Aug. 8, 2008, accessed May 25, 2012, http://seedmagazine.com/content/article/a_new_state_of_mind/.
3. Ibid.
4. Antonio Damasio, *Descartes' Error* (New York: G.P. Putnam's Sons, 1994), pp. 34-51.
5. Robin Hanson, "Bias and Power," overcomingbias.com, March 7, 2008, accessed May 25, 2012, http://www.overcomingbias.com/tag/standard-biases/page/6.
6. Bhavna Mistry, "Case Study: Andrex Says Thank You," brandrepublic.com, October 1, 2003, accessed May 25, 2012, http://www.brandrepublic.com/news/191551/.
7. Gerry Everding, "Brain Region Learns To Anticipate Risk, Provides Early Warnings, Suggests New Study In *Science,*" wustl.com, March 2, 2005, accessed May 25, 2012, http://news.wustl.edu/news/Pages/4804.aspx.
8. Daniel Goleman, "The Power of Mindsight," *Greater Good,* March 3, 2008, accessed May 25, 2012, http://greatergood.berkeley.edu/article/item/the_power_of_mindsight.
9. Burt Helm, "Which Ads Don't Get Skipped?," businessweek.com, September 3, 2007, accessed May 25, 2012, http://www.businessweek.com/magazine/content/07_36/b4048026.htm.
10. John Seabrook, "How To Make It: James Dyson Built A Better Vacuum. Can He Pull Off A Second Industrial Revolution?" *New Yorker,* September 20, 2010, accessed May 25, 2012, http://www.newyorker.com/reporting/2010/09/20/100920fa_fact_seabrook#ixzz1vZH6DteI
11. Julia Finch, "Dyson's Profits Rise To £190m," guardian.co.uk, May 26, 2010, accessed May 25, 2012, http://www.guardian.co.uk/business/2010/may/26/dyson-profits-rise.
12. Ibid.
13. Daniel Kahneman, *Thinking, Fast and Slow* (New York: Farrar, Straus and Giroux, 2011), p. 81.
14. Robert Krulwich and Jad Abumrad, "Why Is it So Hard to Do the Right Thing?" npr.org, January 26, 2010, accessed May 25, 2012, http://www.npr.org/templates/story/story.php?storyId=122781981.
15. Kahneman, *Thinking, Fast and Slow,* p. 87.
16. Editor, "5126 Failures—The Dyson Brand Story," brandstory.typedpad.com, April 18, 2007, http://brandstory.typepad.com/writer/innovation/.
17. Kahneman, *Thinking, Fast and Slow,* p. 284.
18. Ibid., pp. 61-68.
19. Jonah Lehrer, "Why Are Easy Decisions So Hard?" wired.com, March 2, 2011, accessed May 25, 2012, http://www.wired.com/wiredscience/2011/03/why-are-easy-decisions-so-hard/.

20. Media Awareness Network, "Advertising: It's Everywhere," media-awareness.ca, accessed May 25, 2012, http://www.media-awareness.ca/english/parents/marketing/advertising_everywhere.cfm.

21. Christopher Caldwell, "Select All: Can You Have Too Many Choices?" *New Yorker,* March 1, 2004, accessed May 25, 2012, http://www.newyorker.com/archive/2004/03/01/040301crbo_books#ixzz1vZIijS6h.

22. Cara Feinberg, "The Mindfulness Chronicles," harvardmagazine.com, September-October 2010, accessed May 25, 2012, http://harvardmagazine.com/2010/09/the-mindfulness-chronicles?page=all.

23. Associated Press, "Microsoft Funded 'Grass Roots' Campaign," usatoday.com, August 23, 2001, accessed May 25, 2012, http://www.usatoday.com/tech/news/2001-08-23-microsoft-letters.htm.

24. Prakash Ranjan, "Honda Product Manager Gets Caught Astroturfing," e-marketing stories.com, December 27, 2010, accessed May 25, 2012, http://e-marketingstories.com/2010/12/27/honda-product-manager-gets-caught-astroturfing/.

25. Kashmir Hill. "Chick-fil-A Has Completely Lost Control of Its Facebook Page," Forbes.com, July 25, 2012, accessed August 1, 2012, http://www.forbes.com/sites/kashmirhill/2012/07/25/chick-fil-a-has-completely-lost-control-of-its-facebook-page/

CHAPTER 9

1. Michael Marriott, "The Short Life of a Rap Star, Shadowed by Many Troubles," nytimes.com, March 17, 1997, accessed May 25, 2012, http://www.nytimes.com/1997/03/17/nyregion/the-short-life-of-a-rap-star-shadowed-by-many-troubles.html.

2. Marc Spiegler, "Marketing Street Culture Bringing Hip-Hop Style to the Mainstream," businessresearchsources.com, accessed May 23, 2012, http://www.businessresearchsources.com/business-school/American-Demographics_234/.

3. "Tommy Hilfiger," *Minneapolis Star Tribune,* June 22, 1996, accessed May 25, 2012, http://www.answers.com/topic/tommy-hilfiger#ixzz1m70tXdLW.

4. Editor, "Tommy Hilfiger Corporation," accessed May 23, 2012, http://www.fundinguniverse.com/company-histories/Tommy-Hilfiger-Corporation-Company-History.html.

5. Editor, "History and Background of Tommy Hilfiger," fragrancex.com, accessed May 25, 2012, http://www.fragrancex.com/products/_bid_Tommy—Hilfiger-am-cid_perfume-am-lid_T__brand_history.html.

6. IBS Center for Management Research, "Tommy Hilfiger—The Struggles of an American Fashion Icon," icmrindia.org, accessed May 23, 2012, http://www.icmrindia.org/casestudies/catalogue/Marketing/Tommy%20Hilfiger-Marketing.htm.

7. Editor, "Tommy Hilfiger," answers.com, accessed May 23, 2012, http://www.answers.com/topic/tommy-hilfiger.

8. Erin Barrett and Jack Mingo, ed., *W.C. Privy's Original Bathroom Companion* (New York: St. Martin's Press, 2003), pp. 407–410.

9. Mary Morgan, "A History in Marketing of Marlboro Brand Cigarettes," yahoo.com, February 19, 2007, accessed May 25, 2012, http://voices.yahoo.com/a-history-marketing-marlboro-brand-cigarettes-204451.html?cat=9.

10. Kathleen Schalch, "Present at the Creation: The Marlboro Man," NPR, October 21, 2002.

11. Stacy Flaherty and Mimi Minnick, "Marlboro Oral History And Documentation Project, Ca. 1926-1986," November 2000, accessed May 25, 2012, http://americanhistory.si.edu/archives/d7198.htm.

12. Jessica Jaffe, "The Imagery, Fantasy, and Symbolism of the Marlboro Man," rochester.edu, accessed May 23, 2012, http://www.rochester.edu/College/ANT/faculty/foster/ANT226/Spring01/papers/jaffe_imagery.html.

13. *Advertising Age,* "The Marlboro Man," adage.com, March 29, 1999, accessed May 25, 2012, http://adage.com/century/icon01.html.

14. Kenneth Roman, *The Kings of Madison Avenue* (New York: Palgrave Macmillan, 2009).

15. *Advertising Age,* "The Marlboro Man."

16. Philip Morris USA, "Market Information," philipmorrisusa.com, accessed May 23, 2012, http://www.philipmorrisusa.com/en/cms/Company/Market_Information /default.aspx.

17. Geoffrey Miller, *Spent* (New York: Viking Adult, 2009).

18. Ibid.

19. Ibid.

20. David Linden, *The Accidental Mind* (Cambridge: Belknap Press, 2007), p. 24.

21. Daniel Kahneman, *Thinking, Fast and Slow* (New York: Farrar, Straus and Giroux, 2011), p. 52.

22. David Kiley, "Can You Name That Slogan?" October 14, 2004, accessed May 25, 2012, http://www.businessweek.com/bwdaily/dnflash/oct2004/nf20041014_4965 _db035.htm.

23. Barrett and Mingo, ed., *W.C. Privy's Original Bathroom Companion,* pp. 407-410.

24. Kahneman, *Thinking, Fast and Slow.*

25. Russell A. Dewey, Ph.D., "Priming," intropsych.com, accessed May 23, 2012, http:// www.intropsych.com/ch06_memory/priming.html.

26. L. L. Jacoby, "Perceptual Enhancement: Persistent Effects of an Experience," *Journal of Experimental Psychology: Learning, Memory, and Cognition* 9 (1), 1983, pp. 21-38.

27. University of Chicago Press Journals, "I Like It, But I Don't Know Why: How Does Conditioning Affect Consumer Choice?" *ScienceDaily,* May 18, 2010.

28. Roger Dooley, *Brainfluence* (Hoboken, N.J.: John Wiley & Sons, Inc., 2012), p. 59.

29. Timothy D. Wilson, *Strangers to Ourselves* (Cambridge: Belknap Press, 2002), p. 185.

30. Ibid., p. 187.

31. Stuart Whitewell, "Ingredient branding case study: Intel," intanglebusiness.com, July 11, 2005, accessed May 25, 2012, http://www.intangiblebusiness.com/Brand -Services/Marketing-services/News/Ingredient-branding-case-study-Intel~466.html.

32. Dr. Damon Walia, Ashank Dayal Mathur, Abhinaw Shrivastava and Evenpreet Singh, "Inside Intel Inside," scribd.com, accessed May 23, 2012, http://www.scribd .com/doc/38851337/Inside-Intel-Inside.

33. Intel, "Intel Inside Program," intel.com, accessed May 23, 2012, http://www.intel .com/pressroom/intel_inside.htm.

34. Ibid.

35. Charles R. Harness, "The Other White Meat," naldc.com, accessed May 23, 2012, http://naldc.nal.usda.gov/download/IND89023175/PDF.

36. Tom Dougherty, "Pork: It's No Longer the Other White Meat. Sadly," stealing share.com, March 8, 2011, accessed May 25, 2012, http://www.stealingshare.com /blog/?p=2271.

37. "The Other White Meat Brand," porkbeinspired.com, accessed May 24, 2012, http://www.porkbeinspired.com/towm_promo_heritage_page.aspx.

38. A. K. Pradeep, *The Buying Brain* (Hoboken, NJ: Wiley, 2010).

39. Tom Dougherty, "How to Avoid Being the Shack," stealingshare.com, accessed May 24, 2012, http://www.stealingshare.com/pages/How%20to%20Avoid%20 Being%20The%20Shack.htm.

40. Jim Edwards, "Pizza Hut Plan to Change Name to 'The Hut' Meets With Ridi- cule," cbsnews.com, June 20, 2009, accessed May 25, 2012, http://www.cbsnews .com/8301-505123_162-42741949/pizza-hut-plan-to-change-name-to-the-hut -meets-with-ridicule/.

41. Elizabeth A. Smith, Ph.D. and Ruth E. Malone, Ph.D., "Altria Means Tobacco: Philip Morris's Identity Crisis," April 2003, accessed May 25, 2012, http://www .ncbi.nlm.nih.gov/pmc/articles/PMC1447789/.

42. NBA, "Michael Jordan," nba.com, accessed May 23, 2012, http://www.nba.com /history/players/jordan_bio.html.

43. Editor, "The Media Business; Pepsi Drops Michael Jackson," nytimes.com, November 15, 1993, accessed May 25, 2012, http://www.nytimes.com/1993/11/15/business/the-media-business-pepsi-drops-michael-jackson.html.

CHAPTER 10

1. Francis Glebas, *Directing the Story* (Waltham, MA: Focal Press, 2008), p. 123.
2. Timothy D. Wilson, *Strangers to Ourselves* (Cambridge: Belknap Press, 2002), p. 212[0].
3. Maureen Morrison, "Starbucks Forges 'Moments Of Connection' By Offering Experience," adage.com, November 7, 2011, accessed May 25, 2012, http://adage.com/Article/Special-Report-Marketer-Alist/Marketer-A-List-Starbucks/230837/.
4. Al Ries, "Have We Killed Brand Advertising?," adage.com, June 2, 2011, accessed May 24, 2012, http://adage.com/Article/Al-Ries/Viewpoint-Killed-Brand-Advertising/227893/.
5. Howard Shultz, "Looking Forward to Starbucks Next Chapter," Starbucks.com, January 5, 2011, accessed May 24, 2012, http://www.starbucks.com/Blog/Looking-Forward-To-Starbucks-Next-Chapter.
6. Wilson, *Strangers to Ourselves*, p. 212.
7. World Jewish Daily, "Science Confirms What Rabbis Understood: Jewish Practice Makes You Happier And More Fulfilled," worldjewishdaily.com, accessed May 24, 2012, http://www.worldjewishdaily.com/Wisdom-Judaism.Php.
8. Leda Cosmides and John Tooby, *Evolutionary Psychology: A Primer* (Santa Barbara: University Of California, Santa Barbara, 1997), p. 12.
9. Jacques Henri Taylor, "Why Your Brain Is Made for Movement," huffingtonpost.com, August 1, 2011, accessed May 27, 2012, http://www.huffingtonpost.com/Jacques-Henri-Taylor/Mindful-Movement_B_892955.Html.
10. Ibid.
11. Bruno Dubuc, "The Brain From Top To Bottom," mcgill.ca, accessed May 24, 2012, http://thebrain.mcgill.ca/flash/D/D_07/D_07_Cr/D_07_Cr_Tra/D_07_Cr_Tra.Html.
12. Craig Freudenrich, Ph.D. and Robynne Boyd, "How Your Brain Works," howstuffworks.com, accessed May 24, 2012, http://science.howstuffworks.com/Environmental/Life/Human-Biology/Brain2.Htm.
13. George I. Viamontes and Bernard D. Beitman, "Mapping The Unconscious In The Brain," *Psychiatric Annals* 37, pp. 243-258.
14. Ibid.
15. Leslie Bilderback, "An Explanation of Taste," February 6, 2009, accessed May 25, 2012, http://leslie-bilderback.suite101.com/An-Explanation-Of-Taste-A94569.
16. Gerhard Gschwandtner, *Everything I Know About Sales Success* (New York: McGraw-Hill, 2006), p. 124.
17. Ibid., p. 133.
18. Kerry A. Dolan, "The Soda with Buzz," forbes.com, March 28, 2005, accessed May 25, 2012, http://www.forbes.com/global/2005/0328/028_print.html.
19. Ibid.
20. Gschwandtner, *Everything I Know About Sales Success*.
21. Charles C. Manz, *Emotional Discipline* (San Francisco: Berrett-Koehler Publishers, 2003).
22. Gschwandtner, *Everything I Know About Sales Success*, p. 124.
23. Ibid., 135.
24. Dolan, "The Soda with Buzz."
25. Duff Mcdonald, "Red Bull's Millionaire Maniac," businessweek.com, May 19, 2011, accessed May 25, 2012, http://www.businessweek.com/magazine/content/11_22/B4230064852768.htm.
26. Dolan, "The Soda with Buzz."
27. "Company Figures," redbull.com, accessed May 24, 2012, http://www.Redbull.com/Cs/Satellite/En_INT/Company-Figures/001242939605518?Pcs_C=PCS_Article&Pcs_Cid=1242937556133.

28. McDonald, "Red Bull's Millionaire Maniac."
29. Annie Layne Rodgers, "It's a (Red) Bull Market After All," fastcompany.com, September 30, 2001, http://www.fastcompany.com/Articles/2001/10/redbull.html.
30. Gad Saad, *The Consuming Instinct* (Amherst, NY: Prometheus Books, 2011).
31. D. G. Dutton and A. P. Aron, "Some Evidence For Heightened Sexual Attraction Under Conditions Of High Anxiety," *Journal Of Personality And Social Psychology* 30, pp. 510–517.
32. A. Dan Ariely, *Predictably Irrational* (New York: Harper Collins, 2010), pp. 78-88.
33. Sandra Blakeslee, "Cells That Read Minds," nytimes.com, January 10, 2006, http://www.nytimes.com/2006/01/10/Science/10mirr.html?_R=1&pagewanted=all.
34. V. S. Ramachandran, Speech, "The Neurons That Shaped Civilization," TED India, November 2009, accessed May 25, 2012, http://blog.ted.com/2010/01/04/The_Neurons_Tha/.
35. Ibid.
36. Ibid.
37. Ibid.
38. Saad, *The Consuming Instinct*.
39. Gerd Gigerenzer, *Gut Feelings* (New York: Viking Adult, 2007), p. 79.
40. Daniel Kahneman, *Thinking, Fast And Slow* (New York: Farrar, Straus and Giroux, 2011), p. 409.

INDEX